# Read-Aloud Handbook

Grade **4**

# Table of Contents

# Introduction

## The Value of Reading Aloud to Students

Reading aloud to students is one of the best ways to engage them with the text. Students of all ages love to be read to, and as teachers read stories, poems, and informational texts to their students, they model the joy of reading and the range of genres and text types students will encounter in their own reading.

Interactive read-alouds serve the added purpose of providing teachers with opportunities to demonstrate thinking while reading a text to students. In the *Benchmark Advance* program, teachers are encouraged to use classic and contemporary read-alouds to model the metacognitive strategies all readers use.

Metacognitive strategies support readers to develop and deepen their comprehension of a text before, during, and after they read. Through the application of metacognitive strategies in the classroom, students think about thinking and develop as readers.

In the *Benchmark Advance* Read-Aloud Handbook, the instruction supports teachers to model and guide practice with these strategies. From grade level to grade level, as well as throughout each grade level, students review previously taught metacognitive strategies and learn how to integrate them into their reading. Through instruction and practice, students can develop the ability to draw on multiple metacognitive strategies during every reading experience.

## Supporting Common Core Standards Through Read-Alouds

The read-aloud selections and instruction in this handbook support a range of Common Core Standards. Teachers support students' foundational reading skills as they model reading prose and poetry with accuracy, appropriate rate, and expression. As students listen with purpose and understanding, paraphrase the texts, and discuss ideas with peers, they enhance their speaking and listening skills. The interactive read-aloud prompts also support students' ability to use text evidence to answer a range of text-dependent questions.

## Using the Read-Alouds

Within the *Benchmark Advance* program, the Read-Aloud Handbook is listed in the Suggested Pacing Guide and in the Whole Group overview pages.

This handbook provides read-alouds for each of the 10 units in *Benchmark Advance*, Grade 4. You may use the read-alouds in any order you choose. Think of them as a resource to draw from to extend content knowledge beyond the selections in the Texts for Close Reading units.

# Modeling the Metacognitive Strategies

As you use the Read-Aloud Handbook, you can guide instruction with the following model prompts.

## Introduce the Passage

Read the title, share information about the author, invite students to share their ideas on what the passage is about, and engage students with additional information.

## Explain the Strategy

Each unit's selections reinforce a specific metacognitive strategy. Explain to students that as you read, you will model the strategy. At least one of the interactive read-aloud prompts per selection supports the metacognitive strategy.

## Read and Think Aloud

Read aloud the text with fluent expression. As you read, stop occasionally to think aloud and model the target metacognitive strategy. Use the sample prompts during reading to help you formulate think-alouds for the passages you are reading.

You may wish to write thoughts on self-stick notes and place the notes on the page as students watch. In order to keep students engaged, the Read-Aloud Handbook provides four think-alouds during the reading. More frequent interruptions may lead to confusion.

## After Reading

You may ask questions to focus conversation on the habits of readers. For example:

• What did you see me do as I read the passage?

• What kinds of questions did you see me ask?

• What kinds of inferences did I make?

• Where did I find the important information?

• How did I summarize and synthesize information as I read? How did that help me?

• What information in the text helped me visualize?

• What did I do to "fix up" my comprehension?

Create a class Metacognitive Strategies Anchor Chart based on the information generated during your discussions in each unit. Save this anchor chart and add to it each day as you continue to focus on the same strategy.

**Turn and Talk.** Invite students to share examples of metacognitive strategies they used as they listened to the text. Ask partners to share their ideas with the whole group.

**Connect and Transfer.** Remind students that readers need to be active and engaged with the text whenever they read and that you would like them to consciously practice using this strategy until it feels natural and automatic.

# Metacognitive Strategies at a Glance

| | |
|---|---|
| **Ask Questions** | Readers ask questions before they read. They often pause during reading to ask questions that help them understand and stay involved in what they are reading. Readers sometimes ask questions after they read. Readers ask the following kinds of questions:<br><br>• Questions about unfamiliar words or confusing information<br><br>• Questions that have answers right in the text<br><br>• Questions that have answers that can be inferred from the text<br><br>• Questions that are not answered in the text and will need further research or discussion |
| **Visualize** | Readers visualize when they form pictures in their minds to help them "see" and understand characters, settings, objects, and actions they are reading about. Readers visualize by using the following kinds of information:<br><br>• Vivid verbs that describe actions<br><br>• Adjectives that describe size, shape, color, and other details<br><br>• Graphic aids that tell size, shape, length, distance, time, and other information (such as charts, maps, time lines, diagrams, etc.)<br><br>• Similes and metaphors that compare one thing to another<br><br>• Sensory language that evokes how something feels, sounds, smells, or tastes |
| **Determine Text Importance** | Readers identify big ideas, themes, and specific information when they read. They may also evaluate the author's purpose and point of view. Readers determine text importance in the following ways:<br><br>• Activate and build prior knowledge<br><br>• Determine what is important versus what is interesting<br><br>• Distinguish between what to read carefully and what to ignore<br><br>• Highlight important words and nonfiction text features (captions, labels, bullets, etc.)<br><br>• Make notes and drawings in the margin to understand and remember the text<br><br>• Determine author's perspective, point of view, and/or opinion |

| | |
|---|---|
| **Make Inferences and Predictions** | Readers make inferences when they use clues and information in a text to figure something out that the author isn't directly telling them. Sometimes they also use their prior knowledge to help them. Readers make inferences in the following ways:<br><br>• Using story clues to figure out what is happening or why it is happening<br><br>• Using clues about characters (their actions, words, thoughts) to figure out what they are like and what they might do next<br><br>• Using clues to figure out the book's themes, or big ideas |
| **Summarize and Synthesize** | Synthesizing is the opposite of analyzing. While analyzing requires readers to take text apart, synthesizing requires readers to put text together to form a new idea or perspective. Readers summarize and synthesize information in the following ways:<br><br>• Summarize information by stating the big ideas<br><br>• Make generalizations, judgments, and opinions<br><br>• Distinguish between more important ideas and less important ideas<br><br>• Stop to collect their thoughts about a topic before, during, and after reading |
| **Make Connections** | Readers make connections when they link what they are reading to something they already know. Readers make three types of connections to texts:<br><br>• Text to self: readers make a personal connection with the text<br><br>• Text to text: readers make a connection between the text they are reading and a text they have already read<br><br>• Text to world: readers make a connection between the text and something in the world at large |
| **Fix-Up Monitoring** | When comprehension breaks down, readers use fix-up monitoring strategies to repair their comprehension. Readers use the following fix-up monitoring strategies:<br><br>• Stop and reread to clarify meaning<br><br>• Read ahead to clarify meaning<br><br>• Talk about what is confusing in the text<br><br>• Write about what is confusing in the text |

**Objective**

• Model asking questions

**Set the Stage**

**Introduce the Text** *Today I'm going to read aloud an article about the responsibilities of the president of the United States. The article begins by describing how our federal government works. It then tells about the various jobs the president has as the chief executive of our government.*

**Engage Thinking** *What jobs do you think the president performs? Turn to a partner to share your prediction.*

**Engage with the Text**

Read aloud the text at a fluent, expressive pace. Use the suggested prompts to model your thinking, clarify events, and elicit student interaction.

**1.** *The article says that the president has plenty of help. What kind of help might the president need? Who helps the president? I'll read on to determine if these questions are answered in this article.* (Ask questions)

**2.** *Three branches run the United States. I know* run *has many meanings. For example, it can mean "to move quickly," "manage," or "campaign in an election." In this sentence "manage" is the meaning that makes sense.* (Determine word meaning)

**3.** *Each paragraph contains a main idea along with details that support that main idea. For example, the main idea that the president recommends new laws is supported by examples such as adding new reading programs or making it easier for sick people to buy medicine.* (Determine main idea)

# Hail to the Chief

## by John P. Riley

1   Is the president of the United States the most powerful person in the world? Some people think so, because he or she is the chief executive of a mighty nation. An executive is responsible for managing an organization or business. The chief executive of the nation is responsible for managing our government. That is a big responsibility! But the president has plenty of help. **1**

2   In our country, the government is divided into three branches, or parts. The president is in charge of the executive branch. Another branch— Congress—makes laws. This is the legislative branch. (*Legislate* means "to make laws.") The third branch of our government is the judicial branch. The Supreme Court and other federal judges and courts in the judicial branch make sure the decisions made by the president and Congress follow the Constitution of our country.

3   All three branches work together to run the United States. For example, the president is the commander in chief of the armed services of the United States—the person who leads our military forces. But Congress has the power to declare war and provide the money to pay for it. So the president and Congress have to work together. **2**

4   Of all the public officials that voters select—mayor, governor, senator— the president is the only person that all voters can choose when they vote on Election Day. So the president must work for all the people, not just those from a certain city or state.

## What work does the president do?

5   **The president recommends new laws to Congress.** The president and his or her staff suggest new ways to solve problems and to improve the lives of American citizens through legislation. The president might want to add new reading programs to help schoolchildren, or make it easier for sick people to buy medicine. For the president's ideas to become law, Congress must pass the law (agree to it) and provide the money to make it work. Congress also has ideas for new laws. If the president disagrees with those ideas, he or she can try to prevent them by using the power to veto. *Veto* means "to refuse to agree to something." **3**

6　**The president enforces the law.** The president is the top law officer in the nation, with the power to make sure citizens obey the laws of our country. In rare—but dramatic—times, the president can also order army troops to enforce laws. For example, in 1962, President John F. Kennedy sent troops to the University of Mississippi to protect a black student from angry crowds who didn't want him there.

7　**The president is host to other nation's leaders.** The president invites other world leaders to his home, the White House, to have meetings and to show off American hospitality. When the White House hosts a dinner party for important visitors, the dinner menu usually includes favorite foods from the guest's country. When President and Mrs. George W. Bush invited President Vicente Fox of Mexico to dinner, dessert included ice cream with red chili pepper sauce.

8　**The president is a symbol of American leadership.** He or she is the one person who represents our nation at home and around the world. Some countries admire the U.S. president; others do not. Being president of the United States is a difficult job, with many tough choices to make. Great power comes with great responsibility. **4**

---

**4.** *Turn and talk to a partner. Take turns telling each other what you learned about the president and the government.* (Summarize)

## Extend Thinking Questions

Pose one or more questions to engage students more deeply with the text.

• *The president and Congress make and pass laws. What are examples of how laws have influenced the way you live?*

• *Which job of the president do you think is most important? Why?*

**iELD Paraphrase to Support Comprehension**

After paragraph 2: *Our government has three branches. The president is the head of the executive branch. Congress makes up the legislative branch. The Supreme Court makes up the judicial branch.*

After paragraph 3: *The president is the head of the military. Congress can declare war and provide money. The president works for all of the people in the country.*

After paragraph 5: *The president recommends new laws to Congress. Then Congress decides whether or not to pass the law. Also, Congress can have ideas for new laws, and then the president can veto the ideas.*

**CCSS**
**RI.4.1, RI.4.2, RI.4.3, RI.4.4, SL.4.2, L.4.4a**

## Set the Stage

**Introduce the Text** *Today I'm going to read aloud from the book* The Kid Who Ran for President *by Dan Gutman. The novel is about twelve-year-old Judson Moon, who is running for the office of President of the United States. This part opens when Judson is about to speak to students at his school. He will give his first speech that his campaign manager, Lane, wrote for him.*

**Engage Thinking** *What do you think Judson will say to fellow students in this speech? Turn to a partner to share your prediction.*

## Engage with the Text

Read aloud the text at a fluent, expressive pace. Use the suggested prompts to model your thinking, clarify events, and elicit student interaction.

**1.** *I know Judson is about to give his first speech. Why didn't he write his own speech? What will he talk about? Will the speech be a success? What other questions do you have so far?* (Ask questions)

**2.** *So far it looks like everyone thinks Judson is a great candidate. The principal complimented him, Lane told him he would be great, and the students all cheered for him.* (Make inferences)

# Give the People What They Want, Part 1

1  JUDSON MOON FOR PRESIDENT read the huge banner strung across the stage. It looked like every American flag in the school had been moved into the auditorium. I peeked from behind the curtain and saw my classmates sitting out there, buzzing with excitement. The school band was playing "Hail to the Chief." The podium looked like a lonely place to be.

2  Lane straightened my tie for me and handed me some sheets of paper.

3  "What does it say?" I asked. "It's a pretty standard political speech," he replied. "You know, the flag, patriotism. Stuff like that."

4  "I'm scared, Lane. What am I doing here?"

5  "Starting the adventure of a lifetime," he said with a smile. "You'll be great. Can you feel the energy out there? Feed off it! Throw their energy right back at them!"

6  I didn't have any time to read Lane's speech. Principal Berlin got up onstage. He held his hand up and made the V-sign with his fingers, which in our school means everybody has to stop talking right away. **1**

7  "Students," the principal said when everybody calmed down, "I have been at O'Keeffe School for eighteen years. In that time I have met many remarkable young men and women. But never in my years here have I run across a student with the ambition of this young man. I asked him here today to give his first public speech and kick off his campaign. I hope he will be an example to you all. Let's give a big hand for the next President of the United States, our own...Judson Moon!"

8  Lane gave me a little shove and I walked to the podium.

9  The applause was deafening. I've heard applause before, of course. But never for *me*. When the applause is for *you*, it somehow sounds different. You hear the hands clapping with your ears, but it just washes over you. You can't tell how loud it is or how long it goes on. You go into a sort of trance state.

10  Finally, the kids hushed themselves. The whole school was staring at me. I fumbled for the papers Lane had given me. It took all my concentration to read the words. It didn't matter what they said. I just didn't want to make any dumb mistakes.

11  "Fellow students," I began, "we are making history today. Never, in the history of the United States of America, has a *child*—one of *us*—run for

the office of President. That's what I am doing, and I come here today to ask for your support."

12  Some kids started cheering and hooting. A chant of "MOON! MOON! MOON! MOON!" swept across the auditorium. The teachers did their best to shush the kids. I waited until everybody calmed down before continuing. "I'm sure you're aware of the problems our country faces today. Crime. Environmental disaster. Unemployment. Racism. Inflation. Too much homework…" **2**

13  That got a laugh.

14  "Let me ask you this," I continued. "Who is responsible for these problems? Is it Congress? Foreigners? Rich people? Poor people? Black people? White people? Women? Men? No, there is one group who is totally to blame for all the problems in our country today, and I'll tell you who that group is."

15  I paused for a moment to find my place on the page.

16  "Grown-ups!" I shouted.

17  The kids went nuts. A cheer went up. Kids were stomping their feet. The teachers began to look around at each other nervously.

18  "*That's* who's responsible for the problems of our country. Tell me, who's responsible for housing discrimination, sex discrimination, and race discrimination?"

19  "Grown-ups!" they screamed.

20  "Who ripped a hole in the ozone layer, cut down the rain forests, made our water unsafe to drink, and our air unsafe to breathe?"

21  "Grown-ups!" they screamed even louder.

22  "Who brought on the health care crisis?"

23  "Grown-ups!"

24  "Who caused every war in the history of this planet?"

25  "Grown-ups!"

26  "That's right! Kids had nothing to do with *any* of these problems. Tell me this—are grown-ups going to solve all these problems they created?"

27  "No!" the whole school shouted.

28  "That's right," I said, more confidently. "In this young millennium, it's gonna be up to us to solve the problems created in the last millennium. And the way I look at it, the first step is for a kid to run for President in 2008. And win!" **3 4**

3. *Judson refers to the last millennium. I know* millennium *comes from two Latin roots:* mille, *which means 1,000, and* annum, *which means "year." So* millennium *means "1,000 years."* (Determine word meaning)

4. *Turn and talk to a partner. Ask each other questions about what you visualize as Judson is giving this speech.* (Visualize/Ask questions)

## Extend Thinking Questions

Pose one or more questions to engage students more deeply with the text.

• *According to Judson, what are some ways that grown-ups have impacted the people of the country?*

• *How has Judson changed from the beginning of this part of the story to the end of this part of the story?*

### iELD Paraphrase to Support Comprehension

After paragraph 7: *Judson is running for President of the United States. Principal Berlin has introduced him, and Judson is about to give his first campaign speech to the entire school.*

After paragraph 11: *The audience applauds loudly. Judson steps up to the podium. He tells students that he is the first child to run for president. He names some problems our country faces. Students laugh when he mentions too much homework.*

After paragraph 25: *Judson says that all of the problems in the country were caused by one group: Grown-ups. He says it's up to kids to solve these problems and that the first step is for a kid to run for President.*

CCSS
RL.4.1, RL.4.3, RL.4.4, L.4.4b

# Give the People What They Want, Part 2

1    They were in the palm of my hand now. I could feel it. Every student was silent and staring at me, even the eighth-grade jerks who *never* shut up for anything....

2    "Now, we all know that none of us can vote yet," I continued. "The grown-ups made sure of that, didn't they? What I want each of *you* to do is convince your parents to vote for *me*. You may have to beg them. You may have to put a little pressure on them. But if you want to solve these problems I've been talking about, do whatever you can to get your moms and dads to vote for me. Because if they vote for another grown-up, we'll only have the same old problems grown-ups caused over the last two centuries."

3    "MOON! MOON! MOON! MOON! MOON! MOON!" they chanted. It took a while before I could continue.

4    "My fellow students, I know what you're thinking. You're thinking, 'What's in it for *me*?' Well, I'll *tell* you what's in it for you. In appreciation for your support, my first official act as President of the United States will be to abolish homework, now and forever!"

5    A huge roar of approval went up across the auditorium. Clapping. Screaming. Foot stomping. The whole room was shaking. It felt like a football game. The teachers were flipping out. **❶**

6    I felt an exhilarating surge of power I had never experienced before. They were cheering because of *me*. They were whipped up because of what *I* was saying. It was a rush.

7    "If your parents vote for me," I bellowed into the microphone, "homework will go the way of the horse and buggy." Fists were pumping in the air.

8    "Homework will become a quaint reminder of what life was like back in the twentieth century!"

9    Kids were jumping up and down on their seats.

10    "In the twenty-first century, the only place you'll see homework will be in museums!" **❷**

11    It was pandemonium. I paused to allow them to calm down a little. I didn't want to incite a riot or anything.

12 I noticed a boy standing in the middle of the auditorium, raising his hand and shouting insistently, "Excuse me!" Peering at him, I could see it was that jerk Arthur Krantz.

13 "Yes, Mr. Krantz," I called out. "You have a comment?"

14 "First of all, the President of the United States has no power to abolish homework. None. Zero. Second, we *need* homework. Doing homework is how students reinforce what we learn at school! Homework is a *good* thing."

15 I glanced over to Lane at the side of the stage for some advice. He was mouthing some words to me, but I couldn't make them out. I was never any good at reading lips. But watching him gave me an idea. **3**

16 "READ MY LIPS, BOOGER BOY!" I bellowed. "NO…MORE… HOMEWORK!"…

17 "You're just making empty promises to get votes!" Krantz shouted at me. "Your candidacy is a joke! Your running mate is a grown-up, you hypocrite! You don't know anything about *anything*. You're going to make all kids look bad!"

18 A group of boys jumped on Krantz and started punching him. Some teachers rushed over to pull the boys off him. Krantz was taken out of the auditorium holding his hand over his eye.

19 I glanced at my speech and saw I was almost at the bottom.

20 "Fellow students, our grandparents had their chance to save America. They blew it! Our parents had their chance to save America. They blew it! Now it's a new millennium and our generation is going to get our chance. Let's not blow it!… Kids are the only hope for America. Thank you."

21 "NO MORE HOMEWORK!" the kids chanted as I left the podium. "NO MORE HOMEWORK!"

22 As I came off the stage, Principal Berlin looked at me like I was an insect. The teachers looked like they were in shock.

23 The kids, of course, looked thrilled. The dumbest guys seemed particularly happy, slapping me on the back and saying stuff like, "Awesome, dude."

24 "Looks as if you've got the kids' vote," Lane said, giving me a hug. "Don't you think that went a little too far, Lane?" I asked. "Krantz was right, you know. I can't promise to get rid of homework! That's crazy!"

25 "It's the first rule of politics, Judd. Give the people what they want."

**4**

3. *I can tell that Judson wants to please the students. But he doesn't necessarily know the facts or have his own ideas, so he has to look to his friend Lane for advice.* (Describe characters)

4. *Turn and talk to a partner. Tell each other your opinion of Arthur Krantz. Give evidence from the story to support your opinion.* (Describe characters)

## Extend Thinking Questions

Pose one or more questions to engage students more deeply with the text.

• *What does Lane mean when he says, "Give the people what they want"?*

• *What impact did Judson's speech have on the students?*

### iELD Paraphrase to Support Comprehension

**After paragraph 5:** *Judson tells the students to convince their parents to vote for him. If he wins, he will do away with homework forever. The audience jumps up and down clapping and screaming.*

**After paragraph 18:** *Arthur Krantz tells Judson he cannot keep his promise because the president has no power to end homework. The other students tell Krantz to shut up. They jump on Krantz. Teachers take him out of the auditorium.*

**After paragraph 25:** *The teachers and principal were not happy about the speech. The students were. Judson realizes he can't keep his promise to do away with homework. Lane tells him to "give the people what they want" even if he can't keep his promise.*

**CCSS**
**RL.4.1, RL.4.3, RL.4.4, L.4.4a, L.4.5b**

## Objective

• Model asking questions

## Set the Stage

**Introduce the Text** *Today I'm going to read aloud an article about the importance of voting. The article tells why voting is important and what responsibilities voters have.*

**Engage Thinking** *Why do you think it is important for citizens to vote? Turn to a partner to share your prediction.*

## Engage with the Text

Read aloud the text at a fluent, expressive pace. Use the suggested prompts to model your thinking, clarify events, and elicit student interaction.

**1.** *The article begins by saying the citizens of the United States have the right to vote. Do all citizens have the right to vote? What do we vote for in the United States? How do people decide whom to vote for? I'll read on to see if the article answers any of these questions.* (Ask questions)

**2.** *The article says that our country is a democracy. The next sentence gives a context clue that is a definition. A* democracy *means "our government is chosen by the people."* (Determine word meaning)

# Let Your Voice be Heard!

## by Ann Jordan

1 One of the privileges we have as citizens of the United States is the right to vote. Many people have worked hard to win that right for us. **1**

2 Our country is a democracy. That means our government is chosen by the people. In a famous speech, President Abraham Lincoln said that we have "a government of the people, by the people, and for the people." Lincoln was proud of the fact that the people of our country can participate in our government. One way we do that is to vote. **2**

3 When citizens vote, they are saying, "I want my voice to be heard." When citizens vote, they are helping decide who makes the laws of our country and what kinds of laws are made. Voters make decisions about many different things, such as buying land for parks, making new roads, and building hospitals. The people in your community might have voted to build your school, for example.

4 Voters make decisions about other things, too. In your classroom, you might vote for members of the Student Council, or which story to read, or what kind of snack you want. What would happen if only a few students in your class voted? Those few students would be the ones making the decisions for the whole class. The nonvoting students would have to accept the decisions made by the few who voted.

5 The same thing is true of our country. When people don't vote, they are allowing those who do vote to make important decisions that affect everyone. They are not taking part in what we call "the democratic process." They are not making their voices heard.

6 Sean, a fifth grader, is the president of the Student Council at his school in San Antonio, Texas. To become a council member originally, he made a speech that outlined what he planned to do if elected. Sean thinks it's important for students to learn about the democratic process at school. He says, "It teaches us that it is our responsibility to vote, and it helps us learn how to select the right person to represent us."

7    Eighteen-year-old Kelsey, a student in Richardson, Texas, is excited about being old enough to vote in the next presidential election. She says, "Being able to vote for the president of the United States is really cool. I will have a voice in what goes on in our country." She has been preparing for the privilege of voting by listening to the candidates speak on television. "I'm voting for the first time, and I want to be sure I make the right choices." **3**

8    Being an educated voter is important. Voters need to know what the candidates plan to do if they are elected. Listening to the candidates on television, as Kelsey is doing, is one way to learn. Reading about them in newspapers, watching news shows on television, and checking out the candidates' websites are other ways to become informed. An organization called the League of Women Voters also provides information for voters. **4**

9    Whenever you have an opportunity to vote, remember that it is your right and your privilege. Let your voice be heard!

**3.** *The author believes that voting is important. One reason is because citizens who vote help decide who makes the laws. For example, voters decide on the president of the Student Council and the President of the United States.* (Cite reasons and evidence)

**4.** *Turn and talk to a partner. How can voters learn about candidates?* (Summarize)

## Extend Thinking Questions

Pose one or more questions to engage students more deeply with the text.

• *How do elected officials impact our lives?*

• *What are the effects of voting? What are the effects of not voting?*

### iELD Paraphrase to Support Comprehension

After paragraph 2: *Our country is a democracy. Its citizens can choose its government. One way to choose the government is to vote.*

After paragraph 5: *Voters make many decisions. They decide who makes the laws and what kinds of laws are made. When people do not vote, they let those who do vote make all of the decisions.*

After paragraph 9: *Voters need to learn what candidates plan to do if they are elected. They can listen to candidates speak. They can read about them in newspapers or check out their websites. Voting is both a right and a privilege.*

CCSS
RI.4.1, RI.4.2, RI.4.4, RI.4.8, SL.4.2, L.4.4a

# The Quilt

## by Sachi Oyama

1   Dressed in colonial clothes and long hoop skirts, Miss Masako Hirata's students danced the minuet. They made hornbooks and held spelling bees. Miss Hirata's fourth graders were learning the ways of colonial America in the 1700s. **1**

2   Now they had a very special assignment.

3   Each student was to stitch his or her name with needle and thread on a square piece of cloth. Miss Hirata would take the patches and sew them together to make a large quilt like the ones made in early America. When they finished, they would have a quilt with the names of all the students.

4   Each name had a story. The children of Miss Hirata's class spoke English, but many of their names were Japanese. Their parents had emigrated from Japan. The students themselves had all been born in **2** America, though. Most came from cities along the California coast or in the valleys. Some students came from Los Angeles, some from San Diego, others from Brawley or Fresno. Many of the children's parents were shopkeepers, many were farmers, and some were ministers.

5   Miss Hirata's fourth graders were many miles from the homes they knew. They lived in a camp surrounded by barbed wire, watched by guards in towers. Why? Japan, the country their parents came from, was at war with America. In 1941, Japan had attacked Pearl Harbor in Hawaii. A Japanese attack on the West Coast of the United States seemed possible. Many people thought that Japanese Americans might be loyal to Japan instead of America. They feared Japanese Americans might help Japanese forces attack the United States. Many politicians, newspaper writers, and ordinary citizens in California and other states said that Japanese Americans were dangerous. They urged the United States Army to gather all Japanese Americans in California and on the rest of the West Coast and intern them.

6   President Franklin D. Roosevelt gave General John L. DeWitt, the man in charge of defending the West Coast against enemy attack, permission to carry out this plan in February 1942. Soon after, Japanese Americans were ordered to leave their homes and jobs and report to an internment camp. This meant that most Japanese American families had to sell their homes and almost all their possessions quickly, for very little money.

7   Most lost nearly everything they had worked for.

8   Today, we recognize that interning Japanese Americans was unfair. Japanese Americans showed their loyalty to the United States in many ways during World War II. For example, thousands of young Japanese American men joined the U.S. armed forces. Even though many had families in internment camps, the Japanese American soldiers fought bravely for the United States. The United States government has officially apologized for its wartime treatment of Japanese Americans. **3**

9   The American colonists that Miss Hirata's class was studying fought a war for independence from Britain. After the war, their leaders wrote in the Constitution a list of rights held by all citizens of the United States. One of those rights is the right to a fair trial before being imprisoned. Miss Hirata's students were American citizens. They had never been put on trial, but they were imprisoned in the camp. Their constitutional rights had been violated.

10  Still, the students loved their country, and worked hard studying its history. They busily stitched the small patches of cloth for their colonial quilt. Miss Hirata's lessons were always interesting, always fun. What would their names look like spread across a large quilt? Finally the patches were finished. Miss Hirata sewed them together. The quilt showing the names of all the fourth graders was proudly hung on the classroom wall.

11  Many years later, when the war was long over and the students of Miss Hirata's class were parents and grandparents themselves, they would see the quilt again. It had become part of a traveling exhibit for the Smithsonian Institution, the most famous museum in America. The quilt traveled to cities across the United States, where it was seen by thousands of people. Miss Hirata's class had made the quilt in order to learn about the colonial period in United States history. Now the quilt was helping to teach others about another chapter in United States history: World War II and the difficult experiences of Japanese Americans in that era. Miss Hirata's former students felt proud to see that their history project had itself become a part of America's history. **4**

**4.** *Turn and talk to a partner. Ask each other questions about how the quilt represented two different periods of American history.* (Make inferences/Ask questions)

## Extend Thinking Questions

Pose one or more questions to engage students more deeply with the text.

• *How did government decisions impact the lives of Japanese Americans during World War II?*

• *How did the quilt help demonstrate Miss Hirata and her students' loyalty to America?*

### iELD Paraphrase to Support Comprehension

**After paragraph 4:** *Miss Hirata's fourth graders were studying colonial history. They worked together to make a quilt. Most of them came from California.*

**After paragraph 6:** *Japan attacked Pearl Harbor in 1941. Americans were afraid Japanese Americans would be loyal to Japan. In 1942, President Roosevelt ordered all Japanese Americans be placed in internment camps. This is where Miss Hirata's students were when they made their quilt.*

**After paragraph 9:** *The citizens at the internment camps had a constitutional right to a fair trial before being imprisoned, but this right was violated. The U.S. government has apologized for this unfair treatment.*

CCSS
RI.4.1, RI.4.2, RI.4.3, RI.4.4, RI.4.8, SL.4.2, L.4.4b

## Objective

• Model asking questions

## Set the Stage

**Introduce the Text** *Today I'm going to read aloud a selection about how Mariano Vallejo, a general, worked to help California become a state. This first part tells about the challenges Vallejo had to overcome in order to convince people to accept California as a state.*

**Engage Thinking** *What issues do you think people worried about when considering statehood? Turn to a partner to share your prediction.*

## Engage with the Text

Read aloud the text at a fluent, expressive pace. Use the suggested prompts to model your thinking, clarify events, and elicit student interaction.

**1.** *This first paragraph says that big issues had been worked out. What issues were they? How were they resolved? What other questions do you think might be answered as we read on?* (Ask questions)

**2.** *Not everyone believed in Vallejo's vision. Vision can mean "eyesight" or "a dream." In this context, "dream" makes sense. Not everyone believed in Vallejo's dream.* (Determine word meaning)

**3.** *José Antonio Carrillo was against Vallejo's vision. He was a large property owner. He did not want California to become a state because he wanted to avoid the taxes statehood might bring.* (Describe relationships)

# Mariano Vallejo: A Californio for Statehood, Part 1

## by Diane Brooks

1   The date was September 3, 1849. Tall, proud General Mariano Guadalupe Vallejo left Monterey's Colton Hall in a hopeful mood. He and his fellow delegates to California's Constitutional Convention had completed their work swiftly. Big issues had been worked out in just three days. Now when Congress voted to accept California as a state, all would be ready for its government to begin working. **1**

2   Why did the general feel hopeful? Since he was a small boy, Mariano Vallejo had dreamed of California becoming a great country. Though he was a Californio and had grown up under Spanish and later Mexican rule, Vallejo believed that the region would have its best chance at greatness as part of the United States. America was a democratic nation, a country in which people elect governors and representatives to make laws.

3   Not everyone agreed with Vallejo's vision. Pío Pico, a leader in the **2** south, had at one time wanted California to become part of Britain. Some Californios with large property holdings in southern California, such as José Antonio Carrillo, wanted the southern part of California to become a United States territory rather than a state. That way they could avoid the heavy taxation that statehood might bring. Carrillo proposed that only the northern part of California be made a state. **3**

4   There was also much anxiety about the future. Would Californios be able to keep their vast ranches? Would there be taxes? What would happen to California's Mexican culture? Vallejo had worked to ease these concerns and help newcomers and Californios understand each other. His standing as an influential leader was demonstrated when he was chosen, along with his friend Johann Sutter, to escort Dr. Robert Semple to the chair of the Convention.

5   One notable law written into the constitution had existed in Mexican California but had yet to be enacted anywhere in the United States: All land or money owned by a woman before she married, or received by her as a gift afterwards, would remain her property. Would this attract wealthy unmarried women to the new state?

6   Another law forbade slavery. In California, African Americans would not be denied freedom.

7   The delegates also debated where California's eastern boundary should be. Some delegates wanted the state to extend all the way to the Rocky Mountains. The final decision was to call for a boundary just to the east of the Sierra Nevada mountains and then down the middle of the Colorado River. This compromise included the gold fields and the agricultural lands in a large but not enormous state. After all, Californians did not want to ask for more than Congress might approve.

8   Another issue considered was the design for the state seal. It ended up a collection of images, among them a crouching grizzly bear feeding on grapes. Vallejo strongly objected to the bear. He had no good memories of his imprisonment at Sutter's Fort during the Bear Flag Revolt, and he wanted that animal removed unless it was shown in a lasso with a man holding the other end of the rope. Vallejo was finally convinced that a standing bear would be respectful to those Californios who had supported the United States. **4**

*4. Turn and talk to a partner. Take turns asking each other questions about what issues had to be worked out for California to become a state.* (Summarize/Ask questions)

## Extend Thinking Questions

Pose one or more questions to engage students more deeply with the text.

• *How does a democratic government influence the way a country is run?*

• *Which law written into the California Constitution do you think was most important? Why?*

**iELD  Paraphrase to Support Comprehension**

After paragraph 1: *General Mariano Vallejo believed California should become part of the United States. In 1849 California drew up its constitution. Congress would now be able to accept California as a state.*

After paragraph 4: *Not everyone wanted California to become a state. They were worried they would have to pay high taxes and lose their property and their culture. Vallejo was able to ease their worries.*

After paragraph 8: *One law written into the California constitution was that women could keep their property. Another forbade slavery. Two others issues were the state boundaries and the state seal.*

**CCSS**
**RI.4.1, RI.4.3, RI.4.4, SL.4.2, L.4.4a**

**Set the Stage**

**Introduce the Text** *Today I'm going to read more about Mariano Vallejo. Let's first summarize what you remember from the part I read before.* (Have volunteers give a summary.) *In this next part, you will learn about Vallejo as California changed under four different governments.*

**Engage Thinking** *How do you think life in California changed as its governments changed? Turn to a partner to share your prediction.*

**Engage with the Text**

Read aloud the text at a fluent, expressive pace. Use the suggested prompts to model your thinking, clarify events, and elicit student interaction.

**1.** *This second paragraph includes the phrase "California under four flags." I wonder what that means. How did this affect Vallejo's life? What other questions do you have?* (Ask questions)

**2.** *Vallejo learned the skills of a vaquero. I'm not sure what a* vaquero *is. Context clues say he learned to lasso and ride. So a vaquero is probably like a cowboy. I can check a dictionary to confirm that meaning.* (Determine word meaning)

**3.** *This selection describes how California changed governments four times from 1818 until it became a state. The information is organized chronologically, in time order.* (Determine sequence of events)

# Mariano Vallejo: A Californio for Statehood, Part 2

1  A public celebration was held to celebrate the coming together of Californios and Americans to create a new constitution. There was music, dancing, and tables of Mexican and American foods.

2  What a moment for Mariano Vallejo to reflect on times past. His life in California under four flags was like a history of the region. The red and yellow flag of Spain flew over the presidio of Monterey in 1818 when this ten-year-old boy and his friends watched for pirate ships. **❶**

3  With few defenses, townspeople usually fled when a pirate ship was spotted. Spain was at war and too far away to help. Yet Vallejo was grateful for the opportunities he had to acquire knowledge in that era. He learned to ride, lasso, and develop the other skills of a vaquero. He read every book he could get his hands on. He learned French and English from sailors on the trading ships that occasionally put into port. He hoped someday to help make his country great and strong. **❷**

4  But times changed. Mexico declared itself free from Spain and claimed all of California. Now there was a green, white, and red flag flying. Mariano joined the army, determined to help make California's defenses strong. He got his first taste of politics as secretary to the governor and learned about the land and its people.

5  He fell in love with and married the beautiful Francisca Benicia Carrillo of San Diego. They settled on a land grant in the Sonoma Valley, north of San Francisco. Vallejo's duties, as commander of the northern region, were to keep an eye on the Russians at Fort Ross, protect Mexico's northern holdings, and handle Indian affairs. He carried out these duties successfully. He and Francisca raised a large family, entertained friends and an increasing number of foreigners, and were supportive of settlers.

6　But times were changing again. Some Californios wanted to revolt against Mexico. Governors were frequently changed, defenses were weak, and Mexico was too far away to help with problems with all the new foreigners. The Mexican governor aroused the anger of settlers by decreeing that all who were not Mexican citizens must leave California. Vallejo was named a general of Northern California but later dismissed his troops in order to remain neutral.

7　Then, on June 14, 1846, Vallejo was arrested by a band of American settlers and imprisoned at Sutter's Fort. Americans who wanted California to become a state felt that this Mexican general was an obstacle to their plan. Having captured Vallejo, they raised the Bear Flag at Sonoma to signify California's independence. Vallejo was distressed and displeased. Didn't Americans understand that he was one of the Californios who wanted to be a fellow citizen? But the revolt was short-lived, and soon afterward Vallejo began being treated with the respect he deserved. **3**

8　Now, with a constitution drafted and application for statehood imminent, Vallejo looked toward a prosperous future for California under the Stars and Stripes. Recognizing Vallejo's knowledge and wisdom, the new governor named him to a committee to decide county boundaries and names. There would be a need for a state capital, and Mariano Vallejo offered a portion of his 175,000 acres to be used for that purpose. Mariano Vallejo would be elected a state senator in the new government. He was a proud Californio who had helped to build a magnificent state. **4**

**4.** *Turn and talk to a partner. What are some details that support the main idea that California changed governments four times? (Determine main idea)*

## Extend Thinking Questions

Pose one or more questions to engage students more deeply with the text.

• *How were people's lives in California impacted by Spain when California was under its rule?*

• *Do you admire Mariano Vallejo? Why or why not?*

### iELD Paraphrase to Support Comprehension

**After paragraph 3:** *In 1818 California was ruled by Spain. Pirates would attack California. However, Spain was at war. It was too far away to help protect the people.*

**After paragraph 5:** *Mexico declared itself free from Spain. It claimed all of California. At this time Vallejo joined the army and married. He became commander of northern California. He raised a large family there.*

**After paragraph 8:** *Some Californios revolted against Mexico. In 1846 American settlers arrested Vallejo. Eventually the revolt ended and he was released. The settlers realized he also wanted California statehood. Vallejo would become a state senator for California.*

CCSS
RI.4.1, RI.4.2, RI.4.3, RI.4.4, RI.4.5, SL.4.2, L.4.4a, L.4.4c

## Objective

• Model asking questions

## Set the Stage

**Introduce the Text** *Today I'm going to read aloud the story, "And the Citizenship Award Goes To..." In this story the teacher, Mr. Rubinett, gives an award each month to the student in class who is an outstanding citizen.*

**Engage Thinking** *What do you think a student does to earn the Citizenship Award? Turn to a partner to share your prediction.*

## Engage with the Text

Read aloud the text at a fluent, expressive pace. Use the suggested prompts to model your thinking, clarify events, and elicit student interaction.

**1.** *The narrator says he is an invisible chico. What is a chico? Does the narrator get the award? What do you get if you win the award? I'll read on to find out.* (Ask questions)

**2.** *I know* invisible *means "unable to be seen." But I think in this story, it does not literally mean that no one can see the person. I think it means that this person is shy and people do not notice him or her.* (Determine word meaning)

# And the Citizenship Award Goes To. . .

1   At my old school, I was the invisible chico. **1** But in this school, things are very different. Nobody can get away with being invisible. So when Mr. Rubinett says that he is about to announce this month's outstanding citizen, everyone in the classroom looks up excitedly. I never thought I would get the award because even though I'm not invisible here, I don't speak all that much. I mean, I say hello to a few kids in my class and in the lunchroom, but that's it. **2**

2   "This month, the award goes to a new student at Sunshine School," says Mr. Rubinett. There are four new students in my class, so I think I am still in the clear. Then he goes on. "This person is someone who always says 'please' and 'thank you' while standing in the lunch line. This person does not push or shove. This person is a good citizen. I have watched this person on the playground. I think we can all learn a thing or two from this person."

3   Mr. Rubinett says that the prize for this month's award is a pizza lunch with Mr. Rubinett, and a fancy pen and pencil set. Mr. Rubinett is everyone's favorite teacher, and when he shows the class the sleek pen and pencil set, everyone says, "Oh, nice writing utensils, Mr. R!"

4    Mr. Rubinett goes on about the outstanding citizen award in a very serious tone. "On two different days, I saw this person hand the swing over to a girl who had been waiting. I also watched this person speak very kindly to a group of kindergartners. This person also picked up a milk container and lunch tray from the floor. A very impressive move, boys and girls."

5   I could feel a horrible lump in my throat. I didn't know if I was happy or sad about the possibility of being in the spotlight. The room was quiet with anticipation. Inside my head, I was exploding with possibility.

6    "The citizenship award goes to . . . Manuel Perez."

7   The room filled with the sound of applause. I could tell that my face was beat red, because it was hotter than the sun. Mr. Rubinett asked me to stand and say a few words, but I forget how to speak. I just smiled and took it all in. Mr. Rubinett shook my hand, then he took my photo, and presented me with the pen and pencil set.

8  "Thank you, everyone," I said. Again, everyone applauded.

9  I was beaming because I knew that my mom and dad were going to be proud of me. My abuela, too, would be over the moon about this. Suddenly, I thought of something to say.

10  Everyone waited for me to gather my thoughts.

11  "It is my abuela, my grandmother, who taught me about manners. Always say 'please' and 'thank you,'" I said with a smile. "Today, it has paid off," I said.

12  As Mr. Rubinett patted me on the back, I realized that this day was a new beginning for me.

**3.** *I can tell Manuel Perez is shy and kind by his actions and his words. For example, he could not speak at first when he got the award. He speaks kindly to kindergartners.* (Describe characters)

**4.** *Turn and talk to a partner. Ask your partner questions about what happened up to the point when the winner was announced. Then listen to your partner summarize the rest of the story.* (Summarize/Ask questions))

## Extend Thinking Questions

Pose one or more questions to engage students more deeply with the text.

• *How can being a good citizen impact others?*

• *Why was this a new beginning for Manuel?*

### iELD Paraphrase to Support Comprehension

After paragraph 1: *Mr. Rubinett, the teacher, is about to announce the winner of the award for outstanding citizen of the month. The narrator is new in the school. He does not expect to get the award.*

After paragraph 6: *The narrator, Manuel Perez, wins the award. It is because Mr. Rubinett has seen him be helpful, polite, and kind to other students all month.*

After paragraph 11: *At first Manuel is too shy to say anything. Then he tells everyone that it was his grandmother who taught him about manners.*

**CCSS**
**RI.4.1, RL.4.2, RL.4.3, RL.4.4, SL.4.2, L.4.4a, L.4.5b**

## Objective
• Model visualizing

## Set the Stage

**Introduce the Text** *Today I'm going to read aloud the first half of Chapter 2, from the book* Out of My Mind. *The author, Sharon Draper, wrote about what goes on in the mind of a child who cannot communicate with the outside world. She writes from the experience of having a developmentally disabled daughter herself.*

*This chapter begins with Melody, who has cerebral palsy, explaining what her world is like. She describes what she thinks others see when they look at her.*

**Engage Thinking** *What do you think others think of Melody when they see she is unable to talk, walk, or care for herself? Turn to a partner to share your prediction.*

## Engage with the Text

Read aloud the text at a fluent, expressive pace. Use the suggested prompts to model your thinking, clarify events, and elicit student interaction.

**1.** *The beginning of this excerpt gives a detailed description of Melody's physical characteristics. I can easily picture what ten-year-old Melody looks like as she sits in her pink wheelchair. I see her dark hair and eyes, her head wobbling, her thin legs that sometimes flail out of control.* (Visualize)

**2.** *In the video Melody has a look of contentment on her face. I know that the base word* content *means "satisfied." The suffix* -ment *means the state or condition. So Melody has a look of being satisfied on her face.* (Determine word meaning)

# An excerpt from
# Out of My Mind, Part 1
## by Sharon Draper

1   I can't talk. l can't walk. I can't feed myself or take myself to the bathroom. Big bummer.

2   My arms and hands are pretty stiff, but I can mash the buttons on the TV remote and move my wheelchair with the help of knobs that I can grab on the wheels. I can't hold a spoon or a pencil without dropping it. And my balance is like zip—Humpty Dumpty had more control than I do.

3   When people look at me, I guess they see a girl with short, dark, curly hair strapped into a pink wheelchair. By the way, there is nothing cute about a pink wheelchair. Pink doesn't change a thing.

4   They'd see a girl with dark brown eyes that are full of curiosity. But one of them is slightly out of whack.

5   Her head wobbles a little.

6   Sometimes she drools.

7   She's really tiny for a girl who is age ten and three quarters.

8   Her legs are very thin, probably because they've never been used.

9   Her body tends to move on its own agenda, with feet sometimes kicking out unexpectedly and arms occasionally flailing, connecting with whatever is close by—a stack of CDs, a bowl of soup, a vase of roses.

10  Not a whole lot of control there.

11  After folks got finished making a list of my problems, they might take time to notice that I have a fairly nice smile and deep dimples—I think my dimples are cool.

12  I wear tiny gold earrings.

13  Sometimes people never even ask my name, like it's not important or something. It is. My name is Melody.

14  I can remember way back to when I was really, really young. Of course, it's hard to separate real memories from the videos of me that Dad took on his camcorder. I've watched those things a million times.

15 Mom bringing me home from the hospital—her face showing smiles, but her eyes squinted with worry.

16 Melody tucked into a tiny baby bathtub. My arms and legs looked so skinny. I didn't splash or kick.

17 Melody propped with blankets on the living room sofa—look of contentment on my face. I never cried much when I was a baby; Mom swears it's true. **2**

18 Mom massaging me with lotion after a bath—I can still smell the lavender—then wrapping me in a fluffy towel with a little hood built into one corner.

19 Dad took videos of me getting fed, getting changed, and even me sleeping. As I got older, I guess he was waiting for me to turn over, and sit up, and walk. I never did.

20 But I did absorb everything. I began to recognize noises and smells and tastes. The *whump* and *whoosh* of the furnace coming alive each morning. The tangy odor of heated dust as the house warmed up. The feel of a sneeze in the back of my throat. **3**

21 And music. Songs floated through me and stayed. Lullabies, mixed with the soft smells of bedtime, slept with me. Harmonies made me smile. It's like I've always had a painted musical sound track playing background to my life. I can almost hear colors and smell images when music is played.

22 Mom loves classical. Big, booming Beethoven symphonies blast from her CD player all day long. Those pieces always seem to be bright blue as I listen, and they smell like fresh paint.

23 Dad is partial to jazz, and every chance he gets, he winks at me, takes out Mom's Mozart disc, then pops in a CD of Miles Davis or Woody Herman. Jazz to me sounds brown and tan, and it smells like wet dirt. Jazz music drives Mom crazy, which is probably why Dad puts it on.

24 "Jazz makes me itch," she says with a frown as Dad's music explodes into the kitchen.

25 Dad goes to her, gently scratches her arms and back, then engulfs her in a hug. She stops frowning. But she changes it back to classical again as soon as Dad leaves the room. **4**

---

**3.** *Melody recalls how she began to recognize noises, smells, and tastes. The use of sensory language helps me visualize this as well. I can hear the "whump" and "whoosh" of the furnace, I can smell the heated dust, and I can taste and feel the sneeze that Melody feels in the back of her throat.* (Visualize)

**4.** *What have you learned so far about Melody?* (Describe characters)

## Extend Thinking Questions

Pose one or more questions to engage students more deeply with the text.

• *It was almost impossible for Melody to reveal herself to others. What does Melody want others to know about her?*

• *Besides telling others what you are like, what are some other ways you can reveal yourself to others?*

### iELD Paraphrase to Support Comprehension

After paragraph 10: *Melody is a ten-year-old girl who cannot talk, walk, or care for herself. She is confined to a wheelchair. She is very tiny, with thin legs. She does not have much control of her body.*

After paragraph 21: *Melody recalls memories and videos of her coming home as a baby. She never learned to walk. She did absorb everything, including noises, smells, and tastes.*

After paragraph 25: *Music is Melody's greatest enjoyment. She feels she can hear colors and smell images when she hears music. Her mom loves classical music. Her dad loves jazz.*

**CCSS**
**RL.4.1, RL.4.3, RL.4.4, L.4.4b**

Unit 2

- Model visualizing

## Set the Stage

**Introduce the Text** *Today I'm going to read aloud the second half of Chapter 2, from the book* Out of My Mind. *In this part we learn how frustrated Melody is that she cannot share words.*

**Engage Thinking** *Why do you think Melody is so frustrated that she cannot share words with her parents? Turn to a partner to share your prediction.*

## Engage with the Text

Read aloud the text at a fluent, expressive pace. Use the suggested prompts to model your thinking, clarify events, and elicit student interaction.

**1.** *In the first paragraph of this part, the narrator describes country music in such detail I can almost see, hear, and smell it just like she can. Words like "loud", "sugar sweet," and "fresh lemonade" help me visualize what she sees and hears.* (Visualize)

**2.** *Melody says there are millions of words and everyone was able "to bring them out." I don't think she literally means people were bringing out words. I think the phrase means everyone was able to speak except her.* (Determine phrase meaning)

# An excerpt from
# Out of My Mind, Part 2
## by Sharon Draper

1   For some reason, I've always loved country music loud, guitar-strumming, broken-heart music. Country is lemons—not sour, but sugar sweet and tangy. Lemon cake icing, cool, fresh lemonade! Lemon, lemon, lemon! Love it. **❶**

2   When I was really little, I remember sitting in our kitchen, being fed breakfast by Mom, and a song came on the radio that made me screech with joy.

3   *So I'm singin'*

4   *Elvira, Elvira*

5   *My heart's on fire, Elvira*

6   *Giddy up oorn poppa oom poppa mow mow*

7   *Giddy up oom poppa omn poppa mow mow*

8   *Heigh-ho Silver, away*

9   How did I already know the words and the rhythms to that song? I have no idea. It must have seeped into my memory somehow—maybe from a radio or TV program. Anyway, I almost fell out of my chair. I scrunched up my face and jerked and twitched as I tried to point to the radio. I wanted to hear the song again.

10  But Mom just looked at me like I was nuts.

11  How could she understand that I loved the song "Elvira" by the Oak Ridge Boys when I barely understood it myself? I had no way to explain how I could smell freshly sliced lemons and see citrus-toned musical notes in my mind as it played.

12  If I had a paintbrush. . .wow! What a painting that would be!

13  But Mom just shook her head and kept on spooning applesauce into my mouth. There's so much my mother doesn't know.

14  I suppose it's a good thing to be unable to forget anything—being able to keep every instant of my life crammed inside my head. But it's also very frustrating. I can't share any of it, and none of it ever goes away.

15 I remember stupid stuff, like the feel of a lump of oatmeal stuck on the roof of my mouth or the taste of toothpaste not rinsed off my teeth.

16 The smell of early-morning coffee is a permanent memory, mixed up with the smell of bacon and the background yakking of the morning news people.

17 Mostly, though, I remember words. Very early I figured out there were millions of words in the world. Everyone around me was able to bring them out with no effort.

18 The salespeople on television: *Buy one and get two free! For a limited time only.*

19 The mailman who came to the door: *Mornin', Mrs. Brooks. How's the baby?*

20 The choir at church: *Hallelujah, hallelujah, amen.*

21 The checkout clerk at the grocery store: *Thanks for shopping with us today.*

22 Everybody uses words to express themselves. Except me. And I bet most people don't realize the real power of words. But I do.

23 Thoughts need words. Words need a voice.

24 I love the smell of my mother's hair after she washes it.

25 I love the feel of the scratchy stubble on my father's face before he shaves.

26 But I've never been able to tell them. **3** **4**

**3.** *I think the theme of this part of the story is the importance of words. Melody says that thoughts need words. She shares how much she wishes she could use words to tell her parents how she feels.* (Determine theme)

**4.** *Turn and talk to a partner. What characteristics about Melody most impressed you? Why?* (Describe characters)

## Extend Thinking Questions

Pose one or more questions to engage students more deeply with the text.

• *How did Melody try to reveal to her mother how she felt about the song "Elvira?" What was the result?*

• *What characters in other stories you have read did you admire? Why? Did any remind you of Melody?*

### iELD Paraphrase to Support Comprehension

**After paragraph 13:** *Melody hears, smells, and sees the song "Elvira." She tries to show her mother that she wants to hear it again. Her mother does not understand. She just keeps feeding Melody.*

**After paragraph 14:** *Melody feels that it is good that she remembers everything in her life. She also feels it is frustrating because she cannot share what she remembers.*

**After paragraph 26:** *Mostly Melody remembers words. She feels words have power. They can tell what your thoughts are. Melody wishes she could speak so she could share her thoughts about her parents, but she cannot.*

CCSS
RL.4.1, RL.4.2, RL.4.3, RL.4.4, L.4.5b

# Mirror, Mirror!

## Characters

**Queen** from "Snow White and the Seven Dwarfs"

**Mirror**

**Huntsman**

1   The Queen from "Snow White and the Seven Dwarfs" stares blankly into a mirror on the wall. The mirror is surrounded by a bright red light. The Queen poses as if she is being photographed. She makes very dramatic faces to try to highlight her good looks. She spends a moment trying to fix her hair. One minute, her hair is up, the next minute it is tightly secured in a bun. She peers into the mirror, making various facial expressions. To the left, on the wall is a picture of a beautiful young girl. The girl is Snow White.

2   **Queen**: Mirror, mirror, on the wall, who in this land is fairest of all? (*The Queen eagerly waits for a response from the mirror, but does not receive one. She becomes very agitated.*)

3   **Queen**: I said, Mirror, mirror—

4   **Mirror**: (*in a weak voice, from off stage*) Well—

5   **Queen**: Speak up! (*The Queen claps her hands, and becomes enraged with the mirror. She moves in close as if she is trying to figure out how to take the mirror off the wall and break it.*) **❶**

6   **Mirror**: (*in a small, sweet voice*) You, my queen, are fair, it is true.

7   **Queen**: That's better. (*The Queen smiles, resumes a more natural pose, as if she is in control once again.*)

8   **Mirror**: However, Queen, (*changes the tone of her voice to be commanding and intimidating*) Snow White is the fairest of all. **❷**

9   (*The Queen gasps with surprise, then she looks at the mirror with disbelief.*)

10  **Mirror**: You are turning green!

11  (*The Queen focuses on the mirror and studies herself. A green tint washes over her face. The Queen is horrified. She keeps looking at herself from different angles, desperately trying to see something other than what she sees.*)

12  **Mirror**: (*almost laughing*) Green with envy, Queen.

13  **Queen**: Do not speak to me! (*The Queen reaches for her makeup on her dressing table. She begins dusting herself with white powder, desperately trying to wipe away the green. At first, her face is definitely turning whiter, but after a few seconds the green tint becomes a rich color.*)

14  **Mirror**: (*in an innocent-sounding tone*) But you have asked me who is the fairest, and I have spoken the truth. **3**

15  **Queen**: (*The Queen is disgusted by the mirror. She stomps her feet.*) What do you know? You are just a mirror!

16  **Mirror**: I am the…truth. (*The word "truth" seems to stop the Queen in her tracks. She is not sure what to do. Again she looks in the mirror, and searches for answers.*) **4**

17  (*The Queen turns to the picture of Snow White, which hangs on the wall. At first, she looks at it innocently. She brings her fingers to the picture and traces the outline of the girl's face. But then her eyes become filled with fire. Her breath becomes labored. Her heart flutters as if it's about to break through her chest. The Queen puts her hand on her heart, but as she does, it's as if her own flesh is burning her palm. She shakes her hand and blows on it. The Queen makes a piercing sound as if a knife is coming through her heart. Just then, a huntsman appears and stands facing the Queen.*)

18  **Huntsman**: Your majesty?

19  **Queen**: (*delirious*) Take Snow White into the woods. Do away with her. I never want to see her again. Bring me proof that she is dead.

20  (*The huntsman nods and exits. The Queen stands before the mirror, void of emotion, and looking like a statue.*)

**3.** *At first I thought the Mirror was afraid of the Queen because the stage directions said the Mirror spoke in a small sweet voice. But as I read on I see that the Mirror is not afraid of the Queen at all. The Mirror tells the Queen the truth and almost laughs at her.* (Make inferences)

**4.** *Think about how the Queen acts after the Mirror says "I am the…truth." What do you visualize using your sense of seeing, feeling, and hearing?* (Visualize)

## Extend Thinking Questions

Pose one or more questions to engage students more deeply with the text.

• *What details are given about the setting in this scene?*

• *What actions or words show the Queen is angry? Jealous? Cruel?*

### iELD  Paraphrase to Support Comprehension

After paragraph 5: *The Queen asks the Mirror who the fairest in the land is. The Mirror does not answer. The Queen asks again, demanding the Mirror speak up. She tries to break the Mirror.*

After paragraph 13: *The Mirror tells the Queen that Snow White is the fairest. The Queen turns green with envy.*

After paragraph 20: *The Mirror tells the Queen that she speaks the truth. The Queen is enraged. She calls for the Huntsman. She orders the Huntsman to kill Snow White.*

CCSS
**RL.4.1, RL.4.3, RL.4.4, RL.4.5, SL.4.2, L.4.4**

## Set the Stage

**Introduce the Text** *Today I'm going to read aloud a dramatic scene based on the children's book* The Wonderful Wizard of Oz *written by the same author of* The King of the Polar Bears, *L. Frank Baum. In this play, Dorothy is on her way to the Emerald City to ask the Wizard to help her get back to Kansas. On her way there she meets the Scarecrow.*

**Engage Thinking** *The Scarecrow asks Dorothy if the Great Oz will help him. What help do you think he needs? Turn to a partner to share your prediction.*

## Engage with the Text

Read aloud the text at a fluent, expressive pace. Use the suggested prompts to model your thinking, clarify events, and elicit student interaction.

**1.** *The beginning stage directions help me visualize the old Scarecrow leaning against a tree. I can feel what it must be like when Dorothy presses on his belly and hears the Scarecrow speak loudly as he wakes up.* **(Visualize)**

**2.** *The Scarecrow has a hard time speaking and standing. I think this is because he has been asleep for so long. When he finally begins to practice talking and standing, he comes alive.* **(Cause and effect)**

# Let's Go!

## A scene based on "The Wonderful Wizard of Oz"

### Characters

**Dorothy**, a young girl traveling on the yellow brick road

**Scarecrow**, a stuffed man who doesn't have a brain

1   The scene opens with Dorothy standing in the center of the yellow brick road. The road, which is well-lit, zigzags quite a bit, and gives the audience the feeling that it goes on forever. There is a frumpy old scarecrow leaning against a tall tree. Dorothy is staring at it, checking for signs of life. Slowly, she places her hand on the Scarecrow's belly and presses down to see if it moves. Dorothy is just about to give up on the stuffed figure, when it speaks, loudly and with a touch of sleep in its voice. **❶**

2   **Scarecrow**: Good day!

3   **Dorothy**: (*surprised to see that he speaks, she covers her mouth with her hand*) Good day!

4   **Scarecrow**: Good day!

5   **Dorothy**: Good day!

6   **Scarecrow**: Good day!

7   **Dorothy**: Can you say anything else?

8   **Scarecrow**: Can you say anything else?

9   **Dorothy**: No, Scarecrow, I am asking if you can say anything else.

10  **Scarecrow**: No, Scarecrow, I am asking if you can say anything else.

11  **Dorothy**: Well, that's strange!

12  **Scarecrow**: Huh? What's strange?

13  **Dorothy**: So you can talk?

14  **Scarecrow**: Certainly. (*He is trying to get off his post against the tree, but he seems to be stuck to the tree. Dorothy rushes to help the Scarecrow. She manages to unfasten him at the back. Scarecrow is adjusting to having been stiff and asleep for many hours. Scarecrow continues stretching to loosen his limbs and get them in working order. He ends up falling into a split on the middle of the road. He cannot get up from the position. He raises his arm to Dorothy for some help. She takes it, and helps him up. Eventually, he is able to stand upright.*) How do you do?

15  **Dorothy**: I'm pretty well, thank you. (*Relieved to have some company, Dorothy relaxes in Scarecrow's company.*)

16  **Scarecrow**: (*still flexing his joints and yawning quite a bit*) I feel like a new man. Who are you? **2**

17  **Dorothy**: My name is Dorothy and I am going to the Emerald City to ask the Great Oz to send me back to Kansas.

18  **Scarecrow**: (*looking very confused, scratching his head*) Where is the Emerald City and who is Oz?

19  **Dorothy**: Why don't you know?

20  **Scarecrow**: (*Sits down on the curb, slowly and stiffly. Then he rises. He makes several attempts to speak to Dorothy, but he is frustrated because he cannot think of the words. Dorothy patiently waits for him to speak*). I... don't...know... anything. You see, I am stuffed, so I have no brains at all. (*He grabs a part of his right arm with his left hand and squeezes it to demonstrate that he is made of stuffing.*)

21  **Dorothy**: (*putting her arm around Scarecrow to comfort him*) I'm awfully sorry for you.

22  **Scarecrow**: Do. . .you. . .think. . .um (*struggling to remember what he is trying to say*) if I go to the Emerald City with you, that, um. . . Oz would. . .give me some brains? **3**

23  **Dorothy**: (*grabbing Scarecrow's hand*) I cannot tell, but you may come with me, if you like. If Oz will not give you any brains you will be no worse off than you are now. (*Dorothy smiles warmly at Scarecrow, and he seems to stand taller than before. Arm in arm they go down the yellow brick road. The audience can hear them talking and laughing. The sound of their conversation dies down as they become more distant. Lights fade.*) **4**

**3.** *Turn and talk to a partner. Ask and answer questions about the Scarecrow. Use words like "Why", "How", and "What" to ask each other questions.* (Ask questions)

**4.** *At the end of the play the stage directions say that the conversation "dies down." When someone is far away, his or her voice gets lower. I think "dies down" means that their conversation gets lower and lower as they get further away.* (Determine word meaning)

## Extend Thinking Questions

Pose one or more questions to engage students more deeply with the text.

• *Describe the setting of this play. Use evidence from the play, including dialogue and stage directions.*

• *What do Dorothy's reactions to the Scarecrow show you about Dorothy?*

### iELD Paraphrase to Support Comprehension

After paragraph 1: *Dorothy pokes a Scarecrow. The Scarecrow wakes up and speaks in a sleepy voice.*

After paragraph 15: *Dorothy helps the Scarecrow down from the tree. Then she helps him stand upright. The Scarecrow asks Dorothy how she is. She answers that she is well.*

After paragraph 23: *The Scarecrow learns that Dorothy is going to Emerald City to ask the Great Oz to help her get back to Kansas. The Scarecrow joins Dorothy on the road to Emerald City. He hopes that the Great Oz will give him brains.*

CCSS
RL.4.1, RL.4.3, RL.4.4, RL.4.5, SL.4.1c, L.4.5b

## Objective
• Model visualizing

## Set the Stage

**Introduce the Text** *Today I'm going to read aloud an excerpt from the fairy tale* The King of the Polar Bears. *The author, L. Frank Baum published his famous children's book* The Wonderful Wizard of Oz *in 1900. This new kind of children's literature helped Baum become a best-selling children's author. In this part of the book, the polar bears discover that their present King is covered in feathers rather than fur.*

**Engage Thinking** *How do you think the polar bears reacted when they saw their King covered in feathers? Why do you think they had this reaction? Turn to a partner to share your predictions.*

## Engage with the Text

Read aloud the text at a fluent, expressive pace. Use the suggested prompts to model your thinking, clarify events, and elicit student interaction.

**1.** *The narrator describes how the King went toward the two polar bears "with deep growls and a stately tread." This description appeals to my sense of hearing and seeing. It helps me hear and see how loud and scary the King was.* (Visualize)

**2.** *The King knocks the mocker lifeless. I know the one polar bear made fun of the King. So a* mocker *must mean "one who makes fun of someone." The suffix* less *means "without." So* lifeless *means "without life." Now I know the King killed the polar bear who made fun of him.* (Determine word meaning)

# The King of the Polar Bears, Part 1

## by L. Frank Baum

1   When the moon fell away from the sky and the sun came to make the icebergs glitter with the gorgeous shades of the rainbow, two of the polar bears arrived at the King's cavern to ask his advice about the hunting season. But when they saw his great body covered with feathers instead of hair they began to laugh. For this was not their great and wonderful King, one who could rule the polar bears. This was a silly bird King. So one said:

2   "Our mighty King has become a bird! Who ever before heard of a feathered polar bear?"

3   This remark made the King very angry. His people should not make fun of the King. He advanced upon them with deep growls and a stately tread. **❶** For he may be covered with feathers, but he still acted like the king he was. And with one swift blow of his monstrous paw, the proud King knocked the mocker lifeless at his feet. **❷**

4   The other ran away to his fellows and carried the news of the King's strange appearance. The polar bears quickly called a council. The meeting took place on a broad field of ice, where they talked gravely of the remarkable change that had come upon their monarch. Was he still fit to be King? That was the debate.

5   "He is, in reality, no longer a bear," said one. "Nor can he justly be called a bird. But he is half bird and half bear, and so he cannot remain our King."

6   "Then who shall take his place?" asked another.

7   "He who can fight the bird-bear and overcome him," answered an aged and wise member of the group. "Only the strongest is fit to rule our race."

8   There was silence for a time, but at length a great bear moved to the front and said:

9   "I will fight him; I, Woof, the strongest of our race! And I will be King of the Polar Bears."

10 They voted. The others nodded assent in agreement. They then dispatched a messenger to the King to say he must fight the great Woof and master him or resign his sovereignty. If he lost, he would no longer be King.

11 "For a bear with feathers," added the messenger, "is no bear at all, and the king we obey must resemble the rest of us."

12 "I wear feathers because it pleases me," growled the King. "Am I not a great magician? But I will fight, nevertheless, and if Woof masters me he shall be king in my stead."

13 Then he visited his friends, the gulls, who were feasting, and told them of the coming battle. **3**

14 "I shall conquer," he said, proudly. "Yet my people are in the right, for only a hairy one like themselves can hope to command their obedience."

15 The queen gull said:

16 "I met an eagle yesterday, which had made its escape from a big city of men. And the eagle told me he had seen a monstrous polar bear skin thrown over the back of a carriage that rolled along the street. That skin must have been yours, oh king, and if you wish I will send a hundred of my gulls to the city to bring it back to you." **4**

**Unit 2**

**3.** *The setting in this excerpt changes several times. At first the polar bears and the King are in the King's cavern. Then the polar bears meet on a "broad field of ice." Next the messenger returns to the King's cavern. Finally, the King goes near water where the gulls are eating fish. (Describe setting)*

**4.** *Turn and talk to a partner. Based on the last paragraph, what conclusions can you draw about why the King has feathers? (Draw conclusions)*

## Extend Thinking Questions

Pose one or more questions to engage students more deeply with the text.

- *Think about the characters in this story. What actions or words show that strength is a trait the polar bears value?*

- *What did the messenger tell the King? How did the King react to the message? What does this show about the King?*

### iELD Paraphrase to Support Comprehension

After paragraph 3: *The King of the polar bears got so angry at his subject for making fun of his feathers that he knocked him dead.*

After paragraph 10: *The polar bears listened to the wise, old bear. They will choose the strongest bear to fight their King. Now the messenger will tell the King that if he loses the fight he will no longer be king.*

After paragraph 16: *The King agrees that he must win the fight. He visits the gulls. They were the ones who probably gave him the feathers to cover his body. A hunter must have taken the King's fur. The gulls say they will try to get it back for him.*

CCSS
RL.4.1, RL.4.3, RL.4.4, SL.4.2, L.4.4a, L.4.4b

**Set the Stage**

**Introduce the Text** *Today I'm going to continue reading an excerpt from* The King of the Polar Bears. *What happened in the first part of this story?* (Have volunteers summarize part 1.)

*In this excerpt we learn about the skin and the results of the fight between the King and Woof.*

**Engage Thinking** *What do you think will happen when the King and Woof fight? Turn to a partner to share your predictions.*

**Engage with the Text**

Read aloud the text at a fluent, expressive pace. Use the suggested prompts to model your thinking, clarify events, and elicit student interaction.

1. *The author describes the city. I can visualize the streets. I can see an old-fashioned carriage with a white bear skin robe on the opened back seat. Then I see the gulls swooping down together, grabbing the skin and flying away with it.* (Visualize)

2. *The birds swooped down in unison. The root* uni *means "one." So I can tell that the gulls swooped down as one group to seize the skin from the carriage.* (Determine word meaning)

# The King of the Polar Bears, Part 2

1    "Let them go!" said the King, gruffly. And the hundred gulls were soon flying rapidly south towards the city of men.

2    For three days they flew straight as an arrow, until they came to scattered houses, to villages, and finally to the city. Then their search began.

3    The gulls were brave, and cunning, and wise. Upon the fourth day they hovered over the city streets until a carriage rolled along with a great white bear robe thrown over the back seat. One of the gulls pointed to the skin. In unison, the birds swooped down. They seized the skin in their beaks. And rejoicing, they flew quickly away. **①** **②**

4    There was no time to lose, for six days had passed. The King's great battle was upon the seventh day, and they must fly swiftly to reach the Polar Regions by that time.

5    Meanwhile the bird-bear was preparing for his fight. He sharpened his claws in the small crevasses of the ice. He caught a seal and tested his big yellow teeth by crunching its bones between them. And the queen gull set her band to pluming the King bear's feathers until they lay smoothly upon his body.

6    But every day they cast anxious glances into the southern sky, watching for the hundred gulls to bring back the King's own skin.

7    The seventh day came, and all the Polar bears in that region gathered around the King's cavern. Among them was Woof, strong and confident of his success.

8    "The bird-bear's feathers will fly fast enough when I get my claws upon him!" he boasted. The others laughed and encouraged him.

9    The King was disappointed at not having recovered his skin, but he resolved to fight bravely without it. He advanced from the opening of his cavern with a proud and kingly bearing, and when he faced his enemy he gave so terrible a growl that Woof's heart stopped beating for a moment, and he began to realize that a fight with the wise and mighty King of his race was no laughing matter.

10 After exchanging one or two heavy blows against the King, Woof's courage returned. Still, his blows seemed not to affect the King at all. So Woof determined to overcome his adversary by bluster. He would fool the King.

11 "Come nearer, bird bear!" he cried. "Come nearer, that I may pluck your plumage!" It was clear to all that Woof was defying the King.

12 The defiance filled the King with rage. He ruffled his feathers as a bird does, till he appeared to be twice his actual size. Then he strode forward and struck Woof so powerful a blow that his skull crackled like an eggshell and he fell prone upon the ground. **3**

13 While the assembled bears stood looking with fear and wonder at their fallen champion, the sky became darkened.

14 An hundred gulls flew down from above. They dropped a skin covered with pure white hair that glittered in the sun like silver on the King's body. **4**

15 And behold! The bears saw before them the well-known form of their wise and respected master. And with one accord, they bowed their shaggy heads in homage to the mighty King of the Polar Bears.

3. *Turn and talk to a partner. Woof had a plan to fool the King. In your own words, tell your partner what the plan was and why it failed.* (Summarize)

4. *When the gulls return with the skin they drop it onto the King's body. The author says it glittered "like silver." This simile helps me visualize just how beautiful and shiny the King now looks.* (Use similes)

## Extend Thinking Questions

Pose one or more questions to engage students more deeply with the text.

• *Do you think the ending to this part of the story was a good ending? Why or why not?*

• *In this story we learn what the King is like by his words and actions. What are some actions you do to reveal what you are like?*

### iELD Paraphrase to Support Comprehension

**After paragraph 3:** *The gulls fly down to take the skin from the carriage. They grab the skin with their beaks. They fly away with it.*

**After paragraph 10:** *The King got ready for his fight. He fought bravely in his feathers. The King scared Woof with a big growl. Woof would try to fool the King.*

**After paragraph 15:** *Woof mocked the King. This made the King even angrier. The King struck Woof in the head and killed him. Then the gulls dropped the skin onto the King's body. The King had won. The bears all bowed to him.*

CCSS
RL.4.1, RL.4.3, RL.4.4, SL.4.2, RL.4.4b, RL.4.5a

## Set the Stage

**Introduce the Text** *Today I'm going to read aloud a poem called "Ode to La Tortilla." An ode is a poem praising a person or object. The author, Gary Soto, decided to become a writer when he was twenty years old. His stories and poems reflect his own life growing up as a Mexican American. This poem is a tribute to a popular Mexican food called "tortilla."*

**Engage Thinking** *What questions about tortillas do you think will be answered in this poem? Turn to a partner to share your prediction.*

## Engage with the Text

Read aloud the text at a fluent, expressive pace. Use the suggested prompts to model your thinking, clarify events, and elicit student interaction.

**1.** *The introduction gives context clues that tell me exactly what a tortilla is. It is a flat, round bread that is a popular food in Mexico.* (Determine word meaning)

**2.** *The narrator describes what he is doing, where he is, and what he sees. I can visualize him eating the tortilla with butter dripping down his arm. I can see him standing on a lawn watching a sparrow hopping.* (Visualize)

# Ode to La Tortilla

## by Gary Soto

The tortilla dates back to the 1500s. The name was given by the Spaniards to the unleavened flat bread they found in Mexico among the Aztec in the sixteenth century. *Tortilla* comes from the Spanish word *torta*, which means "round cake." **①**

They are flutes

When rolled, butter

Dripping down my elbow

As I stand on the

5  Front lawn, just eating,

Just watching a sparrow

Hop on the lawn,

His breakfast of worms

Beneath the green, green lawn, **②**

10  Worms and a rip of

Tortilla I throw

At his thorny feet.

I eat my tortilla,

Breathe in, breathe out, **③**

15  And return inside,

Wiping my oily hands

On my knee-scrubbed jeans.

The tortillas are still warm

In a dish towel,

20  Warm as gloves just

Taken off, finger by finger.

Mama is rolling

Them out. The radio

On the window sings,

25 *El cielo es azul*. . .

I look in the black pan:

The face of the tortilla

With a bubble of air

Rising. Mama

30 Tells me to turn

It over, and when

I do, carefully,

It's blistered brown.

I count to ten,

35 *Uno, dos, tres*. . .

And then snap it out

Of the pan. The tortilla

Dances in my hands

As I carry it

40 To the drainboard,

Where I smear it

With butter,

The yellow ribbon of butter

That will drip

45 Slowly down my arm

When I eat on the front lawn.

The sparrow will drop

Like fruit

From the tree

50 To stare at me

With his glassy eyes.

I will rip a piece

For him. He will jump

On his food

55 And gargle it down,

Chirp once and fly

Back into the wintry tree. **4**

**3.** *As I read aloud this poem I can hear its steady rhythm. The pauses and repetition such as "green, green lawn" and "Breathe in, breathe out" show the difference between prose and poetry. I also notice how the language appeals to my senses of seeing and touch.* (Refer to parts of a poem)

**4.** *Turn and talk to a partner. Ask: What are some words that appeal to your senses of touch and seeing?* (Ask questions/Use figurative language)

## Extend Thinking Questions

Pose one or more questions to engage students more deeply with the text.

• *Why does the tortilla "dance" in the narrator's hands as he carries it to the drainboard?*

• *In this poem we learn the narrator likes watching nature as he enjoys eating warm tortillas. What do the things you enjoy reveal about you?*

### iELD Paraphrase to Support Comprehension

**After line 12:** *The narrator is eating a tortilla. He throws down a piece of the tortilla for a sparrow on the lawn.*

**After line 39:** *The narrator finishes the tortilla. He goes inside. His mother is making more tortillas. He helps her make them.*

**After line 57:** *The narrator takes the warm tortilla to the drainboard. He will now start the whole process again. He will smear it with butter, eat it on the lawn. The sparrow will come down for a piece. Then the bird will fly away.*

**CCSS**
**RL.4.1, RL.4.3, RL.4.4, RL.4.5, L.4.4a**

**Set the Stage**

**Introduce the Text** *Today I'm going to read aloud a dramatic scene about the character Peter Pan. The author, J.M. Barrie wrote a play in 1904, about a boy who never grew up. When he died, Barrie left the copyright for his Peter Pan stories to a children's hospital in London. This scene from the beginning of the play takes place at night in Wendy's bedroom. Peter is looking for something he has lost.*

**Engage Thinking** *What do you think Peter is looking for? Will he find it? Turn to a partner to share your prediction.*

**Engage with the Text**

Read aloud the text at a fluent, expressive pace. Use the suggested prompts to model your thinking, clarify events, and elicit student interaction.

**1.** *The beginning stage directions describe Peter's actions in detail. They tell what Peter does in sequence. I can use the details to visualize how Peter looks as he runs around the room trying to catch his shadow. I can picture his face changing slowly from happy to sad to crying.* (Visualize)

**2.** *Peter sobs uncontrollably. I know that the prefix -un means "not" and the suffix able means "able to." So* uncontrollably *must mean "not able to be controlled." I guess Peter cannot stop himself from sobbing.* (Determine word meaning)

# Peter and Wendy
## A dramatic scene based on the story of Peter Pan

### Characters

**Peter**

**Peter's Shadow**

**Wendy**

1  (The young boy Peter is scurrying about in the middle of the night. He is prancing around in Wendy's dark and quiet bedroom, searching for something that he has lost, while Wendy is fast asleep. At once, the boy spies his shadow. He smiles, as if he has just won a game. Peter Pan heads toward his shadow, but he misses somehow, and comes up empty-handed. A shudder of disappointment sweeps through him.

2  Peter leans against the wall and slides down to the floor. Disappointment overwhelms him. Spotlight comes up on Peter's face and the audience watches him go from happy to serious to very sad. He starts to whimper and then gradually, he sobs uncontrollably. Wendy wakes up to the sound of the boy's cries.) **❶ ❷**

3  **Wendy**: Boy, why are you crying?

4  (*Peter, who can be very polite, stands and bows to the little girl. She, in turn nods her head from her bed.*

5  **Peter**: What's your name?

6  **Wendy**: (*happily and with much conviction*) Wendy Moira Angela Darling. What is your name?

7  **Peter**: Peter Pan.

8  **Wendy**: Is that all?

9  **Peter**: *Peter stands up and turns his back to Wendy. He is not sure if he wants to continue the conversation with this girl.*) Yes. (*He begins to second-guess himself and his own name.*)

10  **Wendy**: (*genuinely*) I'm so sorry. **❸**

11  **Peter**: (*He turns to face Wendy. He gulps to try and hide the pain*) It doesn't matter.

12 **Wendy**: Tell me, Peter Pan, where do you live?

13 **Peter**: (*abruptly*) Second to the right, and then straight on till morning. (*Peter begins to pace around the room with his quick feet. He looks in the four corners of the room to search again for his shadow.*)

14 **Wendy**: What a funny address!

15 **Peter**: (*He stands still, doubting himself just a bit, and then feeling a little angry toward Wendy Moira Angela Darling.*) No, it isn't.

16 **Wendy**: (*eager to try to explain herself*) I mean, is that what they put on the letters?

17 **Peter**: (*wishing that Wendy had not just said that, certain that it will add to his already bad mood, he crosses his arms against his chest*) Don't get any letters.

18 **Wendy**: (*cautiously*) But your mother gets letters?

19 **Peter**: (*snarling*) Don't have a mother.

20 **Wendy**: (*full of sympathy*) O, Peter, no wonder you were crying. (*Wendy gets out of bed and runs to Peter to comfort him.*)

21 **Peter**: (*rather indignantly, turning his body away from Wendy*) I wasn't crying about mothers. I was crying because I can't get my shadow to stick on. Besides, I wasn't crying.

22 **Wendy**: (*looking very confused*) It has come off?

23 **Peter**: Yes.

24 (*Then Wendy sees Peter's shadow on the floor. She is surprised and sad for Peter, to think he could be separate from his shadow.*)

25 **Wendy**: How awful! (*Wendy sees that Peter has tried to stick on his shadow with a bar of soap. She smiles and decides that she can fix things.*) It must be sewn on!

26 **Peter**: (*innocently*) What's sewn? **4**

3. *Peter gets upset when Wendy says, "Is that all?" when he tells her his name. Wendy says she is sorry because she didn't mean to make him feel badly. This dialogue shows that the two characters do not understand each other very well at this point of the play.* (Make inferences)

4. *Turn and talk to a partner. What mistake does Peter make about his shadow? What mistake does Wendy make about Peter's crying?* (Describe characters)

## Extend Thinking Questions

Pose one or more questions to engage students more deeply with the text.

• *Think about how we learned about different characters. What actions or words show that Peter is insecure? What actions or words show that Wendy is a kind and caring person?*

• *Is this story realistic fiction or a fantasy? How can you tell?*

### iELD Paraphrase to Support Comprehension

After paragraph 2: *Peter is looking for his shadow. Wendy is asleep. Peter cries because he cannot catch his shadow. Wendy wakes up.*

After paragraph 10: *Peter is embarrassed that his name is so short. Wendy is sorry for making him feel badly.*

After paragraph 25: *Wendy thinks Peter is upset because he does not have a mother. She learns that he is upset because he can't get his shadow to stick to him. Wendy explains that he will need it sewn back on.*

**CCSS**
**RL.4.1, RL.4.3, RL.4.4, RL.4.5, SL.4.3, L.4.4b**

**Objective**

• Model determining text importance

**Set the Stage**

**Introduce the Text** *Today I'm going to read aloud from a book called* Three Bird Summer. *In this story, the narrator tells about a trip to the North to visit his Grandma. As I read the story, use all of your senses to picture in your mind what the narrator sees, hears, feels, and smells on this journey.*

**Engage Thinking** *Nature plays an important part in this story. What do you think the narrator will see, hear, and feel on this trip? Turn to a partner to share your prediction.*

**Engage with the Text**

Read aloud the text at a fluent, expressive pace. Use the suggested prompts to model your thinking, clarify events, and elicit student interaction.

**1.** *The first two paragraphs tell what the narrator sees and feels. There are many interesting details, such as the near-darkness, the pine trees, and the sweet, then skunky smell of the night air. However, I think the most important information in this part of the story is that the narrator loves to visit his Grandma in the North in Hubbard Falls.* (Determine text importance)

**2.** *At first I wasn't sure what the word* illuminated *meant. But I reread the words around it: "It was too dark to see anything except the small area illuminated by the light." Since the opposite of dark is light, I can figure that the area that is not dark has been lit up by the light. So* illuminated *probably means "lit up."* (Use antonyms/Determine word meaning)

# Three Bird Summer

## by Sara St. Antoine

1 There was a moment on the drive to Grandma's cabin when you realized you were finally up north. After counting hay bales for mile after mile of flat farm fields, wondering how long it would take for somebody to invent human teleporting so you would never have to make this boring drive again, you'd suddenly see them: pine trees. Their triangular tops rose up over the horizon—a boundary, a front, a promise—like spindly giants in pointy hats, signaling the beginning of the great North.

2 Now, even in the near-darkness, I could see the familiar silhouette of the pines as we drove up the two-lane highway toward the town of Hubbard Falls. I rolled my window all the way down and let the night air rush against my face. Warm, then cool; sweet, then skunky. **1**

3 We skirted the edge of town and followed one last mile of country road to get to Grandma's property. Only a small mailbox on the right side of the road indicated the presence of any kind of human habitation to our left. The woods were dark, and the drive was just a narrow gap between the trees. Mom turned in and drove carefully with her high beams on. We steered around trees and bumped over roots and ruts for nearly half a mile until the cabin appeared, nestled on a rise, with just one exterior light on.

4 Mom parked our car beside Grandma's old Ford station wagon, and we climbed out into the night. It was too dark to see anything except the small area illuminated by the light, but the smell of pines and damp earth was enough to know we'd made it. **2** I loved arriving at night, when the property felt at its most mysterious, when crazy little bugs whipped through the air and unknown creatures snapped branches beneath the distant trees. But part of what I loved, too, was knowing that when I woke up, the curtains of darkness would be lifted and my summer world would be there, waiting for me.

## [The next morning…]

5 I hopped down the wooden steps of the deck and followed the worn path that curved around the cabin and down to the lake. The smell of dry pine needles tickled my nose. When I reached the shore, I walked out the length of the dock and stood at its end, taking everything in.

6　Three Bird Lake was a long oval—more than two miles from end to end and just over a mile across. Small houses dotted the shoreline for most of its perimeter. When my mom was growing up, this had been a summer cabin community with plenty of untouched wooded land. Now most of the neighbors lived here year-round in real houses with grassy lawns. Only Grandma's property was crowded with pines and birches like a genuine northern forest. Lucky for us, she had more than a hundred acres of woods. If you stuck to her property, you could still feel like you were someplace wild, even if the other people on the lake owned Jet Skis and plastic flamingos.

7　The end of the dock was my favorite place on Grandma's property. I spent hours here doing nothing at all. Grandma teased me about it sometimes. "World's best dock-sitter" she sometimes called me. "The neighbors probably think you're a statue, there to scare off gulls." But I didn't care. I loved the big sky and the big lake rolling out at my feet.

8　A cool breeze crossed the water. I felt like the great North was barreling through me with my every breath. Here's what slipped away: schedules, bus rides, the stale smell of the school cafeteria, algebraic equations, Mom and Dad's phone arguments, girl talk, and Grandma's interrogations. Here's what I got in exchange: water sloshing slowly and steadily against the dock like the heartbeat of a great whale. A pair of black-and-white loons swimming into view. Fresh air and a lake, that, right then, felt like it was all mine. **3** **4**

**3.** *The theme of this story is how the narrator responds to the beauty of nature at Three Bird Lake. The details that support this theme tell the specific things the narrator enjoys. For example, "I loved the big sky and the big lake rolling out at my feet."* (Determine theme)

**4.** *Turn and talk to a partner. Ask: Do you think this story is organized by cause and effect, time order, or description? Give examples.* (Determine structure/Ask questions)

## Extend Thinking Questions

Pose one or more questions to engage students more deeply with the text.

- *What are some examples of how the author described the setting and appealed to readers' sense of sight, smell, and feeling?*

- *How would your respond to Three Bird Lake if you visited it? What would you enjoy most? Why?*

### iELD Paraphrase to Support Comprehension

**After paragraph 4:** *The narrator is driving with his mother to Grandma's house up north in Hubbard Falls. It is night. They drive along narrow roads between the trees. The narrator looks forward to the beauty of the summer world that will begin the next day.*

**After paragraph 6:** *Three Bird Lake is a long oval. Small houses are around the lake. Grandma's cabin and property still remain natural. Most others have lawns and "real houses."*

**After paragraph 8:** *The narrator goes to his favorite place, which is the end of the dock. He thinks of how the peacefulness and beauty of nature and the lake will replace the worries of the school year.*

**CCSS**
**RI.4.1, RL.4.2, RL.4.3, RL.4.4, L.4.4a, L.4.5c**

## Objective

• Model determining text importance

## Set the Stage

**Introduce the Text** *Today I'm going to read aloud two poems by a famous English poet, William Wordsworth. Wordsworth's writings were especially influenced by his love of nature. The poems I will read today tell of his observations of two of nature's most beautiful resources: the daffodil and the butterfly.*

**Engage Thinking** *What do you think the poet will focus on in his poem about daffodils? What will he share about his observations of the butterfly? Turn to a partner to share your prediction.*

## Engage with the Text

Read aloud the text at a fluent, expressive pace. Use the suggested prompts to model your thinking, clarify events, and elicit student interaction.

**1.** *Poems often contain figurative language. The first line of "I Wandered Lonely as a Cloud" contains a simile. The poet compares his loneliness to a cloud floating above "vales and hills." This simile helps me picture a cloud floating above in the big blue sky all alone. It helps me to really share his feeling of loneliness.* (Use similes/Visualize)

**2.** *At first I wasn't sure what* jocund *meant. But when I reread the lines before it I see that the poet describes how happy and lively the waves are. So "jocund company" must mean "happy and lively company."* (Determine word meaning)

# I Wandered Lonely as a Cloud

## by William Wordsworth

I wandered lonely as a cloud
That floats on high o'er vales and hills, **①**
When all at once I saw a crowd,
A host, of golden daffodils;
5 Beside the lake, beneath the trees,
Fluttering and dancing in the breeze.

Continuous as the stars that shine
And twinkle on the milky way,
They stretched in never-ending line
10 Along the margin of a bay;
Ten thousand saw I at a glance,
Tossing their heads in sprightly dance.

The waves beside them danced; but they
Outdid the sparkling waves in glee;
15 A poet could not but be gay
In such a jocund company; **②**
I gazed—and gazed—but little thought
What wealth the show to me had brought.

For oft, when on my couch I lie
20 In vacant or in pensive mood,
They flash upon that inward eye
Which is the bliss of solitude;
And then my heart with pleasure fills,
And dances with the daffodils. **③**

# To a Butterfly

I've watched you now a full half-hour,

Self-poised upon that yellow flower;

And, little Butterfly! indeed

I know not if you sleep or feed.

5   More motionless! and then

How motionless!—not frozen seas

What joy awaits you, when the breeze

Hath found you out among the trees,

And calls you forth again;

10   This plot of orchard-ground is ours;

My trees they are, my Sister's flowers;

Here rest your wings when they are weary;

Here lodge as in a sanctuary!

Come often to us, fear no wrong;

15   Sit near us on the bough!

We'll talk of sunshine and of song,

And summer days when we were young;

Sweet childish days, that were as long

As twenty days are now. **4**

**Unit 3**

**3.** *I can figure out the theme of "I Wandered Lonely as a Cloud" by identifying the important details. For example, the poet was lonely until he saw the daffodils. The daffodils were so beautiful they "outdid the sparkling waves." When he thinks about the daffodils his "heart with pleasure fills." These details support the theme of the beauty and importance of nature.* (Determine text importance/Theme)

**4.** *What do you think the theme is for "To a Butterfly"? What details support your answer?* (Determine text importance/Theme)

## Extend Thinking Questions

Pose one or more questions to engage students more deeply with the text.

- *From whose point of view is each poem told? How can you tell?*

- *What have you observed in nature that made you feel like the poet did when he observed the daffodils?*

### iELD Paraphrase to Support Comprehension

**After stanza 2 of "I Wandered Lonely as a Cloud":** *The poet sees a field of golden daffodils. They look like twinkling stars.*

**After stanza 4 of "I Wandered Lonely as a Cloud":** *The poet does not realize how much joy the daffodils bring at first. Then when he lies alone he remembers them. He realizes what happiness they bring.*

**After the last line of "To a Butterfly":** *The poet watches a butterfly on a tree. The tree is in his and his sister's garden. He invites the butterfly to return to their garden whenever it needs to be safe.*

**CCSS**
**RL.4.1, RL.4.2, RL.4.4, RL.4.5, RL.4.6, SL.4.2, L.4.4a, L.4.5a**

## Set the Stage

**Introduce the Text** *Today I'm going to read aloud an article about the history of Yosemite National Park. This important tourist attraction is visited by millions of people every year. The article begins with how the once secret valley in Yosemite eventually became known to the world for its resources and beauty.*

**Engage Thinking** *Why do you think Yosemite became so popular? Turn to a partner to share your prediction.*

## Engage with the Text

Read aloud the text at a fluent, expressive pace. Use the suggested prompts to model your thinking, clarify events, and elicit student interaction.

**1.** *The beginning of this article tells many facts about Yosemite Valley. Some facts are more important than others. For example, it is interesting that Yosemite Valley is as large at Rhode Island. However, it is more important to understand how after 1851 its walls of granite and rich supply of plants and animals became a tourist attraction.* (Determine text importance)

**2.** *Even though Yosemite became a state park, it was not fully protected. People squatted illegally and destroyed some of the meadows. This caused the government to make it a national park to protect it.* (Cause and effect)

# A Famous Secret Valley

## by Jerry Miller

1   Only one road enters Yosemite Valley. This road circles the narrow, seven-mile-long valley, then exits where it entered. Yet, this small valley, lying in the center of California's Sierra Nevada, is one of the most visited in the world. It forms the very heart of Yosemite National Park—a park almost as large as the state of Rhode Island.

2   For the native people who lived in the valley for thousands of years, it provided the perfect place of safety. Carved by glaciers, the valley's sheer walls of granite—stretching a staggering 4,000 feet high—hid a rich supply of plants, fish, and other animals.

3   The Ahwahneechee Indians kept their valley a secret from European settlers until 1851. The first white people to enter were California militia who followed native raiders back into their valley home after conflicts with gold miners. The soldiers eventually forced the native people to abandon their natural fortress. They also spread the news about the wonders of Yosemite Valley. In 1855, a writer, James Hutchings, and a painter, Thomas Ayres, visited the valley. Publication of their articles and pictures attracted even more writers, artists, and tourists. **①**

4   By 1864, many Californians had decided that the area should be preserved for tourists. In the midst of the Civil War (1861–1865), Congress and President Abraham Lincoln gave the Yosemite Valley and a nearby grove of giant sequoias to the state of California. The area became the nation's first park set aside by the federal government for its scenic value.

5   Becoming a state park, however, did not provide adequate protection for the valley. Settlers continued to squat illegally on park land. Large herds of sheep and pigs nearly destroyed the meadows. In 1899, John Muir, a writer and lover of wilderness, joined with Robert Underwood Johnson, a wealthy magazine editor. They began a campaign to protect Yosemite by making it a national park. The campaign succeeded. An area almost the same size as the present park was set aside for preservation in 1890. **②**

6   However, the battle over the proper use of Yosemite still continues.... As a result, use of the park has changed over time.

7   The bitterest battle began in the early 1900s. After a great earthquake and water shortage in 1906, the city of San Francisco asked to build a dam that would cover the park's magnificent Hetch Hetchy Valley in water. Environmentalists struggled for years to block it, but the dam was finally authorized in 1913, and the valley disappeared beneath an artificial lake by 1923. Today, the dam provides fresh water and electric power to much of San Francisco. But many still argue that the dam should be torn down and the valley restored. **3**

8   In 1984, preservationists won one of their largest victories. That's when the park was declared a World Heritage Site, which means it was identified as having "outstanding value" to humans for its cultural and natural heritage.

9   There are magnificent cliffs, domes, and spires of granite. El Capitan is one of the largest granite monoliths in the world, rising more than 3,000 feet above the valley floor. Half Dome at 8,842 feet high is probably the world's most photographed rock. With a pair of binoculars, you can watch rock climbers from around the world scrambling up these great cliffs....

10  These cliffs are also home to some of the world's tallest and most breathtaking waterfalls.... In addition to rivers, streams, and hundreds of falls, the park has 3,200 lakes.

11  Aside from granite and water, what you see depends on what part you visit. Yosemite ranges from 2,000 to 13,000 feet in altitude. Hiking from the park's lowest to highest places takes you through almost as many landscapes as hiking from Mexico to Alaska. The park has 800 miles of wilderness hiking trails.

12  Do you like wildflowers? Discover 1,400 species of flowering plants, shrubs, and trees.... The world's largest trees, the giant sequoias, are the greatest attraction. Some of these may reach 3,000 years old, 300 feet high, and measure 50 feet around.

13  With 95 percent of Yosemite designated as wilderness, the park provides plenty of space for wild creatures, too.... Two hundred forty-seven species of birds can be found in the park. One of these is the great gray owl, a threatened species in California. With all these attractions, it's no wonder that Yosemite's once-secret valley draws millions of visitors each year. **4**

3. *Environmentalists struggled to prevent the dam from being built. I know the suffix -ist means "a person or people who." So environmentalists are people who are concerned about the environment.* (Build vocabulary)

4. *Turn and talk to a partner. Ask: What are the most interesting facts you learned about Yosemite?* (Summarize/ Ask questions)

## Extend Thinking Questions

Pose one or more questions to engage students more deeply with the text.

• *How did the author of this article organize the information?*

• *What are two different ways people responded to the resources and beauty of Yosemite?*

### iELD Paraphrase to Support Comprehension

**After paragraph 3:** *Yosemite Valley lies in the center of California's Sierra Nevada. For thousands of years the native people lived there. In 1851 California militia forced the native people out.*

**After paragraph 8:** *As the years passed, Yosemite was declared a state park, then a national park. In 1923, a dam was completed and a lake covered the Hetch Hetchy Valley. In 1984 the park was declared a World Heritage Site.*

**After paragraph 13:** *Yosemite is home to thousands of resources. There are granite cliffs, waterfalls, and lakes. Plants include a huge variety of trees, flowering plants, and shrubs. The park provides space for animals such as black bears, river otters, and mountain lions, as well as 247 species of birds.*

CCSS
RI.4.1, RI.4.2, RI.4.3, RI.4.4, SL.4.3, L.4.4b

**Unit 3**

## Objective
• Model determining text importance

## Set the Stage

**Introduce the Text** *Today I'm going to read aloud a biography about a nineteenth-century American artist, Grafton Tyler Brown. The article begins with a description of one of his most famous paintings, "A Canyon River with Pines and Figures." But as you listen to this biography, you will learn that Brown was much more than just an artist.*

**Engage Thinking** *What other accomplishments do you think you will learn about in this biography? Turn to a partner to share your prediction.*

## Engage with the Text

Read aloud the text at a fluent, expressive pace. Use the suggested prompts to model your thinking, clarify events, and elicit student interaction.

**1.** *There was a lot of interesting information about Grafton Tyler Brown in the first two paragraphs. The description of his famous painting helped me picture what it looked like. However, I think the most important information was that Brown was the first African American painter of the American West. This information tells me why his work is so important.* (Determine text importance)

**2.** *Sometimes authors provide definitions for words that are unfamiliar. I didn't know what* lithography *was, but the author included the definition: "a form of printmaking" to help readers understand the term. She also included the definition of* cartography, *which is "mapmaking."* (Determine word meaning)

# Portrait of An Artist: Grafton Tyler Brown

## by Deborah Nevins

1   Steep walls of rock jut up from both sides of a silvery, rushing river. The cliffs are sharp and jagged. Under a white sky, they glow in pale reds, pinks, and creamy sand tones of the minerals that formed them. The reds contrast with the deep greens of the dark pine forests below. Can you picture it?

2   This is a large painting called "A Canyon River with Pines and Figures." The artist, Grafton Tyler Brown, painted it in 1886. Today we recognize Brown as the first African American painter of the American West. **1**

3   Brown was born in Harrisburg, Pennsylvania, in 1841. At that time, slavery was still common in the United States, but Brown was born to a free black family. As he grew up, he learned the art of lithography, which is a form of printmaking, and he also learned cartography, or mapmaking. In the days before photography, artists like Brown provided illustrations and maps for all sorts of products. Newspapers, books, pamphlets, posters, and even advertising used lithographic prints.

4   In the mid-1850s, when he was still a teenager, Brown moved to San Francisco, where he found work at a lithography company. But in the West, the young man found more than a new job—he found a whole new life. He discovered entirely new landscapes; the American West, in those days, was still quite wild and mostly undeveloped. Brown saw vistas unlike anything he had seen back East. The magnificent scenes made a deep impression on him. **2**

5   After a few years, Brown bought the lithography shop he worked for. More and more people were moving west, and Brown used his skills to document new settlements that were rapidly springing up. In 1872, he sold his business so he could travel. He passed through Oregon, Washington, Idaho, Wyoming, Nevada, and British Columbia, Canada. Along the way, the artist produced many maps and illustrations. One of his most important works was a book called *The Illustrated History of San Mateo County* (1878), which featured seventy-two views of the county's communities and ranches.

6    Brown decided to work with paints to better capture the sights that moved him. He painted natural scenes from Yosemite Park in California to Yellowstone Park in Wyoming. He painted Mount Rainier and the Cascade Mountains. And he painted the waterfalls, chasms, rocky cliffs, gentle rolling hills, lakes, rivers, and snow-capped mountains of the Pacific Northwest. Later in his life, Brown worked as a draughtsman for the U.S. Army Engineer's Office in St. Paul, Minnesota. There he charted the upper Mississippi region and remained until his death in 1918. **3**

7    Critics praise Brown's works as honest depictions of the land. Brown's paintings are not romanticized exaggerations of nature like those of some other artists of the Great West. For example, Brown's skies are not always bright blue. Sometimes, they are pale, gray, or cloudy. And although Brown's painting style is realistic, his canvasses are also carefully produced with rhythmic, repetitive shapes, lines, and colors. These design elements create a sense of pattern and motion. At the same time, surprisingly, they give off a sense of quiet and stillness. Although his subjects are often very grand, Brown used soft, muted colors. These contrasts between movement and stillness, awe and quiet reflection, give us an insight into Brown's feelings about nature. **4**

**3.** *The information about Brown's life is organized in time order. The introduction describes his famous painting, but then the important events in his life are told in order from his birth in 1841 to his death in 1918. (Cite structure)*

**4.** *Turn and talk to a partner. How are Brown's works different from some other artists? What details support this statement? (Summarize)*

## Extend Thinking Questions

Pose one or more questions to engage students more deeply with the text.

• *What details support the inference that Brown was skillful and hardworking?*

• *How did Brown respond to the scenes he discovered when he moved out West?*

**iELD  Paraphrase to Support Comprehension**

After paragraph 2: *Grafton Tyler Brown was the first African American artist of the American West. One of his most famous paints is "A Canyon River with Pines and Figures." He painted it in 1886.*

After paragraph 6: *Brown was born in 1841 in Harrisburg, PA. As he grew up, he learned lithography and cartography. After moving west in the mid 1850s, he discovered a new landscape which made a deep impression on him. He made maps and illustrations of new settlements in the West. He then moved on to painting waterfalls, cliffs, and other natural wonders of the West.*

After paragraph 7: *Brown's artwork is realistic with rhythmic repetitive shapes and colors. They have a contrast between movement and stillness. They demonstrate his strong feelings about nature.*

CCSS
RI.4.1, RI.4.2, RI.4.4, RI.4.5, L.4.4a

Unit 3

## Objective

• Model determining text importance

## Set the Stage

**Introduce the Text** *Today I'm going to read aloud from the book* The Secret Garden. *The author, Frances Hodgson Burnett was born in 1894 in England. She became a playwright and author best known for her children's novels.*

The Secret Garden *begins when Mary Lennox loses her parents to malaria. Eventually she is sent to live with a distant uncle in Yorkshire, England. In part 1, we join Mary and the maidservant's son Dickon. Mary decides to share her discovery of the garden with Dickon.*

**Engage Thinking** *How do you think Dickon will react when he sees the secret garden? Turn to a partner to share your prediction.*

## Engage with the Text

Read aloud the text at a fluent, expressive pace. Use the suggested prompts to model your thinking, clarify events, and elicit student interaction.

**1.** *The author says Mary was imperious. I'm not sure what* imperious *means. The sentence before says she was contrary and obstinate but did not care. So since she didn't care, I think she must have felt superior in some way. When I check a dictionary I see* imperious *means "arrogant or superior," so I am correct.* **(Determine word meaning)**

**2.** *The narrator says that Dickon looked around the garden and saw "gray trees with the gray creepers climbing over them and hanging from their branches." This description helps me visualize a creepy, overgrown hidden garden.* **(Visualize)**

# The Secret Garden, Part 1

## by Frances Hodgson Burnett

1  Mistress Mary got up from the log at once. She knew she felt contrary again, and obstinate, and she did not care at all. She was imperious … and at the same time hot and sorrowful. **❶**

2  "Come with me and I'll show you," she said.

3  She led him round the laurel path and to the walk where the ivy grew so thickly. Dickon followed her with a queer, almost pitying, look on his face. He felt as if he were being led to look at some strange bird's nest and must move softly. When she stepped to the wall and lifted the hanging ivy he started. There was a door and Mary pushed it slowly open and they passed in together, and then Mary stood and waved her hand round defiantly.

4  "It's this," she said. "It's a secret garden, and I'm the only one in the world who wants it to be alive."

5  Dickon looked round and round about it, and round and round again.

6  "Eh!" he almost whispered, "it is a queer, pretty place! It's like as if a body was in a dream."

7  For two or three minutes he stood looking round him, while Mary watched him, and then he began to walk about softly, even more lightly than Mary had walked the first time she had found herself inside the four walls. His eyes seemed to be taking in everything—the gray trees with the gray creepers climbing over them and hanging from their branches, the tangle on the walls and among the grass, the evergreen alcoves with the stone seats and tall flower urns standing in them. **❷**

8  "I never thought I'd see this place," he said at last, in a whisper.

9  "Did you know about it?" asked Mary.

10  She had spoken aloud and he made a sign to her.

11  "We must talk low," he said, "or someone'll hear us an' wonder what's to do in here."

12  "Oh! I forgot!" said Mary, feeling frightened and putting her hand quickly against her mouth. "Did you know about the garden?" she asked again when she had recovered herself. Dickon nodded.

13 "Martha told me there was one as no one ever went inside," he answered. "Us used to wonder what it was like."

14 He stopped and looked round at the lovely gray tangle about him, and his round eyes looked queerly happy.

15 "Eh! the nests as'll be here come springtime," he said. "It'd be th' safest nestin' place in England. No one never comin' near an' tangles o' trees an' roses to build in. I wonder all th' birds on th' moor don't build here."

16 Mistress Mary put her hand on his arm again without knowing it.

17 "Will there be roses?" she whispered. "Can you tell? I thought perhaps they were all dead."

18 "Eh! No! Not them—not all of 'em!" he answered. "Look here!"

19 He stepped over to the nearest tree—an old, old one with gray lichen all over its bark, but upholding a curtain of tangled sprays and branches. He took a thick knife out of his pocket and opened one of its blades.

20 "There's lots o' dead wood as ought to be cut out," he said. "An' there's a lot o' old wood, but it made some new last year. This here's a new bit," and he touched a shoot which looked brownish green instead of hard, dry gray. Mary touched it herself in an eager, reverent way. **3**

21 "That one?" she said. "Is that one quite alive—quite?" **4**

22 Dickon curved his wide smiling mouth.

23 "It's as wick as you or me," he said; and Mary remembered that Martha had told her that "wick" meant "alive" or "lively."

24 "I'm glad it's wick!" she cried out in her whisper. "I want them all to be wick. Let us go round the garden and count how many wick ones there are."

3. *The garden seems to be dead at first. But Dickon uses his knife to cut into some old wood to find "brownish green instead of hard, dry gray." He knew this meant the tree had new growth. I think this information is important. It shows that this garden may eventually flourish. (Determine text importance)*

4. *Turn and talk to a partner. Discuss: What mood does the author set as the children enter the garden together? (Determine mood)*

## Extend Thinking Questions

Pose one or more questions to engage students more deeply with the text.

- *Readers learn that Dickon knew about the garden but never saw it. What actions and words revealed this about Dickon?*

- *Why is this garden so important to Mary?*

### iELD Paraphrase to Support Comprehension

After paragraph 3: *Mary tells Dickon about the secret garden she found. Then she invites him to come with her to see it.*

After paragraph 13: *Mary leads Dickon through the door of her secret garden. They both quietly look around at the tangled branches and gray trees. Mary learns that Dickon knew about the garden, but never saw it.*

After paragraph 20: *Mary asks Dickon if all of the growth is dead. Dickon cuts out a piece of dead wood. He shows Mary that there is a little bit of new growth.*

CCSS
RL.4.1, RL.4.3, RL.4.4, L.4.4c

**Unit 3**

**Set the Stage**

**Introduce the Text** *Today I'm going to continue reading aloud from* The Secret Garden. *Let's summarize what we read in part 1.* (Have volunteers summarize part 1.)

*In part 2, we will join Mary and Dickon as they explore the garden together. They will find surprises in the garden as well as about each other.*

**Engage Thinking** *What surprises do you think Mary and Dickon will find? Turn to a partner to share your prediction.*

**Engage with the Text**

Read aloud the text at a fluent, expressive pace. Use the suggested prompts to model your thinking, clarify events, and elicit student interaction.

**1.** *At the end of Part 1 Mary asked Dickon if a shoot from a plant was alive. Dickon said: "It's as wick as you or me." Wick means "alive." As I read on, I expect that word will be used again and will remember its meaning.* (Build vocabulary)

**2.** *As I listen to Dickon and Mary's conversation I can hear the difference in the way they speak. I can tell Dickon's English is not as proper as Mary's. I can also see how excited Dickon is as he learns about Mary's gardening skills.* (Visualize/Describe characters)

# The Secret Garden, Part 2

1 She quite panted with eagerness, and Dickon was as eager as she was. They went from tree to tree and from bush to bush. Dickon carried his knife in his hand and showed her things which she thought wonderful.

2 "They've run wild," he said, "but th' strongest ones has fair thrived on it. The delicatest ones has died out, but th' others has growed an' growed, an' spread an' spread, till they's a wonder. See here!" and he pulled down a thick gray, dry-looking branch. "A body might think this was dead wood, but I don't believe it is—down to th' root. I'll cut it low down an' see."

3 He knelt and with his knife cut the lifeless-looking branch through, not far above the earth.

4 "There!" he said exultantly. "I told thee so. There's green in that wood yet. Look at it."

5 Mary was down on her knees before he spoke, gazing with all her might.

6 "When it looks a bit greenish an' juicy like that, it's wick," he explained. "When th' inside is dry an' breaks easy, like this here piece I've cut off, it's done for. There's a big root here as all this live wood sprung out of, an' if th' old wood's cut off an' it's dug round, and took care of there'll be—" he stopped and lifted his face to look up at the climbing and hanging sprays above him—"there'll be a fountain o' roses here this summer."

7 They went from bush to bush and from tree to tree. He was very strong and clever with his knife and knew how to cut the dry and dead wood away, and could tell when an unpromising bough or twig had still green life in it. In the course of half an hour Mary thought she could tell too, and when he cut through a lifeless-looking branch she would cry out joyfully under her breath when she caught sight of the least shade of moist green. The spade, and hoe, and fork were very useful. He showed her how to use the fork while he dug about roots with the spade and stirred the earth and let the air in.

8 They were working industriously round one of the biggest standard roses when he caught sight of something which made him utter an exclamation of surprise.

9 "Why!" he cried, pointing to the grass a few feet away. "Who did that there?"

10 It was one of Mary's own little clearings round the pale green points.

11 "I did it," said Mary.

12 "Why, I thought tha' didn't know nothin' about gardenin'," he exclaimed. **2**

13 "I don't," she answered, "but they were so little, and the grass was so thick and strong, and they looked as if they had no room to breathe. So I made a place for them. I don't even know what they are."

14 Dickon went and knelt down by them, smiling his wide smile.

15 "Tha' was right," he said. "A gardener couldn't have told thee better. They'll grow now like Jack's bean-stalk. They're crocuses an' snowdrops, an' these here is narcissuses," turning to another patch, "an here's daffydowndillys. Eh! they will be a sight."

16 He ran from one clearing to another.... He was working all the time he was talking and Mary was following him and helping him with her fork or the trowel.

17 "There's a lot of work to do here!" he said once, looking about quite exultantly.

18 "Will you come again and help me to do it?" Mary begged. "I'm sure I can help, too. I can dig and pull up weeds, and do whatever you tell me. Oh! do come, Dickon!"

19 "I'll come every day if tha' wants me, rain or shine," he answered stoutly. "It's the best fun I ever had in my life—shut in here an' wakenin' up a garden." **3** **4**

3. *Mary and Dickon both seem so excited about the garden. Mary asks Dickon to help her work in the garden. She promises that she can help too. He says he will come every day. I think it's important to know that the garden gives them both a sense of safety and happiness.* (Determine text importance/Make inferences)

4. *Turn and talk to a partner. What have Mary and Dickon learned about the garden? About each other?* (Summarize)

## Extend Thinking Questions

Pose one or more questions to engage students more deeply with the text.

• *What did Dickon observe in the garden? What did Mary observe?*

• *How do you think you would respond to the garden if you had been with Dickon and Mary?*

### iELD Paraphrase to Support Comprehension

After paragraph 4: *Mary asks Dickon if the shoots they found are alive. He tells her they are. Dickon then leads Mary around the garden to find other wonders.*

After paragraph 7: *Dickon cuts through lifeless-looking branches to show green life peeking through. They work together to cut dead wood away and stir the earth to let air in and help the growth.*

After paragraph 19: *Dickon discovers that Mary had cleared grass from around green points that would grow to be flowers. They continue clearing weeds. Dickon agrees to help Mary work in the garden whenever she wanted.*

CCSS
RL.4.1, RL.4.3, RL.4.4, L.4.4a

## Set the Stage

**Introduce the Text** *Today I'm going to read aloud a biography about a twentieth-century American biologist and writer, Rachel Carson. Listen closely to learn how Rachel Carson's love of nature led her to help other people understand the importance of caring for our environment.*

**Engage Thinking** *Rachel Carson loved to observe sea life. How do you think her observations may have affected her thoughts about nature? Turn to a partner to share your prediction.*

## Engage with the Text

Read aloud the text at a fluent, expressive pace. Use the suggested prompts to model your thinking, clarify events, and elicit student interaction.

**1.** *I wonder why the author began this article by describing a specific event in Rachel Carson's life. Did she want to show what Rachel Carson was like? Did she want to show why she was famous?* (Ask questions)

**2.** *When Rachel went to college she studied biology. I know bio- means "life" and -logy is "a branch of knowledge or science." So biology must mean a branch of science that deals with the study of life. Rachel Carson became a biologist. She was a scientist who studied living things such as plants and animals.* (Build vocabulary)

# Rachel Carson's World of Wonder

## by Sylvia Salsbury

1    Imagine you're a scientist studying the sea life along the Maine coast. It is early morning and the tide has gone out. A deep pool of cold water, trapped by rocks at low tide, looks like a good place to study the animals that live on the seashore. You step into the tide pool and feel the water cover most of your legs. Soon you are watching a crab. Perhaps you even discover one of the crab's enemies. You might find sea flowers (anemones) with stinging tentacles, green sea urchins, or tiny fish called blennies. You lose track of the time. All you are thinking about is the community of small creatures living in your tide pool.

2    Finally you start to climb out of the water. But your legs are so cold you can't feel them. This happened one morning in 1951 to biologist Rachel Carson. Her excitement and wonder about the mysteries of the sea kept her in the water too long. Luckily, a friend helped her out of the tide pool and found her a warm blanket. **❶**

## Rachel discovers her love of science

3    As a child, Rachel said she was happiest "with wild birds and creatures as companions." She and her mother spent many hours outdoors, walking and observing plants and animals.

4    When she got to college, Rachel found she especially liked learning about biology. She was also becoming a fine writer. Later, she was one of the first two women to be hired as a biologist and writer for the U.S. Fish and Wildlife Service. **❷**

5    Rachel loved the sea. She went to the shore as often as she could to collect and study living samples of sea life. When she finished, she always carried the crabs, starfish, and other creatures back to the exact place where she found them, and set them free. Sometimes at night Rachel used her flashlight to study seashore animals that hid during the day. In her notebook, she wrote down all that she discovered.

6  In a letter to a friend, she described what she saw at the shore one day *. . . where the pink crust of corallines over the rock has become thick and heavy enough that pieces can be chipped off, there is a whole community of creatures living in it and under it. That, again, was a whole evening's work and entertainment at the microscope, the high point of which was the discovery of an exquisitely beautiful worm (don't laugh, and don't shiver; it is the most beautiful worm in the world)...*

## Writing about nature

7  Rachel wrote many articles about nature. She wanted people to know that birds, fish, and all living things need a special area, or habitat, in which to live. She also wrote books, including her famous book, *The Sea Around Us*. Two cats kept her company while she did her writing. "Buzzie in particular used to sleep on my writing table," she said. While planning what to write, she sometimes lightly sketched her cat's face over the words on her paper!

## Rachel warns about pesticides

8  Rachel Carson was one of the first scientists to worry about spraying insects and weeds with poisonous chemicals, called pesticides. Pesticides can help produce more and better crops. But Rachel knew that this good must be balanced against the danger pesticides can cause to other living things. For example, spraying certain chemicals in an area can also kill friendly insects like the bees that pollinate fruit trees.

9  Some scientists believed that they could control nature to suit humans. Rachel warned that changing things in nature without knowing the results could be dangerous. We need to "think of ourselves as only a tiny part of a vast and incredible universe," she said.

10  Rachel decided she must write about the danger of pesticides. She carefully checked all her scientific reports. She knew her book would be attacked for its outspoken point of view.

11  *Silent Spring* was published in 1962. The book started a worldwide discussion about how humans should take care of nature. Soon scientists were asked to develop ways of controlling particular pests without harming other living things. The U.S. government established the Environmental Protection Agency.

12  Rachel's book affected all people, not just scientists. In 1970, our nation celebrated the first Earth Day, a sign that ordinary citizens were beginning to understand and care about the earth. **3** **4**

**Unit 3**

3. *The section called "Rachel warns about pesticides" is mainly about how Rachel Carson's research on the dangers of pesticides helped save nature. For example, after she wrote the book* Silent Spring, *the Environmental Protection Agency was established. Also, the first Earth Day was celebrated.* (Determine main idea/Details)

4. *Turn and talk to a partner. What are two important facts you learned from this article? What are two interesting facts that are not as important?* (Determine text importance)

## Extend Thinking Questions

Pose one or more questions to engage students more deeply with the text.

• *What do you think was Rachel Carson's greatest accomplishment? Why?*

• *How did Rachel Carson respond to nature?*

**iELD** **Paraphrase to Support Comprehension**

After paragraph 5: *Since she was a child, Rachel Carson loved to study nature. She especially liked to study plants and animals in the sea. She became a biologist and writer.*

After paragraph 7: *Rachel wrote many books and articles. She wanted people to know the importance of habitats.*

After paragraph 11: *Rachel Carson warned the world about the dangers of pesticides. Her famous book* Silent Spring *started a worldwide discussion about taking care of nature. Soon scientists began finding ways to control pests without harming nature.*

**CCSS**
**RI.4.1, RI.4.2, RI.4.3, RI.4.4, SL.4.1c, L.4.4b**

## Set the Stage

**Introduce the Text** *Today I'm going to read aloud two poems about nature. "Kindness to Animals" is a lesson for children to never be cruel to animals. The second poem, "Delight in Nature," tells what the poet enjoys about nature.*

**Engage Thinking** *What animals do you think the poet will talk about in "Kindness to Animals?" What objects of nature might the poet describe in "Delight in Nature?" Turn to a partner to share your prediction.*

## Engage with the Text

Read aloud the text at a fluent, expressive pace. Use the suggested prompts to model your thinking, clarify events, and elicit student interaction.

1. *When I read the first six lines of "Kindness to Animals" I can hear the rhythm of the poem. I hear the stress of every other syllable. This rhythm is a characteristic of poetry that prose does not have.* (Cite rhythm)

2. *At first I wasn't sure what a lark was. I reread the words after it, such as "soaring high" and "fluttering on an untired wing." Now I know that a lark is probably a bird.* (Use context clues)

# Kindness to Animals

Little children, never give

Pain to things that feel and live:

Let the gentle robin come

For the crumbs you save at home,—

5 As his meat you throw along

He'll repay you with a song; **1**

Never hurt the timid hare

Peeping from her green grass lair,

Let her come and sport and play

10 On the lawn at close of day;

The little lark goes soaring high.

To the bright windows of the sky,

Singing as if 'twere always spring,

And fluttering on an untired wing,— **2**

15 Oh! let him sing his happy song,

Nor do these gentle creatures wrong. **3**

# Delight in Nature

Isn't it lovely,

the little river cutting through the gorge

when you approach it slowly

while trout are standing

5   behind stones in the stream?


Isn't it lovely,

the river's thick grass banks?

But I shall never again

Meet Willow Twig, my dear friend

10  I long to see again.

Well, that's how it is.

The winding run

of the stream through the gorge

is lovely.


15  Isn't it lovely

The bluish rocky island out there

when you approach it slowly?

What does it matter

That the blowing spirits of the air

20  Stray over the rocks

because the island is lovely

when you approach it

at an easy pace

and haul it in? **4**

Unit 3

**3.** *I can figure out the theme of "Kindness to Animals" by identifying the important details. For example, the poet tells children to "never give pain to things that feel and live" and "never hurt the timid hare." These details support the theme of the importance of treating animals well. (Determine text importance/Theme)*

**4.** *Turn and talk to a partner. Ask: What do you think is the theme of "Delight in Nature"? What details support this? (Determine text importance/Theme/ Ask questions)*

## Extend Thinking Questions

Pose one or more questions to engage students more deeply with the text.

- *What mood did the poet create in each poem? Give examples of specific language that helped create each mood.*

- *Retell in your own words how the narrator of each poem responds to nature.*

### iELD Paraphrase to Support Comprehension

After line 16 of "Kindness to Animals": *The narrator tells children to be kind to animals. For example, children are told to feed a robin, let a rabbit play on the lawn, and let the lark sing.*

After line 14 of "Delight in Nature": *The poet describes how lovely a river and its grassy banks are.*

After the last line of "Delight in Nature": *The poet describes a winding stream. Finally, the poet describes how lovely an island looks as you approach it.*

**CCSS**
**RL.4.1, RL.4.2, RL.4.3, RL.4.4, RL.4.5, SL.4.2, L.4.4a, L.4.5b**

### Objective

• Model making inferences/predictions

### Set the Stage

**Introduce the Text** *Today I'm going to read aloud a poem by Mary Howitt called "The Spider and The Fly." Listen to see how the spider tries to convince the fly to come into his home.*

**Engage Thinking** *How do you think the spider will try to lure the fly? Turn to a partner to share your prediction.*

### Engage with the Text

Read aloud the text at a fluent, expressive pace. Use the suggested prompts to model your thinking, clarify events, and elicit student interaction.

1. *This first verse has a rhyming pattern of the spider trying to lure the fly into his home. The fly refuses because she fears she will not come out. I think each verse will follow this pattern of the spider trying to lure the fly and the fly refusing.* (Make inferences/predictions)

2. *I can hear this is a poem because of the rhythm and rhyme. Each line has a similar beat. Every two lines end in rhyming words.* (Cite rhyme/Rhythm)

# The Spider and The Fly

## by Mary Howitt

1   "Will you walk into my parlor?" said the spider to the fly;

"'Tis the prettiest little parlor that ever you may spy.

The way into my parlor is up a winding stair,

And I have many curious things to show when you are there."

5   "Oh no, no," said the little fly; "to ask me is in vain,

For who goes up your winding stair can ne'er come down again."

"I'm sure you must be weary, dear, with soaring up so high.

Will you rest upon my little bed?" said the spider to the fly.

"There are pretty curtains drawn around; the sheets are fine and thin,

10  And if you like to rest a while, I'll snugly tuck you in!"

"Oh no, no," said the little fly, "for I've often heard it said,

They never, never wake again who sleep upon your bed!" ❷

Said the cunning spider to the fly: "Dear friend, what can I do

To prove the warm affection I've always felt for you?

15  I have within my pantry good store of all that's nice;

I'm sure you're very welcome - will you please to take a slice?"

"Oh no, no," said the little fly; "kind sir, that cannot be:

I've heard what's in your pantry, and I do not wish to see!"

"Sweet creature!" said the spider, "you're witty and you're wise;

20  How handsome are your gauzy wings; how brilliant are your eyes!

I have a little looking-glass upon my parlor shelf;

If you'd step in one moment, dear, you shall behold yourself."

"I thank you, gentle sir," she said, "for what you're pleased to say,

And, bidding you good morning now, I'll call another day."

25 The spider turned him round about, and went into his den,

For well he knew the silly fly would soon come back again:

So he wove a subtle web in a little corner sly, **③**

And set his table ready to dine upon the fly;

Then came out to his door again and merrily did sing:

30 "Come hither, hither, pretty fly, with pearl and silver wing;

Your robes are green and purple; there's a crest upon your head;

Your eyes are like diamond bright, but mine are dull as lead!"


Alas, alas! how very soon this silly little fly,

Hearing his wily, flattering words, came slowly flitting by;

35 With buzzing wings she hung aloft, then near and nearer grew,

Thinking only of her brilliant eyes and green and purple hue,

Thinking only of her crested head. Poor, foolish thing! at last

Up jumped the cunning spider, and fiercely held her fast;

He dragged her up his winding stair, into the dismal den -

40 Within his little parlor - but she ne'er came out again!


And now, dear little children, who may this story read,

To idle, silly flattering words I pray you ne'er give heed;

Unto an evil counselor close heart and ear and eye,

And take a lesson from this tale of the spider and the fly. **④**

**3.** *The spider wove a "subtle" web in a corner. The web would most likely not be noticed because it was in the corner. So* subtle *probably means "not easily seen or noticed."* (Determine word meaning)

**4.** *Turn and talk to a partner. Ask: What is the lesson of this poem?* (Summarize/Ask questions)

## Extend Thinking Questions

Pose one or more questions to engage students more deeply with the text.

• *How did the spider convince the fly to finally agree with his point of view?*

• *What are some traits that describe the spider? The fly? What details support these traits?*

**iELD** **Paraphrase to Support Comprehension**

**After line 18:** *The spider invites the fly into his parlor, bed, and pantry. The fly refuses each invitation. She knows it is too dangerous.*

**After line 32:** *The spider invites the fly to look into his mirror. She refuses. He knows she will be back. He weaves a web. Then he flatters the fly and invites her in again.*

**After last line:** *The fly believes the flattery. The spider catches the fly, who is never seen again. The moral is not to trust someone based on the person's flattering words.*

**CCSS**
**RL.4.1, RL.4.3, RL.4.4, RL.4.5, L.4.4a**

Unit 4

# Capture!
## A chapter from
## Akimbo and the Snakes, Part 1

## by Alexander McCall Smith

1   Then something caught Akimbo's eye. At first he thought he was imagining it, but then he realized he was not. There was a movement just within the hole. Yes, something was there.

2   Uncle Peter saw it, too. "That's it," he whispered to Akimbo. "Now watch."

3   Slowly a head moved out of the hole, followed by a section of lithe, thin snake's body. Akimbo felt Uncle Peter stiffen beside him.

4   "Mamba," his uncle whispered, almost under his breath. "They were right."

5   Akimbo hardly dared breathe. The snake, as it emerged from the hole, showed itself to be immensely long, at least twice his own height. **1** He glanced at his uncle, wondering what he intended to do. Would he really try to chase that? Uncle Peter gestured to Akimbo to stay where he was. Then, rising to his feet, he began to move slowly toward the snake.

6   The mamba seemed unaware of Uncle Peter's approach, lying seemingly inert on the ground in front of the hole. Akimbo saw a large fly land on one of the snake's coils, and this made it twitch, but only slightly. Uncle Peter had the extended pole held out before him. He was now sufficiently close to the snake for the jaws of the pole to be hovering almost around the snake's body.

7   "Now," thought Akimbo. "Now's your chance."

8   It may have been the shadow thrown by the pole, or it may have been some tremor in the ground that alerted the snake. Whatever it was, the head of the snake suddenly whipped around to confront the danger. For a moment, the deadly reptile and its pursuer faced one another, but then in a sudden flash, the snake shot away, flying up the bank like an arrow released from a bow.

9   Uncle Peter gave a cry and began to follow the snake, holding the pole up against his chest. Akimbo sprang to his feet and followed his uncle.

10  "Watch him!" called out Uncle Peter. "See where he goes!"

11 Akimbo knew how easy it was to lose sight of a fleeing snake, so he was not surprised when the snake seemed to vanish completely into a dense clump of trees. **2**

12 Uncle Peter stopped and waited for Akimbo to catch up with him. "Did you see where it went?" he asked, the disappointment clearly showing in his voice.

13 Akimbo pointed to the place where he had last seen the snake. "I think it was in there," he said.

14 Uncle Peter nodded. "I suspect it's gone," he said. "But there's no harm in our just checking up on those trees to see if it's gone up one of them."

15 They approached the clump of trees gingerly. At any moment, the snake could reappear. Mambas were aggressive—Akimbo had read that time and time again. They could stand their ground and attack when other snakes would think only of seeking out safety. Now they were entering the mamba's territory. It was the one that knew the trees, not them. They were the ones who were weak and vulnerable in such terrain. **3**

16 There were about ten or twelve trees in the clump, and Uncle Peter said they should work their way through, looking carefully at every branch. "It may look like a twig up there," he warned. "Look for curves rather than straight lines—that's how you spot a snake in a tree."

17 Akimbo looked at the first tree, holding his hand above his eyes as he peered at each branch. The foliage was dense, and the leaves provided good cover. His heart sank; it was a hopeless task. He stopped. Was that something? Did that branch move? He looked again. No, it was the wind in the leaves—there was nothing there.

18 They moved farther into the trees. In the back of his mind, Akimbo remembered the warning about green mambas falling from trees onto their victims below. The thought made his flesh creep. **4**

**3.** *The author gives details that make the reader feel worried about the characters. For example, "At any moment, the snake could reappear," "It was the one that knew the trees," and "They were the ones who were weak." I think the author wants to convey a suspenseful mood.* (Determine mood)

**4.** *Turn and talk to a partner. What do you think will happen next? Why?* (Make predictions)

**Extend Thinking Questions**

Pose one or more questions to engage students more deeply with the text.

• *What do we learn about Akimbo when we look at the events through his eyes?*

• *What are the important events in this part of the story?*

**iELD** **Paraphrase to Support Comprehension**

After paragraph 6: *Akimbo and Uncle Peter see the snake come out of the hole. Uncle Peter starts to put his pole around the snake's body.*

After paragraph 11: *The snake was startled. It shot away. Uncle Peter tells Akimbo to watch where it goes. He sees it vanish into a clump of trees.*

After paragraph 18: *Uncle Peter and Akimbo walk carefully among the trees. They check each one to see if they can find the snake. Akimbo remembers that mambas can fall from trees onto their victims.*

**Unit 4**

**CCSS**
**RL.4.1, RL.4.2, RL.4.3, RL.4.4, SL.4.2, L.4.4a**

## Set the Stage

**Introduce the Text** *Today I'm going to read aloud part 2 of an excerpt from* Akimbo and the Snakes. *First, let's summarize part 1.* (Have volunteers summarize part 1.) *In this excerpt Akimbo and his Uncle Peter continue to look for the mamba snake they want to capture for the snake farm.*

**Engage Thinking** *Will Akimbo be of any help to Uncle Peter? Why or why not? Turn to a partner to share your prediction.*

## Engage with the Text

Read aloud the text at a fluent, expressive pace. Use the suggested prompts to model your thinking, clarify events, and elicit student interaction.

**1.** *The sentence says the snake might even track them.* Track *can mean "the rails a train rides on" or "to follow." In this sentence the meaning "to follow" makes sense.* (Determine word meaning)

**2.** *Uncle Peter owns a snake farm, so he knows a lot about snakes. I think he will be able to capture the snake when he climbs the tree.* (Make inferences/predictions)

# Capture!
## A Chapter from Akimbo and the Snakes, Part 2

1   They checked up on several more trees, each time without result. But they knew that they could have walked right past the mamba in such conditions. He could have been in any one of dozens of thick clusters of leaves, immobile, save for the flickering tongue, watching silently. Perhaps he would even track them. **❶** Snakes had been known to do that.

2   Suddenly Akimbo stopped. There was something strange about that branch, he was sure of it. He peered at it again. There was a fork in the branch, and then several twigs. There were leaves, some of them green, some ready to fall. And then…he stood absolutely still. There was a movement on the branch, and just below it, the shape of a coil of snake. Then that moved, too.

3   Akimbo looked around him. Uncle Peter was standing a little distance away, looking up into a tree. Akimbo put his fingers to his mouth and gave a quiet whistle. It could have been a bird, or a cicada, but his uncle turned around and looked at him inquisitively.

4   Akimbo mouthed the words "Up there!" and pointed at the branch.

5   Uncle Peter raised a hand in acknowledgment and moved quickly over to his nephew's side. "Where?" he whispered.

6   Akimbo pointed again, and after a few moments Uncle Peter spotted the snake as well.

7   "Right," he said. "I'm going up after it."

8   Akimbo was shocked. "Surely you won't go up…there," he protested. "It's too dangerous."

9   Uncle Peter brushed aside his objection. "I can get quite close to that branch if I go up to where the trunk divides," he said. "Then my pole should be able to reach him."

10   Akimbo stood back as his uncle began to climb up the tree. **❷** As he did so, Akimbo watched the snake, waiting to see if it moved. It was quite still. Slowly, painfully slowly, it seemed to Akimbo, Uncle Peter inched his way up the tree. When he reached the point where the main

trunk of the tree divided, he stopped and steadied himself. Then the pole began to move out slowly toward the mamba. **3**

11 Akimbo watched, fascinated and terrified at the same time. The snake was still moving, but only slightly, and it seemed to Akimbo that even if the snake sensed their presence, it felt safe on the leafy branch. Once again, Uncle Peter moved the pole in a deft downward thrust, and this time it fell upon the snake and the jaws clasped tight. There was a whipping and thrashing commotion of snake and leaves. Then there seemed to be no more movement, and Akimbo wondered whether the snake was truly caught. But then Uncle Peter called out, triumphant, and began to work his way down the tree, bringing the pole behind him.

12 "I've got him," he said. "Get the bag ready."

13 Akimbo unfolded the large canvas bag and made sure that the strings that drew the mouth tight were untangled. Then Uncle Peter was down from the tree, bearing at the end of his pole the long angry body of the captured snake.

14 As Akimbo watched, Uncle Peter moved his grip on the pole higher. Then when he was close enough, he reached forward with his free hand and seized the snake's tail. Now it was ready for bagging. Akimbo held the mouth of the bag wide open, while Uncle Peter pushed in the end of the pole holding the snake just below the head. Once that was inside, he thrust the rest of the snake's squirming body into the bag and drew the strings at the mouth tight around the pole.

15 "Now," he said, "I'll release the clasp and pull out the pole. The moment that happens, pull the strings tight. But don't touch the bag itself."

16 Akimbo did as he was told. As soon as the jaws of the pole appeared, he pulled the strings as tight as he could. Uncle Peter then took them from him and knotted them. The bag itself collapsed, although there were signs of fierce movement within as the snake struggled vainly against the confines of its prison.

17 Uncle Peter sat down and wiped his brow. "That went well!" he said, smiling at his nephew. "Thank you." **4**

3. *The author continues to give details that evoke suspense and worry. For example, Uncle Peter inches up the tree painfully slowly. Akimbo is terrified. The snake is still moving. It was whipping and thrashing. (Summarize)*

4. *Turn and talk to a partner. Ask: How did Uncle Peter and Akimbo finally bag the snake? (Summarize/Ask questions)*

## Extend Thinking Questions

Pose one or more questions to engage students more deeply with the text.

• *How do you think Uncle Peter's point of view of these events might differ from Akimbo's point of view?*

• *What is the structure of this story? How can you tell?*

### iELD Paraphrase to Support Comprehension

After paragraph 4: *Akimbo saw the snake up in a tree. He quietly showed the snake to Uncle Peter.*

After paragraph 11: *Uncle Peter slowly climbed the tree. He captured the snake with his pole.*

After paragraph 17: *Uncle Peter and Akimbo work together to carefully drop the dangerous snake into a large canvass bag. Uncle Peter ties the bag closed. He thanks Akimbo for his help.*

CCSS
RL.4.1, RL.4.2, RL.4.3, RL.4.4, SL.4.2, L.4.4a

Unit 4

## Set the Stage

**Introduce the Text** *Today I'm going to read aloud a poem about the different movements a sleeping dog makes as he dreams. Pay particular attention to the rhythm and sensory language as you listen to this entertaining poem.*

**Engage Thinking** *What are some things the dog probably dreams about? Turn to a partner to share your prediction.*

## Engage with the Text

Read aloud the text at a fluent, expressive pace. Use the suggested prompts to model your thinking, clarify events, and elicit student interaction.

1. *The poem starts off slowly as the dog sleeps quietly. But then his feet begin to twitch, his tail trembles, and he starts making sounds. I think the dog is starting to have some exciting dreams. I'll read on to see what they are.* (Make inferences/predictions)

2. *The poet tells of "wolf dreams" and "wild themes", then uses the word* feral *to describe not so mild schemes. So I think* feral *goes along with the theme in this part of the poem. It probably is a synonym for* wild. (Determine word meaning)

3. *Throughout the poem the poet uses poetic devices such as repetition of sounds such as -ing endings, and quick rhythm to match the quickness of the actions.* (Cite poetic devices)

# The Dreams of a Dog

Stretching out on the hearth, asleep.

Black lip hanging, soft nose puffing,

Feet are twitching, tail a-trembling,

Gurgling, growling, throat a-rumbling,

5  Snoring softly, dreaming deep…

woof. **1**


Running, barking, running, barking!

Balls and branches, darts and dashes

Frisbees flying, children crying,

10  "Get the toy, go get it boy!"

Running, marking, catching, barking…

Woof!


Rustling, crackling, branches snapping

There's panic in the long grasses!

15  A flip of a tail, a young deer dashes

Chase it, chase it! Breathe it, taste it!

Leaping, soaring, tongue a-flapping…

Woof!

Running, panting, sniffing, sighing,

20  Frisbees crying, children flying,

Wolf dreams, wild themes,

Feral, not-so-mild schemes,

Licking, digging, sniffing, spying…

Woof. **2**

25  Dreaming, snoring, asleep on the flooring,

Soft lip hanging, black nose breathing, **3**

Slack and silent, limp and groggy,

Quiet now, that's a good doggie,

Drooling, sighing, sleeping, snoring…

30  woof. **4**

**4.** *Turn and talk to a partner. Ask: What are some things the dog dreams of?* (Summarize/Ask questions)

## Extend Thinking Questions

Pose one or more questions to engage students more deeply with the text.

• *From whose point of view is this poem written? How can you tell?*

• *What do we learn when we look at the dreams from the narrator's point of view? from the dog's point of view?*

**iELD** **Paraphrase to Support Comprehension**

**Unit 4**

After line 12: *The dog stretches out and falls asleep. He begins to dream about playing Frisbee as he runs and barks.*

After line 24: *The dog continues to have exciting dreams. He dreams of chasing a deer, running after wild animals as he licks, digs, and spies on them.*

After last line: *The dog goes back to a peaceful sleep quietly drooling, sighing, and snoring.*

**CCSS**
**RL.4.1, RL.4.2, RL.4.4, RL.4.5, L.4.4a, L.4.5c**

## Set the Stage

**Introduce the Text** *Today I'm going to read aloud part 1 of an excerpt from Doctor Dolittle, a book from a series written by Hugh Lofting, beginning in 1920. The series follows the doctor who learns how to talk to animals. In this excerpt we find out how Doctor Dolittle learns about animal language.*

**Engage Thinking** *How do you think Doctor Dolittle learns that animals talk among themselves? Turn to a partner to share your prediction.*

## Engage with the Text

Read aloud the text at a fluent, expressive pace. Use the suggested prompts to model your thinking, clarify events, and elicit student interaction.

**1.** *When the Cat's-meat-Man starts to talk to Doctor Dolittle about becoming an animal doctor, Polynesia stops singing and starts to listen. I think this means that the parrot can understand people.* **(Make inferences)**

**2.** *At first I wasn't sure what a Cat's-meat-Man was. But at the end of paragraph 4 the man says, "I could put something in the meat I sell 'em." So a Cats-meat-Man sells cat food to cat owners.* **(Determine word meaning)**

# Animal Language
## An excerpt from Doctor Dolittle, Part 1

### by Hugh Lofting

1 It happened one day that the Doctor was sitting in his kitchen talking with the Cat's-meat-Man who had come to see him with a stomach-ache.

2 "Why don't you give up being a people's doctor, and be an animal-doctor?" asked the Cat's-meat-Man.

3 The parrot, Polynesia, was sitting in the window looking out at the rain and singing a sailor-song to herself. She stopped singing and started to listen. **1**

4 "You see, Doctor," the Cat's-meat-Man went on, "you know all about animals—much more than what these here vets do. That book you wrote—about cats, why, it's wonderful! I can't read or write myself—or maybe I'd write some books. But my wife, Theodosia, she's a scholar, she is. And she read your book to me. Well, it's wonderful—that's all can be said—wonderful. You might have been a cat yourself. You know the way they think. And listen: you can make a lot of money doctoring animals. Do you know that? You see, I'd send all the old women who had sick cats or dogs to you. And if they didn't get sick fast enough, I could put something in the meat I sell 'em to make 'em sick, see?" **2**

5 "Oh, no," said the Doctor quickly. "You mustn't do that. That wouldn't be right."

6 "Oh, I didn't mean real sick," answered the Cat's-meat-Man. "Just a little something to make them droopy-like was what I had reference to. But as you say, maybe it ain't quite fair on the animals. But they'll get sick anyway, because the old women always give 'em too much to eat. And look, all the farmers 'round about who had lame horses and weak lambs—they'd come. Be an animal-doctor."

7 When the Cat's-meat-Man had gone, the parrot flew off the window on to the Doctor's table and said,

8 "That man's got sense. That's what you ought to do. Be an animal-doctor. Give the silly people up—if they haven't brains enough to see you're the best doctor in the world. Take care of animals instead—THEY'll soon find it out. Be an animal-doctor."

9 "Oh, there are plenty of animal-doctors," said John Dolittle, putting the flower-pots outside on the window-sill to get the rain.

10 "Yes, there ARE plenty," said Polynesia. "But none of them are any good at all. Now listen, Doctor, and I'll tell you something. Did you know that animals can talk?"

11 "I knew that parrots can talk," said the Doctor.

12 "Oh, we parrots can talk in two languages—people's language and bird-language," said Polynesia proudly. "If I say, 'Polly wants a cracker,' you understand me. But hear this: Ka-ka oi-ee, fee-fee?"

13 "Good Gracious!" cried the Doctor. "What does that mean?"

14 "That means, 'Is the porridge hot yet?'—in bird-language."

15 "My! You don't say so!" said the Doctor. "You never talked that way to me before."

16 "What would have been the good?" said Polynesia, dusting some cracker-crumbs off her left wing. "You wouldn't have understood me if I had."

17 "Tell me some more," said the Doctor, all excited; and he rushed over to the dresser-drawer and came back with the butcher's book and a pencil. "Now don't go too fast—and I'll write it down. This is interesting—very interesting—something quite new. Give me the Birds' A.B.C. first—slowly now." **3**

18 So that was the way the Doctor came to know that animals had a language of their own and could talk to one another. And all that afternoon, while it was raining, Polynesia sat on the kitchen table giving him bird words to put down in the book. **4**

**3.** *Doctor Dolittle is a good doctor. He is very interested to learn the bird's language. I think he will eventually give up being a people doctor and become an animal doctor.* (Make inferences/predictions)

**4.** *Turn and talk to a partner. How do the different characters feel about Doctor Dolittle becoming an animal doctor?* (Describe characters)

## Extend Thinking Questions

Pose one or more questions to engage students more deeply with the text.

• *What are the different characters' points of view about animal doctors?*

• *What do Dr. Dolittle's actions and words say about him?*

### iELD Paraphrase to Support Comprehension

After paragraph 4: *The Cat's-meat-Man tries to talk Dr. Dolittle into becoming an animal doctor instead of a people doctor. He tells him his is a good doctor and can make lots of money.*

After paragraph 12: *Polynesia the parrot agrees. She tells Dr. Dolittle other animal doctors are not any good. Then she tells him animals can talk. Parrots have two languages: animal languages and people language.*

After paragraph 18: *Dr. Dolittle asks the parrot to teach him bird words. She does. He writes them down in a book.*

**CCSS**
**RL.4.1, RL.4.3, RL.4.4, L.4.4a**

## Set the Stage

**Introduce the Text** *Today I'm going to read aloud part 2 of an excerpt from Doctor Dolittle. Let's summarize what we read in part 1.* (Have volunteers summarize part 1.)

*In this excerpt we learn what happens when Doctor Dolittle becomes an animal doctor.*

**Engage Thinking** *Why do you think Doctor Dolittle finally becomes an animal doctor? Turn to a partner to share your prediction.*

## Engage with the Text

Read aloud the text at a fluent, expressive pace. Use the suggested prompts to model your thinking, clarify events, and elicit student interaction.

**1.** *Spec- is a root that means "to see." Also the horse said there is no reason why he shouldn't wear glasses. So I know spectacles are eyeglasses.* (Determine word meaning)

**2.** *The horse asked for green glasses. He said they would keep the sun out of his eyes. So I think what he actually wanted were sunglasses.* (Make inferences)

**3.** *The horse was so happy that Doctor Dolittle could understand him. Now he will get the glasses he needs. He kicked the boy who tried to put a mustard plaster on him, but the boy just landed in the pond. He didn't get hurt.* (Summarize)

# Animal Language
## An excerpt from Doctor Dolittle, Part 2

1  At tea-time, when the dog, Jip, came in, the parrot said to the Doctor, "See, HE'S talking to you."

2  "Looks to me as though he were scratching his ear," said the Doctor.

3  "But animals don't always speak with their mouths," said the parrot in a high voice, raising her eyebrows. "They talk with their ears, with their feet, with their tails—with everything. Sometimes they don't WANT to make a noise. Do you see now the way he's twitching up one side of his nose?"

4  "What's that mean?" asked the Doctor.

5  "That means, 'Can't you see that it has stopped raining?'" Polynesia answered. "He is asking you a question. Dogs nearly always use their noses for asking questions."

6  After a while, with the parrot's help, the Doctor got to learn the language of the animals so well that he could talk to them himself and understand everything they said. Then he gave up being a people's doctor altogether.

7  As soon as the Cat's-meat-Man had told every one that John Dolittle was going to become an animal-doctor, old ladies began to bring him their pet pugs and poodles who had eaten too much cake; and farmers came many miles to show him sick cows and sheep.

8  One day a plow-horse was brought to him; and the poor thing was terribly glad to find a man who could talk in horse-language.

9  "You know, Doctor," said the horse, "that vet over the hill knows nothing at all. He has been treating me six weeks now—for spavins. What I need is SPECTACLES. I am going blind in one eye. There's no reason why horses shouldn't wear glasses, the same as people. But that stupid man over the hill never even looked at my eyes. He kept on giving me big pills. I tried to tell him; but he couldn't understand a word of horse-language. What I need is spectacles." **1**

10  "Of course—of course," said the Doctor. "I'll get you some at once."

11 "I would like a pair like yours," said the horse. "Only green. They'll keep the sun out of my eyes while I'm plowing the Fifty-Acre Field."

12 "Certainly," said the Doctor. "Green ones you shall have." **2**

13 "You know, the trouble is, Sir," said the plow-horse as the Doctor opened the front door to let him out. "The trouble is that ANYBODY thinks he can doctor animals—just because the animals don't complain. As a matter of fact it takes a much cleverer man to be a really good animal-doctor than it does to be a good people's doctor. My farmer's boy thinks he knows all about horses. I wish you could see him—his face is so fat he looks as though he had no eyes—and he has got as much brain as a potato-bug. He tried to put a mustard-plaster on me last week."

14 "Where did he put it?" asked the Doctor.

15 "Oh, he didn't put it anywhere—on me," said the horse. "He only tried to. I kicked him into the duck-pond."

16 "Well, well!" said the Doctor.

17 "I'm a pretty quiet creature as a rule," said the horse. "Very patient with people—don't make much fuss. But it was bad enough to have that vet giving me the wrong medicine. And when that red-faced booby started to monkey with me, I just couldn't bear it any more."

18 "Did you hurt the boy much?" asked the Doctor.

19 "Oh, no," said the horse. "I kicked him in the right place. The vet's looking after him now. When will my glasses be ready?" **3**

20 "I'll have them for you next week," said the Doctor. "Come in again Tuesday—Good morning!"

21 Then John Dolittle got a fine, big pair of green spectacles; and the plow-horse stopped going blind in one eye and could see as well as ever.

22 And soon it became a common sight to see farm-animals wearing glasses in the country round Puddleby; and a blind horse was a thing unknown. **4**

---

**4.** *Turn and talk to a partner. How did life change in the country because of Doctor Dolittle? (Make inferences/predictions)*

## Extend Thinking Questions

Pose one or more questions to engage students more deeply with the text.

• *Why did Doctor Dolittle and the vet the horse saw at first have different points of view?*

• *What did Doctor Dolittle learn when he looked at the horse's problem through the eyes of the horse?*

**Unit 4**

**iELD** **Paraphrase to Support Comprehension**

After paragraph 6: *The parrot teaches Doctor Dolittle that animals talk with movements. Doctor Dolittle learns how to talk with animals and becomes an animal doctor.*

After paragraph 19: *A horse comes in to see Doctor Dolittle. He tells him that the old vet gave him pills but he did not need them. He needs glasses. The horse also tells how he kicked the farmer's boy into a duck pond when the boy tried to put a mustard-plaster on him. The boy did not get hurt.*

After paragraph 22: *Doctor Dolittle tells the horse he will get his glasses. After that, farm animals all around Puddleby wore glasses.*

**CCSS**
**RL.4.1, RL.4.2, RL.4.3, RL.4.4, SL.4.2, L.4.4a, L.4.4b**

## Set the Stage

**Introduce the Text** *Today I'm going to read aloud part 3 of an excerpt from Doctor Dolittle. Let's summarize what we read in part 2.* (Have volunteers summarize part 2.)

*In this excerpt we will learn how Doctor Dolittle's medical practice grew.*

**Engage Thinking** *How do you think Doctor Dolittle's medical practice for the animals grows? Turn to a partner to share your prediction.*

## Engage with the Text

Read aloud the text at a fluent, expressive pace. Use the suggested prompts to model your thinking, clarify events, and elicit student interaction.

**1.** *After reading this first paragraph I learn that Doctor Dolittle could talk to all the animals that were brought to him. I think that these animals might tell others since they all can talk to each other. I predict more and more animals will come to Doctor Dolittle.* (Make inferences/predictions)

**2.** *The macaw couldn't "stand" the professor who taught Greek incorrectly. I know* stand *can mean "to get up," "be in one place," or "put up with." In this sentence the meaning "put up with" makes sense. The macaw couldn't put up with the professor.* (Determine word meaning)

# Animal Language
## An excerpt from Doctor Dolittle, Part 3

1    And so it was with all the other animals that were brought to him. As soon as they found that he could talk their language, they told him where the pain was and how they felt, and of course it was easy for him to cure them. **❶**

2    Now all these animals went back and told their brothers and friends that there was a doctor in the little house with the big garden who really WAS a doctor. And whenever any creatures got sick—not only horses and cows and dogs—but all the little things of the fields, like harvest-mice and water-voles, badgers and bats, they came at once to his house on the edge of the town, so that his big garden was nearly always crowded with animals trying to get in to see him.

3    There were so many that came that he had to have special doors made for the different kinds. He wrote "HORSES" over the front door, "COWS" over the side door, and "SHEEP" on the kitchen door. Each kind of animal had a separate door—even the mice had a tiny tunnel made for them into the cellar, where they waited patiently in rows for the Doctor to come round to them.

4    And so, in a few years' time, every living thing for miles and miles got to know about John Dolittle, M.D. And the birds who flew to other countries in the winter told the animals in foreign lands of the wonderful doctor of Puddleby-on-the-Marsh, who could understand their talk and help them in their troubles. In this way he became famous among the animals—all over the world—better known even than he had been among the folks of the West Country. And he was happy and liked his life very much.

5    One afternoon when the Doctor was busy writing in a book, Polynesia sat in the window—as she nearly always did—looking out at the leaves blowing about in the garden. Presently she laughed aloud.

6    "What is it, Polynesia?" asked the Doctor, looking up from his book.

7    "I was just thinking," said the parrot; and she went on looking at the leaves.

8    "What were you thinking?"

9  "I was thinking about people," said Polynesia. "People make me sick. They think they're so wonderful. The world has been going on now for thousands of years, hasn't it? And the only thing in animal-language that PEOPLE have learned to understand is that when a dog wags his tail he means 'I'm glad!'—It's funny, isn't it? You are the very first man to talk like us. Oh, sometimes people annoy me dreadfully—such airs they put on—talking about 'the dumb animals.' DUMB!—Huh! Why I knew a macaw once who could say 'Good morning!' in seven different ways without once opening his mouth. He could talk every language— and Greek. An old professor with a gray beard bought him. But he didn't stay. He said the old man didn't talk Greek right, and he couldn't stand listening to him teach the language wrong. I often wonder what's become of him. That bird knew more geography than people will ever know.—PEOPLE, Golly! I suppose if people ever learn to fly—like any common hedge-sparrow—we shall never hear the end of it!" **2**

10  "You're a wise old bird," said the Doctor. "How old are you really? I know that parrots and elephants sometimes live to be very, very old."

11  "I can never be quite sure of my age," said Polynesia. "It's either a hundred and eighty-three or a hundred and eighty-two. But I know that when I first came here from Africa, King Charles was still hiding in the oak-tree—because I saw him. He looked scared to death." **3** **4**

**3.** *I think the theme of this part of the story is how grateful the animals are for the kindness and ability of Doctor Dolittle.* (Determine theme)

**4.** *Turn and talk to a partner. Ask: What details support the theme?* (Summarize/Ask questions)

## Extend Thinking Questions

Pose one or more questions to engage students more deeply with the text.

• *What does Doctor Dolittle learn from Polynesia's point of view about people?*

• *How did Doctor Dolittle become world famous with the animals?*

### iELD Paraphrase to Support Comprehension

After paragraph 4: *Animals from all over the world learned about Doctor Dolittle. They came to the only doctor who could speak their language and actually cure them. Doctor Dolittle was happy with his life.*

After paragraph 9: *Polynesia talks about how dumb people are. They have been around for thousands of years and still cannot talk with animals.*

After paragraph 11: *Doctor Dolittle tells Polynesia she is wise. He asks her how old she is. She says she is either 183 or 182 years old.*

**CCSS**
**RL.4.1, RL.4.2, RL.4.3, RL.4.4, SL.4.2, L.4.4a**

## Objective

• Model making inferences/predictions

## Set the Stage

**Introduce the Text** *Today I'm going to read aloud a poem about what geese do to prepare for their flight south.*

**Engage Thinking** *What are some things geese must do before they fly south for the winter? Turn to a partner to share your prediction.*

## Engage with the Text

Read aloud the text at a fluent, expressive pace. Use the suggested prompts to model your thinking, clarify events, and elicit student interaction.

**1.** *This first verse has an inconsistent rhyming pattern. The text tells how the geese work together to prepare for their migration. I think each verse will follow this inconsistent rhyming pattern and will describe other ways the geese work together to prepare for their journey.* (Make inferences/predictions)

**2.** *The poet uses poetic devices such as repetition and rhyme. For example, the line "We are the geese" is repeated throughout the poem. Rhyming lines such as "We navigate–/Not too early,/Not too late" are used throughout.* (Supply meaning with repetition)

# We Are the Geese

## by Amy Imbody

We are the geese:

We navigate—

Not too early,

Not too late—

5  To make our migration

We calibrate

Our comings and goings

To match the chill

Of air, the kill

10  Of leaf; the frost.

We are the geese:

We do not get lost.

We are the geese:

We orchestrate

15  Our departure date.

We collaborate

To form the "V"

That cuts the wind

To give us speed.

20  We do not debate

Choreography,

But take our turn

To follow, to lead.

We are the geese:

25 We congregate

At edge of pond.

We contemplate

The great beyond:

Southerly places

30 Are our choice—

We lift our wings,

We lift our voice,

A wild, high

Honking cry

35 We are the geese:

We take to sky! **4**

**3.** Col- *is a prefix that means "together."* Labor *is a root that means "work." So when the geese collaborate to form the V, they work together to form the V.* (Determine word meaning)

**4.** *Turn and talk to a partner. What are some things the geese do to prepare for their flight south?* (Summarize)

## Extend Thinking Questions

Pose one or more questions to engage students more deeply with the text.

- *How do you think this poem would differ if it were told from the point of view of a person watching the geese?*

- *What is the theme of this poem? What details support this theme?*

### iELD Paraphrase to Support Comprehension

**After line 12:** *The geese work together. They get ready at just the right time to migrate. They figure out their movement based on the cold weather. They do not get lost.*

**After line 23:** *The geese decide when they will leave. They work together to form the V as they fly. They take turns leading and following.*

**After last line:** *The geese meet at the pond. They think about flying South. They honk together as they take off on their journey South.*

**CCSS**
**RL.4.1, RL.4.2, RL.4.4, RL.4.5, L.4.4b**

## Objective

• Model summarizing/synthesizing

## Set the Stage

**Introduce the Text** *Today I'm going to read aloud a selection about what a house might be like in the near future. In this article you will learn how technology is used in a "smart house" to make a person's life easier while helping to save our planet.*

**Engage Thinking** *What are some technological advances that could be described in this selection? Turn to a partner to share your prediction.*

## Engage with the Text

Read aloud the text at a fluent, expressive pace. Use the suggested prompts to model your thinking, clarify events, and elicit student interaction.

**1.** *The article says that this is a smart house of the future. So I can infer that some of the technology I will read about is not available yet, but may be some day. I'll read on to see if I am correct.* (Make inferences)

**2.** *This smart house is able to diagnose a person's health just by scanning a face. I know that today, doctors use technology such as x-rays and CAT scans to diagnose the health of patients. So, I think that the technology described in this article may be a reality in the near future.* (Summarize)

# Blame It on the House

## by Carmelle LaMothe

1   As you step off the school bus and your feet hit the sidewalk, your house springs to life. Technologically speaking, that is.

2   This is a smart house of the future and it knows you well. **❶** No need for keys jangling in your pocket. Just scan your thumbprint at the door and step inside.

3   As you drop your backpack on the floor, a voice reminds you that there is math homework to be done. (Yes, the house can even read the homework assignments in your backpack!) Your favorite music plays as you enter the kitchen. The wallpaper changes from your little brother's fire engine pattern to something a little more your style.

4   It's snack time, but what's in the fridge? Touch a screen and it will give you suggestions from what's available. Pop into the bathroom and take a peek in the mirror—this one seems almost magic. After a quick scan of your face, it will let know the state of your health: from whether you've got a fever to whether you need a drink of water. **❷**

5   Sounds like science fiction? Actually, this is a glimpse into the future.

6   With the help of computers, timers, and sensors, this smart house seems to think for itself. To save energy, the house is programmed to control the lights and temperature. No more leaving the lights on—your house will turn them on when you enter a room, and turn them off when you leave.

7   Smart houses will get power from alternative energy sources: solar, wind, and geothermal (heat from inside the Earth). **❸** These are all renewable energy sources, so they help the environment. (They are much less polluting than energy sources such as coal, gasoline, and natural gas.)

8   This house is smart in more than one way. Not only does it think, it's built of smart materials. Trash, for example. Yes, trash.

9   An engineer named John Forth, from the University of Leeds in England, has invented a new type of building material called the Bitublock. This material is made of things that usually get thrown out. Bitublocks are six times stronger than concrete blocks, and by using them, we can keep a lot of trash out of landfills.

10  In the future, kids might have a new excuse for not turning in their homework. Instead of blaming it on the dog, kids might say, "My house didn't remind me." What would your teacher think about that? **4**

**3.** *The author provides a definition in parentheses to help readers understand that geothermal means "heat from inside the Earth."* (Determine word meaning)

**4.** *Turn and talk to a partner. How does this smart house save energy? How do you save energy in your house?* (Summarize/Synthesize)

## Extend Thinking Questions

Pose one or more questions to engage students more deeply with the text.

• *What kind of new technology do you think scientists should develop next? Why?*

• *If you could have one technological invention described in this smart house, which would you want? Why?*

**Unit 5**

**iELD  Paraphrase to Support Comprehension**

**After paragraph 4:** *The smart house of the future will be filled with new technology. For example, it will read your thumbprint to unlock the door. It will scan your face to check your health.*

**After paragraph 7:** *The smart house of the future will use computers, timers, and sensors to save energy. It will automatically control temperature and lights. It will use energy sources that are renewable.*

**After paragraph 9:** *The smart house of the future can be built of materials that already exist. The Bitublock is a building material made of trash. It is six times stronger than concrete blocks.*

**CCSS**
**RI.4.1, RI.4.2, RI.4.3, RI.4.4, SL.4.2, L.4.4a**

## Objective

• Model summarizing/synthesizing

## Set the Stage

**Introduce the Text** *Remember, technology is when we use scientific knowledge to help improve lives in some way. Today I'm going to read aloud a selection that tells how scientific knowledge and technology can help keep cities comfortable and still be environmentally friendly.*

**Engage Thinking** *This article is called "How Green Is My City?" What do you think the word "green" refers to in the title? Turn to a partner to share your prediction.*

## Engage with the Text

Read aloud the text at a fluent, expressive pace. Use the suggested prompts to model your thinking, clarify events, and elicit student interaction.

**1.** *The author used examples and description to explain "the heat island effect." I can use these context clues to understand that the heat island effect means that the trapped heat in cities makes cities hotter than surrounding areas.* (Determine word meaning)

**2.** *The article says that buildings with white rooftops will be cooler inside than those with black rooftops. When I wear light clothes in hot weather, I am cooler than when I wear dark clothes. I bet if playground surfaces were painted white they would be cooler too!* (Summarize/Synthesize)

# How Green Is My City?

## by Marcia Amidon Lusted

1   When we think about cities, sometimes all we can picture is pollution and heat and smog. We might wonder, "Is it possible to live a clean life when you're a city person?"

2   Cities are hot places. Masses of concrete, narrow streets, and tall buildings trap the heat from the sun, cars, trucks, buses, and other machines. Scientists call this the heat island effect. It makes cities as much as ten degrees hotter than surrounding areas. On a summer day, it's possible for the roof of a tall building to get as hot as 190 degrees Fahrenheit. You actually could fry an egg up there! **❶**

3   As the global climate heats up, it's getting more and more difficult to keep cities cool. But thanks to some new (and not-so-new) ideas for building rooftops, city buildings might get the chill they need.

## When Color Counts

4   In hot parts of the world, people have known for a long time that houses with rooftops painted white or a light color will be cooler inside. That's because light colors reflect sunlight. Dark colors do the opposite: They absorb heat, like a sponge absorbs water. Thinking about roof color is a simple idea that's catching on in other parts of the world. **❷**

## It's Cool to be Green!

5   Another way to stay cool is to be green—literally. Instead of covering flat roofs with asphalt (what usually happens in cities), some builders are starting to make rooftops green. And we're not talking about paint color here. Green roofs are covered with living plants—grass, leafy plants, even vegetables and herbs. Some even have blooming flowers for a touch of color.

6   Once a green roof has been in place for a few years, the root systems grow thicker and act like a blanket. Buildings stay cooler in the summer and warmer in the winter. Green roofs also absorb a lot of rainwater. This solves a problem builders have had to deal with in other ways.

7   Green roofs can be more than just energy savers, too. Imagine how nice it would be to take the elevator up to the roof and enjoy a picnic in the grass!

8   But installing a green roof can't be done without a lot of planning and information. The roof has to be relatively flat and strong enough to support the weight of the plants, soil, and water that will be absorbed. It must be covered with a tough, waterproof barrier to keep rainwater from leaking through to the spaces below. The soil must be covered so it doesn't blow away, since roofs are very windy places. **3**

9   Some people have designed pre-planted plastic blocks that snap together and rest on top of a waterproof barrier for a fast and easy green roof. So if you live in the city, remember it is possible to live green—and maybe even have a lawn to relax on, high above the hot, busy streets! **4**

**3.** *There are many requirements before a green roof can be installed. Details that support this main idea are that the roof has to be flat, strong, and waterproof.* (Cite details)

**4.** *Turn and talk to a partner. What are some green products or behaviors you have used?* (Make connections)

## Extend Thinking Questions

Pose one or more questions to engage students more deeply with the text.

- *How does this article show that technology can impact people's lives in a positive way?*

- *What are two different meanings for the heading "It's Cool to be Green"?*

**Unit 5**

### iELD Paraphrase to Support Comprehension

After paragraph 4: *Cities are hot places. City buildings get hot inside. Painting roofs white helps keep them cooler.*

After paragraph 7: *Another way to keep buildings cool is to cover roofs with plants. This keeps buildings cooler in summer and warmer in winter.*

After paragraph 9: *Roofs with gardens on top need to be flat and strong. They need to be waterproof too. Plastic blocks with plants in them are a fast way to plant a roof garden. They rest on top of a waterproof barrier.*

**CCSS**
**RI.4.1, RI.4.2, RI.4.3, RI.4.4, SL.4.2, L.4.4a**

## Objective

• Model summarizing/synthesizing

## Set the Stage

**Introduce the Text** *Today I'm going to read aloud a selection about the importance of clean water. Listen to learn about a product researchers developed to clean contaminated water.*

**Engage Thinking** *Millions of people around the world do not have access to clean water. How do you think this affects their lives? Turn to a partner to share your prediction.*

## Engage with the Text

Read aloud the text at a fluent, expressive pace. Use the suggested prompts to model your thinking, clarify events, and elicit student interaction.

**1.** *The opening sentence makes me think of several questions about clean water. Why is it difficult to find? Who does not have access to clean water? What can be done about this problem? I'll read on to see if this article answers these questions.* (Ask questions)

**2.** *The packet is added to contaminated water. Then the water is safe to drink. I think* contaminated *and* safe *are antonyms. Water that is contaminated is the opposite of water that is safe.* (Use antonyms)

# Innovative Packets Save Lives

## by Hugh Westrup

1   Clean water is essential to our lives. But throughout the world, it can be very difficult to find. **❶**

2   In the world's developing countries, people get sick and die every day because of dirty water. About one in nine—or 780 million people—lack access to this vital source. The continent of Africa alone makes up half this number.

3   There are many reasons that water becomes contaminated. The drinking water may come from the same sources that people bathe in or share with farm animals. Or it may be water that is fouled by the runoff from sewage systems. Millions of people don't have sanitary toilets to use.

4   All of this puts the third world, especially children, at greater risk for life-threatening diarrhea. Diarrhea is not a single illness. It has many causes. Most of them are microbes: viruses, bacteria, and tiny parasites in unsanitary water.

5   Clean water is the key to keeping the microbes that cause the illness at bay. That's where the P&G Purifier of Water packets come in. Researchers at the U.S. Centers for Disease Control and Prevention and the Procter & Gamble (P&G) Company invented these small foil packets. More than 780 million packets have been distributed around the world since 2004.

6   Each packet holds a small amount of grayish powder. Add the powder from a packet to about 2.5 gallons of contaminated water and then stir. Pour the mixture through a cloth and allow it to set for 20 minutes. The result is water safe enough to drink. **❷**

7   "There were gasps of excitement when the water turned from this horrible, muddy dark color to crystal clear and safe," recalls Dr. Greg Allgood. He was demonstrating the powder for the first time to residents of a village in Africa. Dr. Allgood travels the world, teaching people how to use the packets. About 1 billion people do not have access to clean drinking water.

8 The powder in each packet works in two ways. One ingredient is calcium hypochlorite, better known as bleach. Calcium hypochlorite is a disinfectant. A disinfectant kills harmful microbes, including the ones that cause diarrhea.

9 Another ingredient is iron sulfate, a powerful flocculant. A flocculant is a substance that makes loose particles in a liquid come together in clumps and sink to the bottom. The clumps are removed when the water is poured through a cloth. In dirty water, flocculants cause toxic metals, such as lead, arsenic, and mercury, and other impurities to clump.

10 The challenge is making the packets available to people around the world who are too poor to afford them. Most Purifier of Water packets are distributed free of charge by the Children's Safe Drinking Water Program. The program is a division of P&G. Dr. Allgood is its director. The packets are given to humanitarian and disaster relief organizations, such as World Vision, the Red Cross, and Save the Children. Some of those organizations provide the packets to communities where clean water is unavailable. Other organizations distribute the packets when hurricanes, floods, and tsunamis destroy clean drinking water supplies.

11 Since 2004, the packets have disinfected more than 2 billion gallons of water worldwide and saved an estimated 43,000 lives. "There is nothing more rewarding," says Allgood, "than giving children their first glass of clean, purified drinking water." **3** **4**

3. *This article is about packets that are given to people where water is contaminated. I know that I use clean water for drinking, bathing, and cooking. So this helps me understand how other people's lives are greatly made better with these packets.* (Make connections)

4. *Turn and talk to a partner. Explain to each other how the water packets work.* (Summarize/Synthesize)

## Extend Thinking Questions

Pose one or more questions to engage students more deeply with the text.

• *Technology is applying scientific knowledge to practical uses. Do you think the packets are an example of technology? Why or why not?*

• *What happened when Dr. Allgood demonstrated the powder for the first time? What caused this to happen?*

**iELD  Paraphrase to Support Comprehension**

After paragraph 4: *Over 780 million people do not have access to clean water. Water gets dirty for many reasons. Dirty water causes diseases.*

After paragraph 9: *Researchers developed a powder that cleans water. Each P&G Purifier of Water packet can clean 2.5 gallons of dirty water. The powder works in two ways: It kills the germs and makes poisonous metals clump together and fall to the bottom.*

After paragraph 11: *The goal is to get these packets to poor people all around the world. Since 2004 the packets have been used to clean more than 2 billion gallons of water and saved about 43,000 lives.*

CCSS
RI.4.1, RI.4.2, RI.4.3, RI.4.4, SL.4.2, L.4.5c

Unit 5

## Objective

• Model summarizing/synthesizing

## Set the Stage

**Introduce the Text** *Today I'm going to read aloud an article about wind energy. "The Clean Power of Wind" explains what wind is, and how it has been used to create energy over the years. The article presents arguments for and against the use of wind energy rather than coal to create electricity.*

**Engage Thinking** *What advantages do you think creating electricity with wind has over creating electricity with coal? Turn to a partner to share your prediction.*

## Engage with the Text

Read aloud the text at a fluent, expressive pace. Use the suggested prompts to model your thinking, clarify events, and elicit student interaction.

1. *Wind energy can be transformed into mechanical energy. I know the prefix* trans- *can mean "to change." So this probably means that wind energy can change its form into mechanical energy.* (Determine word meaning)

2. *One main idea is that wind energy has helped people perform tasks for centuries. Some details that support this are: Ancient Egyptians used wind to move sailboats; Middle Eastern people built windmills to grind wheat.* (Cite main idea)

3. *Wind energy is renewable. It does not harm the environment. I know that some people are not in favor of only using renewable energy sources. So I think it will take a long time before we figure out the best energy sources.* (Summarize/Synthesize)

# The Clean Power of Wind

## by Amber Lanier Nagle

1   On breezy days, wind makes things move. It sways the branches and leaves of the trees and tousles your hair around. It blows clouds and kites across the sky, and during powerful storms, strong winds can even blow the roof off a house.

2   But what exactly is wind? Wind is the movement of air caused by the sun's uneven heating of the earth's surface. During the day, the sun shines and heats the air above land more quickly than it heats the air over water. As the warmer air over the land rises, cooler air from over the water rushes in to take its place, creating wind.

3   Wind energy, the energy obtained from devices powered by the wind, can be transformed into mechanical energy or electrical energy. **❶** For centuries, people have used the wind's energy to accomplish physical tasks. Thousands of years before Christopher Columbus crossed the Atlantic Ocean with his fleet of sailing vessels, ancient Egyptians used wind-catching sails on their ships to navigate the Nile River. The Mayflower's voyage to America in 1620 depended on wind filling its sails with air and pushing the ship through turbulent waters.

4   Wind was also used to perform work on land. Middle Eastern people built wind devices (windmills) that captured wind and turned it into mechanical energy for grinding wheat and other grains. The wind would blow against the windmill blades and cause them to spin like a fan. This turning motion would rotate a shaft, which turned a large grinding stone to crush grain into powdery flour. **❷**

5   Through the centuries, people from other areas of the world designed similar wind machines for other purposes. People of the Netherlands engineered their windmills to pump water and saw wood.

6   Then, in 1887, the first wind machines that could generate electricity were built. Americans used these small wind turbines to generate small amounts of electricity on their rural farms until the 1930s, when the Rural Electrification Administration extended electrical service to very remote areas, making windmills obsolete.

7   But interest in using wind energy to make electricity is growing again due to recent economic and environmental concerns. Most of America's electricity is generated by coal-burning power plants, which pollute the air. Harnessing wind energy to make electricity is much easier on our environment. Wind does not have to be mined from the earth like coal, and wind energy does not produce air or water pollution, because no fuel is burned in the process.

8   Coal and other fossil fuels that are used to make electricity are not in endless supply—they will someday be used up. But wind energy is often referred to as a renewable source of energy, because wind will blow and produce energy forever.

9   Today, wind generates only a small fraction of our nation's electricity via wind farms: large groups of wind turbines that transform wind into electricity. Just like a giant toy pinwheel, blowing wind turns two or three thin blades on a turbine. The spinning blades rotate a series of shafts and gears and then turn a generator that makes electricity. The electricity is transferred to a substation, which is wired to nearby homes and buildings.

10  So why aren't there more wind farms in the United States? Not every city has a windy location nearby, and it is very expensive to transport electricity long distances to the communities that need power. Also, some people do not want wind farms built near their communities, because they feel that wind turbines are ugly and ruin the natural beauty of the land. Some believe that wind farms are harmful to birds and other wildlife, and others argue that the wind turbines' humming sound is bothersome.

11  Our nation is faced with an ever-growing demand for energy, so finding alternative energy sources is important. Creating electricity with wind turbines may not be a perfect solution, but it has many advantages over traditional power generation. Wind is plentiful and easily transformed into electrical energy, but, most of all, wind energy is clean and doesn't harm our environment. **3** **4**

---

**4.** *Turn and talk to a partner. Ask: What is your opinion about using wind energy to create electricity? Support your answer with evidence. (Make connections/Ask questions)*

## Extend Thinking Questions

Pose one or more questions to engage students more deeply with the text.

• *What influenced scientists to develop ways to use wind to produce electricity?*

• *How did the author argue against using wind as an energy source?*

**iELD Paraphrase to Support Comprehension**

After paragraph 5: *People have used energy from the wind for centuries. Wind helped move sailboats. Windmills helped grind wheat into grains. They also pumped water.*

After paragraph 8 : *In 1887 wind machines that could generate electricity were built. This does not pollute the air or water like coal and other fossil fuels. Wind is renewable, but fossil fuels are not.*

After paragraph 11: *Not all areas can generate electricity. Some are not near windy areas. Some people do not want wind turbines near them. Some believe windmills harm birds. However, wind turbines have many advantages over traditional sources.*

**Unit 5**

**CCSS**
**RI.4.1, RI.4.2, RI.4.3, RI.4.4, RI.4.8, SL.4.2, SL.4.3, L.4.4b**

## Set the Stage

**Introduce the Text** *Today I'm going to read aloud one part from the book* Operation Redwood *by S. Terrell French. The novel is about a group of smart friends who work together to stop a company from cutting down trees. This part opens when the friends notice some men spray-painting the trunks of trees in the forest.*

**Engage Thinking** *Where do you think the friends are when they notice the men? Turn to a partner to share your prediction.*

## Engage with the Text

Read aloud the text at a fluent, expressive pace. Use the suggested prompts to model your thinking, clarify events, and elicit student interaction.

**1.** *Two men are spraying paint on some trees. I know the title of the book is* Operation Redwood *and that redwood trees are very rare. So I think the men are marking redwoods.* (Summarize/Synthesize)

**2.** *One of the men says, "This place is a gold mine." I don't think they are in a real gold mine. They are talking about the trees, so I think they mean the trees are worth a lot of money.* (Determine word meaning)

# Intruders

## A chapter from Operation Redwood, Part 1

### by S. Terrell French

1   The sound of the birds woke the children early. In the sunshine, the forest looked bright and ordinary again. For breakfast, they ate the apples and the rest of the chocolate chip cookies and passed around a box of cereal. Danny and Julian started a game of crazy eights and Robin and Ariel joined in after the first round. Molly lay down with her chin in her hands, looking into the forest.

2   "Somebody's coming," she said so softly that only Julian heard. He craned forward and saw two men, dressed in jeans and T-shirts, walking slowly from tree to tree. One had a mustache and was carrying a can of spray paint. The other was older and wore glasses and a camouflage cap.

3   "Everybody down," Julian whispered loudly.

4   Danny and the girls looked up from their cards, and Julian pointed at the two men. Robin crouched down behind one of the storage bins and the others quickly flattened themselves on top of the sleeping bags and peered through the railings.

5   Nobody spoke a word. They watched as the man with the paint can sprayed a blue slash on a giant redwood about twenty feet away. **❶**

6   "Boy, you don't see trees like this anymore," said the older man. He gave the tree an appreciative look and jotted a note on his clipboard.

7   "This place is a gold mine. My granddaddy's place used to look just like this when I was a kid. If he hadn't sold it, I'd be a rich man." **❷**

8   "The rest of the property's not bad either. There must be half a million dollars' worth of fir back on that northern slope."

9   "Yeah, but this here's the real treasure."

10  The spray-painter was standing right underneath them. They could see his brown mustache and the glint of his blue eyes through the cracks in the floorboards. "Hey, look up here," he said. "There's a tree house!"

11  "You better watch out, there might be somebody living up there."

12 Julian felt a sharp poke in his side. Robin was motioning for everyone to stand up. When nobody moved, she gave them a dirty look and stood up tall, her chin thrust out. Julian and Danny jumped up next to her, and Ariel and Molly reluctantly followed.

13 The spray-painter made a long blue streak on one of the trunks below them. **3**

14 "Hey, this is our tree house," Robin yelled down. "What do you think you're doing?" **4**

3. *I can visualize the setting. The five children are up in a tree house with their sleeping bags. The tree is a large redwood. They are in the forest. They can see the two men spraying trees in the forest.* (Describe setting)

4. *Turn and talk to a partner. Why do you think the men are spraying the trunks of the trees?* (Make inferences/ predictions)

## Extend Thinking Questions

Pose one or more questions to engage students more deeply with the text.

• *Do you think trees can be used to develop technology? Why or why not?*

• *What examples of "green" behavior did the children practice in this part of the story?*

**iELD Paraphrase to Support Comprehension**

**After paragraph 4:** *Five children are up in a tree house. They hear some noise in the forest below. They keep silent and watch two men with a can of spray paint.*

**After paragraph 9:** *One man sprays blue paint on a redwood tree. They talk about how valuable all of the trees are.*

**After paragraph 14:** *The men look up. They notice the tree house. The children stand up. The man sprays the trunk of the tree that the children are in.*

**CCSS**
**RL.4.1, RL.4.2, RL.4.3, RL.4.4, SL.4.2, L.4.4a, L.4.5b**

## Objective

• Model summarizing/synthesizing

## Set the Stage

**Introduce the Text** *Today I'm going to read aloud part 2 in a chapter from the book* Operation Redwood. *What happened in part 1? (Have volunteers summarize part 1.) In this part we learn why the men are spraying the trees and what the children's reactions are.*

**Engage Thinking** *One of the friends has a very powerful and influential uncle. Who do you think his uncle might be? Turn to a partner to share your prediction.*

## Engage with the Text

Read aloud the text at a fluent, expressive pace. Use the suggested prompts to model your thinking, clarify events, and elicit student interaction.

**1.** *One of the men pantomimed having a heart attack. The words before this say he grabbed his chest. So I think* pantomime *means "to act out or use gestures." (Determine word meaning)*

**2.** *The children say the tree house belongs to them and they will not leave. The men say that the trees are coming down anyway. I know when people disagree they often fight for what they want. I think the children and the company that wants to cut down the trees will each fight for what they want. (Summarize/Synthesize)*

# Intruders

## A chapter from Operation Redwood, Part 2

1   The spray-painter grabbed his chest and pantomimed having a heart attack. "Holy smokes!" he cried. "What are you doing up there?"

2   "What are you doing spray-painting our tree?" Robin demanded.

3   "The trees you're marking," Julian said, "are those the ones you're cutting down?

4   "That's the way it goes, kids," said the man with glasses.

5   "Sorry. You're going to have to build your tree house someplace else."

6   "We don't want to build it someplace else," Danny said. "We like it right here. Why don't you go cut down trees someplace else?"

7   "Because we've got a THP for these trees, that's how come," the spray-painter said.

8   Ariel stepped forward. "But these trees are so beautiful. You guys just said there's not many of them left."

9   "Listen, kids," the older man said. "The harvest plan's already approved. These trees are worth a bundle. They're coming down."

10  "Well, we're not leaving" said Robin. ❷

11  The spray-painter grinned and glanced back over his shoulder. "Looks like we've got some juvenile tree sitters here."

12  "OK, we'll make a note of that in our report to Mr. Carter," older man responded with mock seriousness, writing something on the clipboard.

13  "You better! You better make a note of it, because Sibley Carter is his uncle!" Robin said, pointing at Julian.

14  The men stared up at them, confused. "What in the world are you talking about?" the older man said.

15  "This boy," Robin grabbed Julian by the arm, "is the nephew of Sibley Carter. *The* Sibley Carter. The CEO of IPX." She pulled Julian forward a little. "And he's not leaving either. Not until you guys agree not to cut down any of these trees."

16  "Are you kidding me?"

17 "No, it's true," Julian said. The squeak in his voice made him wince and he tried again, in a lower tone. "He's my father's brother."

18 "If Sibley Carter was my uncle, I sure wouldn't be living in a tree house," the spray-painter said.

19 "What's your name?" the older man asked.

20 "Julian." And a little louder, "Julian Carter-Li."

21 He started scribbling in his clipboard. "Any of the rest of you claiming to be Mr. Carter's relatives?"

22 They shook their heads. Molly said, "My daddy's Bob Elder."

23 "Oh, you're Bob's kids." The man made another note on his clipboard. "Did your daddy tell you to trespass on this property?"

24 Molly shook her head solemnly.

25 "I didn't think so. You tell him Pete came by." He stepped back and adjusted his cap. "Come on, let's finish up here," he said to the spray-painter. "We'd better make sure there's no other kids hiding up in the trees."

26 Robin watched them walk away. "Tell Carter we're not coming down!" she yelled. "We're serious! He'll have to chop us down!" ❸

27 The spray-painter gave her a thumbs-up. Then the two men walked off into the forest, stopping every so often to mark another tree.

28 "Well, we showed them," Danny said sourly. "They were shakin' in their boots. I'm sure they're going to go back and call the whole project off."

29 Ariel was craning over the side of the railing. "Our beautiful trees," she wailed. "They've put graffiti all over them. Look at that!"

30 They all stared down at the blue marks. The men were now nowhere to be seen.

31 "Maybe we can erase all the marks. So they won't know which trees to cut," Danny suggested.

32 "I don't think you can erase spray paint," Robin said.

33 "Well, paint over it, then," Danny said. "With bark-colored paint."

34 Nobody responded.

35 Ariel began gathering up the scattered cards from their game of crazy eights. "We need to do something else. Just sitting in this tree isn't going to be enough. Not even close." ❹

---

3. *Robin seems to be aggressive and brave. She yells at the men. She tells them they won't leave the tree house. She grabs Julian to pull him forward to show the men his uncle is Sibley Carter. She says Carter will have to chop them down to get them to leave.* (Describe characters)

4. *Turn and talk to a partner. Do you think it is important that one of the children is the nephew of Sibley Carter? Why or why not?* (Make inferences/predictions)

## Extend Thinking Questions

Pose one or more questions to engage students more deeply with the text.

• *Why do you think people decide to cut down redwood trees?*

• *Ariel says, "We need to do something else." What do you think they will do?*

**iELD  Paraphrase to Support Comprehension**

After paragraph 10: *The men confirm that they are spraying trees to be cut down. The children say they won't leave the tree house.*

After paragraph 26: *One of the children is the nephew of Sibley Carter, who owns the company that wants to cut down the trees. The men take notes and leave.*

After paragraph 35: *The children try to think of ways to stop the company from cutting down their trees. None of their ideas will work. They need to think of something else.*

CCSS
RL.4.1, RL.4.2, RL.4.3, RL.4.4, SL.4.2, L.4.4a

**Unit 5**

# Researchers Develop a Cheap Battery to Power Your House—and It's Organic

## by Kristine Wong

1   Here's a dirty little secret about the batteries we increasingly rely on to power our emissions-free cars and store clean, green energy from the sun and wind: They contain metals that must be mined and can contaminate groundwater if they end up in landfills.

2   But an eco-friendly alternative could be coming soon. Researchers at the University of Southern California have developed a first-of-its-kind battery that replaces metal catalysts with quinone—an organic molecule that stores and transfers energy and can be found in fungi, bacteria, and even our bodies. The scientists predict such a battery will be ten times cheaper to make and will last five times longer than a lithium-ion battery. ❶

3   A race is under way to develop battery technology to store electricity from wind farms and solar power plants, the growth of which has been exponential in recent years. Since renewable energy production is intermittent—electricity is generated only when the wind blows and the sun shines—batteries are needed to store that energy and dispatch it to keep the power grid balanced.

4   The problem: Existing battery technology is expensive.

5   "Using organic materials can let you build a very durable system to be scaled up at cost," said Sri Narayan, a chemistry professor at USC who developed the battery with colleague G.K. Surya Prakash. They recently published their research in the Journal of the Electrochemical Society.

6   Here's how their technology—a variant of a redox flow battery—works. First, two types of quinone molecules are modified to make them water soluble; then they're dissolved in separate tanks of water. ❷ The solutions are pumped through a power cell containing a membrane. That triggers a chemical reaction that generates electricity. Reverse the process, and the battery can store electricity. Their organic battery can be recharged 5,000 times, the researchers say, while a standard lithium ion battery can only be recharged 1,000 times. That gives their battery an estimated lifetime of 15 years.

7   Just don't expect an organic battery to power your car or iPhone. Flow batteries' bulk makes them suitable for use only at power plants, though smaller versions could store electricity from your home rooftop solar array.

8   One of the big challenges of developing an organic battery was getting a high concentration of quinone molecules to stay soluble in water. "Mixing the two can be like an oil-water mixture," Prakash said. "There was a lot of thinking and redesigning of molecules."

9   The researchers are working on building a commercial prototype of their laboratory-scale model that could generate electricity at half the cost of current systems.

10  "It's important to have clean energy storage coupled with clean generation," Narayan said. That way, "you're not making clean energy and then putting it into a dirty battery." **3** **4**

**3.** *I know that scientists are trying to develop batteries that hold their charge longer. This article says that scientists predict that this battery can last five times longer than a lithium-ion battery. So I think scientists will continue to research and improve organic batteries.* (Summarize/ Synthesize)

**4.** *Turn and talk to a partner. What are some limitations of the organic battery?* (Summarize)

## Extend Thinking Questions

Pose one or more questions to engage students more deeply with the text.

• *How is the development of the organic battery related to a green future?*

• *What questions do you have about organic batteries? How could you find the answers?*

**Unit 5**

CCSS
RI.4.1, RI.4.2, RI.4.4, SL.4.2, L.4.4a

# The Latest Smog-Eating Weapon Might Just Be Your Roof

Students at the University of California, Riverside, have created a coating that destroys the emissions equivalent of a car driven 11,000 miles

## by Liz Dwyer

1   We all know that getting more pollution-spewing cars off the road is the solution to curbing the globe's dismal air-quality situation. In the meantime, crews of scientists across the world have been busy developing technology that destroys the toxic fumes coming out of automobile tailpipes. The latest effort comes from a team of clever chemical and environmental engineers at the University of California, Riverside. They've come up with a coating for roofs that eats the smog emissions equivalent of a car driven 11,000 miles per year. **1**

2   The roof coating, which is simply a paint made from titanium dioxide, the same chemical found in commercial sunscreens, is photocatalytic. Once it's painted on a surface and particulate matter in air pollution comes in contact with it, the smog turns into harmless inert salts. Architects from Italy to China are constructing buildings made out of these kinds of materials, and the U.K. even has a smog-killing poem. But the UC Riverside solution is perhaps the most practical and cost-efficient of all. Paint can be placed anywhere, and the team estimates that it would cost $5 to produce enough coating to cover the roof of a 2,400-square-foot house.

3   The students hope to expand beyond covering roofs. "Our goal is to apply this coating on any surface that hits direct sunlight," says Jessica Moncayo, one of the students who worked on the project. To that end, the team has big ideas, such as painting freeways with the coating. "Having the coating on freeway dividers allows the coating exposed closer to one [nitrous oxide] emission source—vehicles.

4    So will this pollution-killing technology become available for you to paint on a roof anytime soon? Many students from the UC Riverside team graduated last June. Moncayo says she's not sure how many new students have stepped up to continue the research, and additional funding is needed. It seems like the kind of idea that a paint company would be keen to help out with. **2** However, if a new research crew at UC Riverside is assembled, it'll need to conduct more effectiveness trials and figure out what works best. "Testing additional parameters will allow us to optimize and prove the sustainability of the coating," says Moncayo.

5    Right now, one challenge in bringing the coating to market is that it's only available in white, and not everyone wants a roof painted that color. However, that's not a bad problem to have; it's been proven that a white roof reflects 90 percent of sunlight whereas a black roof reflects just 20 percent. That means our cities could be less smoggy and cooler.

6    Moncayo says that the team's professors have been contacted by government agencies in the U.S. and abroad.

7    "This is good news since our coating was to be cost-effective enough to spread to other countries experiencing poor air quality as well," she says. Getting the public informed of such efforts to improve air quality is crucial, she adds. **3**

8    If the public demands simple solutions, like a coating that can eat smog, politicians and policy makers are more likely to get the ball rolling and make that happen. **4**

**3.** *The roof coating is inexpensive. It helps cut down on air pollution. I know many people are concerned about pollution. This seems like an inexpensive and easy way to control it. So I think this coating will be popular once it comes to market. (Summarize/Synthesize)*

**4.** *Turn and talk to a partner. What is the main idea of this article? Support your answer with details from the article. (Summarize)*

## Extend Thinking Questions

Pose one or more questions to engage students more deeply with the text.

• *What decisions need to be made to continue to develop this technology?*

• *What questions do you have about smog-killing coatings that were not answered in this article? How could you find the answers?*

### iELD Paraphrase to Support Comprehension

After paragraph 2: *Engineers at the University of California have developed a new kind of roof coating. It turns smog particles into harmless salts. It costs only $5 to cover a large roof.*

After paragraph 4: *The team who worked on this coating hope to also use it on freeways. This will help kill pollution emissions from cars. More studies need to be done.*

After paragraph 7: *The team hopes to make improvements to the product such as making more colors. They hope that eventually it will be sold to many countries. This is a simple solution to improve air quality.*

CCSS
RI.4.1, RI.4.2, RI.4.4, SL.4.2, L.4.4a

**Unit 5**

## Objective

• Model making connections

## Set the Stage

**Introduce the Text** *Today I'm going to read aloud a chapter called "Ordinary" from the novel* Wonder *by R.J. Palacio. The book is about Auggie, a ten-year-old boy with a deformed face, who will be going to a mainstream school for the first time. In this excerpt Auggie introduces himself and some of the problems he faces because of his deformity.*

**Engage Thinking** *What obstacles do you think Auggie faces in daily life? Turn to a partner to share your prediction.*

## Engage with the Text

Read aloud the text at a fluent, expressive pace. Use the suggested prompts to model your thinking, clarify events, and elicit student interaction.

**1.** *I remember when I had a black eye from falling. Everyone stared. I felt so embarrassed and uncomfortable around people. So I know how Auggie must feel when people run away or stare at him.* (Make connections)

**2.** *Mom and Dad see Auggie as "extraordinary." Extra- is a Latin affix meaning "beyond." So Mom and Dad see Auggie as "beyond an ordinary boy."* (Determine word meaning)

# Ordinary
## A chapter from Wonder

## by R.J. Palacio

1   I know I'm not an ordinary ten-year old kid. I mean, sure, I do ordinary things. I eat ice cream. I ride my bike. I play ball, I have an Xbox. Stuff like that makes me ordinary. I guess. And I feel ordinary. Inside. But I know ordinary kids don't make other ordinary kids run away screaming in playgrounds. I know ordinary kids don't get stared at wherever they go. **❶**

2   If I found a magic lamp and I could have one wish, I would wish that I had a normal face that no one ever noticed at all. I would wish that I could walk down the street without people seeing me and then doing that look-away thing. Here's what I think: the only reason I'm not ordinary is that no one else sees me that way.

3   But I'm kind of used to how I look by now. I know how to pretend I don't see the faces people make. We've all gotten pretty good at that sort of thing: me, Mom and Dad, Via. Actually, I take that back: Via's not so good at it. She can get really annoyed when people do something rude. Like, for instance, one time in the playground some older kids made some noises.

4   I don't even know what the noises were exactly because I didn't hear them myself, but Via heard and she just started yelling at the kids. That's the way she is. I'm not that way.

5   Via doesn't see me as ordinary. She says she does, but if I were ordinary, she wouldn't feel like she needs to protect me as much. And Mom and Dad don't see me as ordinary, either. They see me as extraordinary. I think the only person in the world who realizes how ordinary I am is me. **❷**

6   My name is August, by the way. I won't describe what I look like. Whatever you're thinking, it's probably worse.

7   Next week I start fifth grade. Since I've never been to a real school before, I am pretty much totally and completely petrified. People think I haven't gone to school because of the way I look, but it's not that. It's because of all the surgeries I've had. Twenty-seven since I was born. **3** The bigger ones happened before I was even four years old, so I don't remember those. But I've had two or three surgeries every year since then (some big, some small), and because I'm little for my age, and I have some other medical mysteries that doctors never really figured out, I used to get sick a lot. That's when my parents decided it was better if I didn't go to school. I'm much stronger now, though. The last surgery I had was eight months ago, and I probably won't have to have any more for another couple of years.

8   Mom homeschools me. She used to be a children's-book illustrator. She draws really great fairies and mermaids. Her boy stuff isn't so hot, though. She once tried to draw me a Darth Vader, but it ended up looking like some weird mushroom-shaped robot. I haven't seen her draw anything in a long time. I think she's too busy taking care of me and Via.

9   I can't say I always wanted to go to school because that wouldn't be exactly true. What I wanted was to go to school, but only if I could be like every other kid going to school. Have lots of friends and hang out after school and stuff like that.

10  I have a few really good friends now. Christopher is my best friend, followed by Zachary and Alex. We've known each other since we were babies. And since they've always known me the way I am, they're used to me. **4**

3. *People think Auggie didn't go to school for all of these years because of the way he looks. But that is not the cause. The cause for not going to school is that he has had so many surgeries. His mother did not want him to get sick.* (Cause and effect)

4. *Turn and talk to a partner. What qualities does Auggie have? Support your answers with details from the story.* (Describe characters)

## Extend Thinking Questions

Pose one or more questions to engage students more deeply with the text.

• *What obstacles will Auggie have to overcome when he goes to school?*

• *One theme of this story is overcoming challenges. Another is supporting those you love. What details support this second theme?*

**iELD  Paraphrase to Support Comprehension**

After paragraph 2: *Auggie is a ten-year-old boy with a facial deformity. He wishes other people did not stare at him. He wishes he was ordinary.*

After paragraph 5: *His sister Via gets annoyed when people stare at him. His parents see him as extraordinary. No one realizes how ordinary he is except him.*

After paragraph 10: *Auggie starts fifth grade in mainstream school next week. So far he was homeschooled by his mother. He is scared about going to school. However, he does have good friends: Christopher, Zachary, and Alex.*

**CCSS**
**RL.4.1, RL.4.2, RL.4.3, RL.4.4, L.4.4b**

**Unit 6**

# The Grand Tour
## A chapter from Wonder

1   Jack Will, Julian, Charlotte, and I went down a big hallway to some wide stairs. No one said a word as we walked up to the third floor.

2   When we got to the top of the stairs, we went down a little hallway full of lots of doors. Julian opened the door marked 301.

3   "This is our homeroom," he said, standing in front of the half-opened door. "We have Ms. Petosa. They say she's okay, at least for homeroom. I heard she's really strict if you get her for math, though." **1**

4   "That's not true," said Charlotte. "My sister had her last year and said she's totally nice."

5   "Not what I heard," answered Julian, "but whatever." He closed the door and continued walking down the hallway.

6   "This is the science lab," he said when he got to the next door. And just like he did two seconds ago, he stood in front of the half-opened door and started talking. He didn't look at me once while he talked, which was okay because I wasn't looking at him, either. "You won't know who you have for science until the first day of school, but you want to get Mr. Haller. He used to be in the lower school. He would play this giant tuba in class."

7   "It was a baritone horn," said Charlotte.

8   "It was a tuba!" answered Julian, closing the door.

9   "Dude, let him go inside so he can check it out," Jack Will told him, pushing past Julian and opening the door. **2**

10  "Go inside if you want," Julian said. It was the first time he looked at me.

11  I shrugged and walked over to the door. Julian moved out of the way quickly, like he was afraid I might accidentally touch him as I passed by him.

12  "Nothing much to see," Julian said, walking in after me. He started pointing to a bunch of stuff around the room. "That's the incubator. That big black thing is the chalkboard. These are the desks. These are chairs. Those are the Bunsen burners. This is a gross science poster. This is chalk. This is the eraser."

13  "I'm sure he knows what an eraser is," Charlotte said, sounding a little like Via. **3**

14 "How would I know what he knows?" Julian answered. "Mr. Tushman said he's never been to a school before."

15 "You know what an eraser is, right?" Charlotte asked me.

16 I admit I was feeling so nervous that I didn't know what to say or do except look at the floor.

17 "Hey, can you talk?" asked Jack Will.

18 "Yeah." I nodded. I still really hadn't looked at any of them yet, not directly.

19 "You know what an eraser is, right?" asked Jack Will. "Of course!" I mumbled.

20 "I told you there was nothing to see in here," said Julian, shrugging.

21 "I have a question...," I said, trying to keep my voice steady. "Um. What exactly is homeroom? Is that like a subject?"

22 "No, that's just your group," explained Charlotte, ignoring Julian's smirk. "It's like where you go when you get to school in the morning and your homeroom teacher takes attendance and stuff like that. In a way, it's your main class even though it's not really a class. I mean, it's a class, but—"

23 "I think he gets it, Charlotte," said Jack Will. "Do you get it?" Charlotte asked me.

24 "Yeah." I nodded at her.

25 "Okay, let's get out of here," said Jack Will, walking away.

26 "Wait, Jack, we're supposed to be answering questions," said Charlotte.

27 Jack Will rolled his eyes a little as he turned around.

28 "Do you have any more questions?" he asked.

29 "Um, no," I answered. "Oh, well, actually, yes. Is your name Jack or Jack Will?"

30 "Jack is my first name. Will is my last name."

31 "Oh, because Mr. Tushman introduced you as Jack Will, so I thought..."

32 "Ha! You thought his name was Jackwill!" laughed Julian.

33 "Yeah, some people call me by my first and last name," Jack said, shrugging. "I don't know why. Anyway, can we go now?"

34 "Let's go to the performance space next," said Charlotte, leading the way out of the science room. "It's very cool. You'll like it, August." **4**

3. *When Auggie says that Charlotte sounds a little like Via I think he feels like Charlotte is trying to protect him. I think Charlotte is not as uncomfortable around him as the others.* (Make inferences)

4. *Turn and talk to a partner. What is the theme of this chapter? What details support this theme?* (Determine theme)

## Extend Thinking Questions

Pose one or more questions to engage students more deeply with the text.

• *What obstacles does Auggie experience on this tour with the other students?*

• *What are some things Charlotte does that shows she is trying to protect and help Auggie?*

### iELD Paraphrase to Support Comprehension

**After paragraph 12:** *Jack Will, Julian, and Charlotte take Auggie on a tour of the school. They show him the homeroom. Then they show him the science lab. He walks in to look around.*

**After paragraph 24:** *Julian points out the desks, chalk, and eraser. Charlotte says Auggie knows what an eraser is. Auggie doesn't know what homeroom is. Charlotte explains what it is to him.*

**After paragraph 34:** *Auggie is uncomfortable but asks Jack if his name is Jack or Jack Will. Julian makes fun of Jack, who seems embarrassed by the question. Then Charlotte suggests going to the performance space. She tells Auggie he will like it.*

**CCSS**
**RL.4.1, RL.4.2, RL.4.3, RL.4.4, SL.4.2, L.4.5b**

## Objective

• Model making connections

## Set the Stage

**Introduce the Text** *Today I'm going to read aloud a story based on a myth about Hercules. In mythology, Hercules is mainly known for his superhuman strength. This story tells about a problem Hercules faces and how he uses his powers to overcome obstacles to solve it.*

**Engage Thinking** *What obstacles do you think Hercules will overcome? Turn to a partner to share your prediction.*

## Engage with the Text

Read aloud the text at a fluent, expressive pace. Use the suggested prompts to model your thinking, clarify events, and elicit student interaction.

**1.** *I know in- means "not" and -ible means "able to be." The root -vinc- comes from* vincere, *which means "conquer." So* invincible *means "not able to be conquered." So if Hercules is not invincible, he is able to be conquered.* (Determine word meaning)

**2.** *I know that Hercules is known for his strength. This story is about a challenge. Hercules has to slay a lion. I think Hercules will use his strength to slay the lion. I'll read on to see if my prediction is correct.* (Make connections/Predictions)

# Hercules and the Lion

1   Hercules, as you probably know, was a very strong man. Indeed, he had superhuman strength, which makes sense because he was more than just a man. Hercules was born to a mortal mother, but his father was Zeus, the immortal god of ancient Greek mythology. So Hercules himself is sort of a half man, half god; in the mythological world, this is apparently not an unusual situation. Whatever he is, Hercules is incredibly strong, but not invincible. **❶**

2   According to the myths, Hercules has an enemy. Unfortunately for him, she is his father's wife, the goddess Hera. Ever since Hercules was born, Hera has been trying to get rid of him. Recently, Hera caused Hercules to lose his mind and do some terrible things. Once he recovered his sanity, he was naturally horrified and anxious to make up for his bad behavior. That's where this story begins.

3   Hercules asks the Oracle at Delphi what he should do. The Oracle orders him to serve his cousin, King Eurystheus, for twelve years. If Hercules succeeds in his servitude, the Oracle says, he will be forgiven and granted immortality. But first, he must obey his cousin, a king for whom Hercules has no respect or fondness.

4   King Eurystheus, who just happens to be a friend of Hera's, devises a plan for his cousin. He orders Hercules to perform a list of twelve tasks, or labors. In each one, Hercules must face incredible danger to kill or retrieve something magical. Naturally, Eurystheus assumes Hercules will never actually carry out these tasks, because surely the first one will kill him. First up, the king tells Hercules he must slay the Nemean lion. **❷**

5   The Nemean lion is a beast that lives in a cave near Nemea. Over the years, it has captured women and held them as hostages in his lair. They lure men to the cave, where the lion then devours them. Naturally, people are anxious to be rid of the Nemean lion.

6   Hercules arms himself with a bow and arrows and sharp spears and goes looking for the beast. But when he finds the lion, he quickly realizes his weapons are useless. The lion's thick golden fur is impenetrable; nothing can get through it. Hercules must depend on his own brute strength.

As the lion lunges at him, Hercules wraps his massive arms around the beast's neck and squeezes with all his might. The lion's razor-sharp fangs and claws tear at Hercules, but in the end, the beast dies in his powerful grasp. **3**

7    Hercules skins the lion using one of its own claws, the only thing that can slice through the fearsome hide. He puts the lion's head over his own like a helmet, and drapes the skin over his shoulders. He returns to Eurystheus, who nearly faints at the sight. Once the king is convinced the creature is really just Hercules in the lion's skin, he is terrified of Hercules and realizes he must make his cousin's next challenge even harder. Meanwhile, Eurystheus orders a huge bronze jar to be made, so he can hide in it when Hercules is around. **4**

**3.** *Hercules cannot use his weapon to slay the lion because the lion's fur is too thick and strong to pierce.* (Cause and effect)

**4.** *Turn and talk to a partner. Tell each other what Eurystheus is like. Support your answers with details from the story.* (Describe characters)

## Extend Thinking Questions

Pose one or more questions to engage students more deeply with the text.

• *What obstacles did Hercules overcome?*

• *How did he overcome them?*

### iELD Paraphrase to Support Comprehension

After paragraph 2: *Hercules is half man and half god. His enemy is his father's wife, the goddess Hera. She causes Hercules to lose his mind and do terrible things. Hercules wants to make up for the things he did.*

After paragraph 4: *If Hercules serves his cousin, King Eurystheus, for twelve years, he will be forgiven and become immortal. Eurystheus orders Hercules to do twelve tasks. The first is to slay the Nemean lion.*

After paragraph 7: *The lion's fur is too thick. Hercules's weapons cannot pierce the fur. So he uses his strength to squeeze and kill the lion. Eurystheus is now terrified of Hercules. He must make the next task harder.*

**Unit 6**

**CCSS**
**RL.4.1, RL.4.2, RL.4.3, RL.4.4, L.4.4a**

## Objective

• Model making connections

## Set the Stage

**Introduce the Text.** *Today I'm going to read aloud part 1 of a story called "The Inca Chasqui." An Inca Chasqui is a runner who delivers messages. In this first part we learn about Natu, a young Inca who dreams of becoming a Chasqui. The story opens with a flashback of an accident Natu has on a suspension bridge.*

**Engage Thinking** *What do you think might have happened as Natu tried to cross the suspension bridge? Turn to a partner to share your prediction.*

## Engage with the Text

Read aloud the text at a fluent, expressive pace. Use the suggested prompts to model your thinking, clarify events, and elicit student interaction.

**1.** *I remember walking across a small suspension bridge. The bridge swayed as I walked. I think it must have been very scary and difficult for Natu to carry a bundle of wool across a bridge like that.* (Make connections)

**2.** *A wind causes the bridge to swing. Natu falls against the side and drops the wool. He almost falls over the side, but his father pulls him to safety.* (Summarize)

# The Inca Chasqui, Part 1

## by Wendi Silvano

1   Natu watched his father unload the wool from the llama's back and divide it into two parts. One part he gave to his son to carry across the bridge that hung suspended high above the raging river, and the other he shouldered himself. Little did Natu know how deeply the bridge before him would affect his dream of becoming an Inca Chasqui. **❶**

2   Without a thought, the young Inca followed his father onto the bridge. The all-white llama plodded behind them. The bridge sagged down into a bowlike curve as they reached the center. Natu balanced his bundle of wool with one hand while he held the thick rope handrail with the other. The mountain wind tousled his straight black hair and dried the sweat that ran in rivulets down his back. Then, without warning, a strong gust of wind burst through the canyon, making the bridge swing sharply to one side. Startled, Natu let go of the handrail and instantly fell against the other side of the bridge just as it was swinging back. The llama's right foot slipped through the openings in the ropes, and it was pulled down to its belly.

3   The sudden weight of Natu's body against the side of the bridge caused it to tip on its side. As his feet swept out over the edge of the walkway, Natu dropped his bundle and grabbed the railing with both hands. He watched in horror as the wool spiraled downward for what seemed like an eternity. The shrill cry of the llama rang in his ears.

4   He squeezed his eyes shut and tightened his grip as the bridge swung back. His stomach flew into his throat. Natu tried to scream for help, but the sound choked in his chest. He was sure that at any moment he would lose his grip and fall to a violent death on the jagged rocks of the river below.

5   Suddenly he felt a strong hand grab the back of his tunic and pull him up. He clasped both arms around his father and sank down. The two of them sat, silently clutching each other, as the swaying gradually slowed. Then Natu's father got up, gently pulled the llama's leg free, and helped it stand. The three of them walked in silence as they carefully made their way to the other side. **❷**

6   Two years later, Natu could remember every detail of that day. But he kept the memory carefully tucked into a back corner of his mind. These days his thoughts were on one thing and one thing only—readying himself to be an Inca Chasqui.

7   Every boy, when he reached the age of fourteen, was expected to train for service in the Inca empire. To pay his mita, or tax requirement, each was assigned a particular service. **3** Some were chosen to be builders or soldiers. Others were servants in the Sapa Inca's household. The fastest and most dependable boys were chosen to be Chasquis.

8   Chasquis were stationed in small, one room huts about every two miles along the rock-paved Inca road system.

9   Each boy carried a message or parcel as fast as he could to the next hut and passed it on to a waiting runner. In this manner, messages could traverse the entire Inca kingdom, from north to south, in just a matter of days. Chasquis had to be strong, loyal, and brave. If even one runner failed to make his delivery, the entire chain would be broken, and the message would never reach its destination.

10  Natu heard the wail of the conch shell, signaling an approaching runner. He scurried up the hill to where his older brother Mayta stood ready. Mayta was the fastest Chasqui in the southeast quarter. Natu loved to see him run. **4**

11  He watched with envy as Mum, the runner, told Mayta the message. Then, like a racing puma, Mayta sped off toward the next hut.

**3.** *The author gives definition clues in two different ways. The definition for* mita *is given within commas, just after the word: a tax requirement.* (Determine word meaning)

**4.** *Turn and talk to a partner. Why does Natu love to see Mayta run?* (Describe characters)

## Extend Thinking Questions

Pose one or more questions to engage students more deeply with the text.

• *How did Natu overcome the obstacles he faced on the suspension bridge?*

• *What kind of challenges do you think the Inca Chasquis faced?*

### iELD Paraphrase to Support Comprehension

After paragraph 5: *Natu is carrying wool across a suspension bridge with his father and a llama. A gust of wind blows. Natu drops the wool. The llama falls and Natu almost falls off the bridge. His father saves them both.*

After paragraph 9: *At fourteen years old, Inca boys train to serve the Inca empire. They can be soldiers, builders, or servants to the Inca leader. Natu dreamed of becoming a Chasqui, or runner who delivers messages.*

After paragraph 11: *Chasquis formed chains in huts all along the Inca road system. Each Chasqui passed a message or parcel to the next. Natu's brother Mayta was the fastest Chasqui in his area.*

**Unit 6**

**CCSS**
**RL.4.1, RL.4.3, RL.4.4, RL.4.5, SL.4.1c, L.4.5b**

Set the Stage

**Introduce the Text** *Today I'm going to read aloud part 2 of "The Inca Chasqui." Let's first summarize part 1.* (Have volunteers summarize part 1.) *In this part you will listen to Mayta, Natu's brother, tell about a danger he faced as he ran to deliver a message to the Sapa Inca.*

**Engage Thinking** *What danger do you think Mayta may have encountered? Turn to a partner to share your prediction.*

## Engage with the Text

Read aloud the text at a fluent, expressive pace. Use the suggested prompts to model your thinking, clarify events, and elicit student interaction.

**1.** *Mayta cleverly threw the meat past the puma to distract him. What other myths can you recall in which a character uses wit to defeat an enemy?* (Make connections)

**2.** *Natu says that Mayta is cunning and brave. I agree. He is cunning because he outsmarted the puma by throwing the meat past him. He is brave because he faced up to the puma rather than running away.* (Describe characters)

# The Inca Chasqui, Part 2

1   Muru stood, looking majestic in his white headdress, his club and sling carefully tucked in the pouch at his side.

2   Natu smiled.

3   "Can you tell me today?" he asked Mum.

4   "Yes, Natu. Today we carry word to the Sapa Inca that the northwest quarter has had an earthquake and needs supplies and men. Tomorrow the governor will send a quipu detailing just what he requires.

5   "Then I will see you tomorrow?" said Natu.

6   "I suppose you will," replied Mum.

7   "Good."

8   For three years Natu had watched Mayta and Muru with admiration. For three years he had longed for the day when it would be he who raced along this rugged stretch on the road to the Inca capital of Cuzco.

9   "Tell me of today's journey," begged Natu the moment Mayta appeared in the doorway that evening.

10   "All right," said Mayta. "Just give me a moment to catch my breath." Natu sat by him on the llama-skin mat that was his bed.

11   "Today was quite exciting. I had only just started up the steep slope when our friend, the puma, decided it liked the smell of the guinea pig Mother had given me for lunch. It glared at me with a look so fierce that I wondered if maybe it wasn't thinking how much more meat there would be on a Chasqui!"

12   Natu laughed. "What did you do?"

13   "For a few moments we both stood frozen, staring at each other like two llamas eyeing the same patch of grass. I carefully reached into my pouch and pulled out my sling and the meat. I slid the meat into the sling and pulled it back as slowly as I could. Then, with a shout that echoed over the mountain and back again, I shot that meat right past our friend's nose and so deep into the brush that I'm sure it took the puma quite some time to find it." **1**

14   "Oh, Mayta!" said Natu, beaming with pride. "You are so cunning and brave. I, too, wish for such adventure!" **2**

15 Natu arose early the next morning. He wanted to take the llamas to pasture at dawn so he wouldn't miss Muru's arrival. He listened to every sound that swept down through the mountain passes, expecting to hear the blow of a conch. What he heard instead made him tighten with fear. It was Mayta's voice yelling for help!

16 Natu ran up the slope, where he found his brother Mayta lying on the ground, writhing and grabbing his ankle. **3**

17 "Mayta!" yelled Natu. "'Are you all right?"

18 "Oh, Natu," grunted Mayta. "I fear I have lost a battle with a lowly stone."

19 Mayta winced with pain as Natu helped him up. Slowly they made their way to the hut, where Mayta rested on the mat. They both looked down at his swollen ankle.

20 "Just wait until Muru sees this," said Mayta. "The tale will reach Cuzco faster than any message ever sent to the Sapa Inca."

21 Natu didn't know whether to laugh or cry. But he knew there was not time for either. In the distance he could hear the sound of the conch. Muru was coming!

22 "Natu," cried Mayta. "You must take the quipu. I cannot run."

23 "But, Mayta—"

24 "No buts. The chain must not be broken. Muru will be too tired to go on. You know the route. You can do it."

25 Natu's heart pounded. This was the chance he had always hoped for— the chance to prove he could be a Chasqui.

26 "I will do it, my brother. I won't let you down."

27 He grabbed Mayta's headdress and pouch.

28 "Mayta is hurt!" called Natu as Muru neared. "Pass me the quipu and go help him."

29 Muru hesitated just a moment. He looked at Natu, then at the hut. **4** "Here," he said. "Be careful."

© Benchmark Education Company, LLC

3. *Natu's brother is "writhing" and grabbing his ankle. As I read on I see Mayta is in pain. I think writhing means he is "squirming in pain" as he grabs his ankle. I'm not sure, so I'll check in the dictionary to confirm the meaning.* (Determine word meaning)

4. *Turn and talk to a partner. Ask: What do you think Muru was thinking as he looked at Natu and then the hut?* (Make inferences/Ask questions)

## Extend Thinking Questions

Pose one or more questions to engage students more deeply with the text.

• *What challenge did Natu face? How did he handle it?*

• *What happened to Mayta just before Natu arrived? What was the effect?*

**iELD Paraphrase to Support Comprehension**

After paragraph 13: *Muru tells Natu that tomorrow they will send a quipu about what supplies people who were in an earthquake need. That night Mayta tells Natu about how he outsmarted a puma on his run that day.*

After paragraph 22: *The next day Natu finds Mayta with a broken ankle. Mayta cannot go on his run. He asks Natu to take the quipu for him.*

After paragraph 29: *Muru brings the quipu to Mayta but sees he cannot run. He agrees to give it to Natu.*

**Unit 6**

CCSS
RL.4.1, RL.4.2, RL.4.3, RL.4.4, RL.4.9, L.4.4a, L.4.4c

## Objective

• Model making connections

## Set the Stage

**Introduce the Text** *Today I'm going to read aloud part 3 of "The Inca Chasqui." Let's first summarize part 2.* (Have volunteers summarize part 2.) *In this part you will hear about a dangerous challenge Natu must face as he runs to deliver the quipu to the Sapa Inca.*

**Engage Thinking** *What danger do you think Natu faces? Turn to a partner to share your prediction.*

## Engage with the Text

Read aloud the text at a fluent, expressive pace. Use the suggested prompts to model your thinking, clarify events, and elicit student interaction.

**1.** *The author provides many details to help me picture the storm coming with the winds and rain getting stronger and stronger. I can hear the roar of the river and see the bridge swinging in the wind.* (Visualize)

**2.** *I remember in part 1 that Natu almost lost his life on that rope bridge. That event helps me understand just how terrified he must be now that he faces having to cross the bridge again, and this time in a storm.* (Make connections)

# The Inca Chasqui, Part 3

1   Natu ran up the path at full speed. It took only minutes to reach the steep section where Mayta had seen the puma. Natu breathed heavily as he pushed himself higher and higher. When he reached the top of the slope, he saw something that could be even more dangerous than a puma. A large dark cloud hung over the adjacent mountaintops—a storm was approaching.

2   The wind and rain began just as he entered the narrow, twisting path that wound down toward the ravine. He had to slow his pace as dirt turned to mud, squishing into his sandals and between his toes with each step. He did his best to listen for falling rocks and mudslides.

3   Natu tried to keep up his speed, but the torrents beat upon him so hard he could barely see the trail. Just one wrong step could mean death. He wiped the water from his eyes and focused sharply on each curve of the narrow path. He tried to stay as close to the rock wall as he could.

4   Natu rounded the last sharp curve, and the roar of the Urubamba River swelled up through the canyon. Just one challenge now separated him from the next hut on the other side of the river. He watched in terror as the rope bridge swung back and forth in the wind.

5   Natu stopped cold. The nightmare of that long-ago day with his father replayed vividly in his mind. He didn't think he could do this. He just couldn't get on that bridge!

6   Then he thought of Mayta. He had promised. If he ever wanted to be a Chasqui, he had to deliver the quipu. Hands trembling, he tied the pouch around his waist so he wouldn't drop it. Then reaching for the right handrail with both hands, he stepped onto the moving bridge and closed his eyes. He slid four paces along.

7   He could hear the raging water far below as it pounded the boulders with tremendous force. The rain pelted his head and streamed down his arms and legs.

8   A gust of wind swung the bridge sharply to the left and back again. Natu halted, his heart racing. When the motion slowed, he moved, step by step—never loosening his grip on the rail. **1 2**

9   He felt the cords beneath him sag and then begin to lift up again. He was more than halfway across! He opened his eyes. He could see the other end of the bridge through the rain.

10  "I can make it," he said aloud. "I'm almost there."

11  Moving quickly but cautiously, Natu stepped off the bridge at last. He instantly sank to his knees with a loud sigh, pounding his thighs with both fists.

12  "I DID IT!" he screamed into the storm. His cry was answered by a bellow of thunder. **3**

13  He waited just long enough to let his pounding heart slow. Then he reached into the pouch and took out the conch shell. He filled his lungs with damp air and put the conch to his lips. Then, blowing with all his might, Natu sprinted down the path toward the next hut. He knew in his heart that nothing would stop him now from becoming a Chasqui.

14  Two months later, a week after his fourteenth birthday, Mayta proudly placed the white headdress on Natu's head and handed him a pouch with a beautiful new conch shell inside. "I am proud of you," he said. "You will be the greatest Chasqui ever known in the Inca empire." **4**

15  Natu smiled. "Even greater than you?" he asked.

16  "Of course," said Mayta. "You've had the best trainer!"

17  Natu laughed. "That I have," he said and he hugged Mayta. "Thanks, big brother."

18  Then the two Inca Chasquis went into the hut to wait for the sound of the conch.

**3.** *The author says Natu's cry was answered by a bellow of thunder. I know thunder makes a loud sound, so bellow must mean the "loud roar" of the thunder.* (Determine word meaning)

**4.** *Turn and talk to a partner. Do you think Natu will make a great Chasqui? Tell why or why not.* (Make inferences)

## Extend Thinking Questions

Pose one or more questions to engage students more deeply with the text.

• *The characters confronted many challenges in this story. Which was the most challenging? How did the character overcome the obstacles?*

• *There are several themes in this story. What is the most important theme that runs throughout parts 1, 2, and 3?*

### iELD Paraphrase to Support Comprehension

**After paragraph 4:** *Natu starts on his journey to deliver the quipu. A storm comes. It gets stronger. Natu comes to the suspension bridge he had to cross two years before.*

**After paragraph 11:** *Natu is afraid to cross the swaying bridge in the storm. He realizes he must. He carefully holds on to the rails. He succeeds in crossing the bridge.*

**After paragraph 18:** *Two months later Natu becomes a Chasqui. His brother tells him he will be great. He and his brother share the hut together to wait for the sound of the conch.*

**Unit 6**

**CCSS**
**RL.4.1, RL.4.2, RL.4.3, RL.4.4, L.4.4a**

# Thornbush, Part 1

## by Carrel Muller

1   Thornbush grew near the path used by children to lead cattle from the village to pasture. It was a small thornbush, hardly a twig, but its thorns were long and sharp.

2   One day while Nama was playing with the other children, he stumbled, and a thorn pierced his side.

3   A year later, Nama was taken to the men's compound to be taught the skills and ways of a warrior. He was quick in learning to shape his spear, and he worked hard learning to throw straight. He learned well the chants, songs, and dances of a warrior. He learned that a warrior must perfect himself for battle. **1** Carelessness could mean death. He did not wish to stumble and, through carelessness, fail. Then he remembered thornbush. He had been careless. He had stumbled.

4   Nama went to Old Man and said, "I fear I will never be a great warrior." He told him about thornbush.

5   "It was long ago," said Old Man. "You were then a child. Do not concern yourself with thornbush." **2**

6   But Nama could not forget.

7   He again walked the children's path. "Thornbush, thornbush, you have given me pain," spoke Nama. "I will cut you down. You will not give pain ever again."

8   Thornbush whispered, "You cannot get rid of me. I am your pain. I am your strength." **3**

9   Nama cut thornbush down.

10   For a while Nama did not think or worry about thornbush. Then he heard the women complaining.

11   "How did that thornbush grow so big?"

12   "It is scratching all who walk the path."

13   "Yes, the children and the cattle."

14   Nama again walked the children's path. There he found not the small thornbush, but a large one with great thorns.

15 "Thornbush, thornbush," he spoke, "you grow stronger. I can bear your presence no longer."

16 Thornbush whispered, "You cannot get rid of me. I am your pain. I am your strength."

17 Nama cut thornbush down.

18 But it grew again, larger and stronger, so Nama returned.

19 "Thornbush, thornbush, I come with great rocks. I will cut you down, and under these stones you will be locked."

20 Thornbush whispered, "Though your heart be rent, under the earth I will not stay. I am your pain. I am your strength." And through the rocks, thornbush returned and grew stronger.

21 Nama's heart was heavy. When he and the other boys practiced the warrior's dance, he could not run as fast or leap as high as the others.

22 Old Man spoke to him. "What is wrong? You are young. You are strong. What weighs you down?"

23 "It is thornbush. It keeps growing. It is important that I get rid of it."
**4**

24 Old Man nodded. "You have made it too big. Go get a thorn and make a pouch to carry it in."

25 Nama did this and tied the pouch around his waist with a leather thong. "How long must I wear this?" he asked.

26 "When you no longer need it, you will throw it away," said Old Man.

27 For a while all went well. Some days Nama could run and leap and toss his spear farther and faster than all the others. Then some task would send him back along the children's path, and he would see thornbush.

28 *I must get rid of it, or I will never be a warrior*, thought Nama.

29 He decided to poison thornbush. He had learned poison for hunting— why not use his skill on thornbush?

30 He had just poured poison over the rocks where thornbush grew when a young girl carrying a water jug came running.

31 "Lioness," she shouted. "Cattle-killed!" she panted.

32 Then others came running. All gathered and discussed the danger to the village. Tomorrow the men would go hunting for the lioness. The boys could follow at a distance but could not participate. Their initiation as warriors was not for another month.

---

**4.** *Because Thornbush keeps growing back, Nama cannot do well in his training as a warrior. Can you recall having any obstacles in meeting certain goals? (Cause and effect/Make connections)*

## Extend Thinking Questions

Pose one or more questions to engage students more deeply with the text.

• *What is Nama's greatest obstacle so far? Has he overcome it? Why or why not?*

• *What do you think will happen with the lioness?*

**iELD Paraphrase to Support Comprehension**

**After paragraph 9:** *Nama walks along the path. Thornbush pierces him. A year later Nama goes off to train as a warrior. Nama is worried he will fail because of Thornbush. The Old Man tells him not to worry. Nama cuts down Thornbush.*

**After paragraph 20:** *Thornbush grows back. Nama tries to cut it down and bury it under rocks but it comes back each time. Thornbush says it is Nama's pain and strength.*

**After paragraph 32:** *Nama could not train well whenever he came across Thornbush. He decides to poison Thornbush. Then a girl warns that a lioness has killed the cattle. The warriors will go after it. Nama and the boys can follow, but not take part yet.*

**CCSS**
**RL.4.1, RL.4.2, RL.4.4, RL.4.9, L.4.4a**

Unit 6

## Objective

• Model making connections

## Set the Stage

**Introduce the Text** *Today I'm going to read aloud part 2 of "Thornbush." First, let's summarize part 1. (Have volunteers summarize part 1.) Two obstacles have been introduced so far: the deadly lioness and the thornbush. In this part Nama encounters another obstacle.*

**Engage Thinking** *What do you think Nama is looking for? Will he find it? Turn to a partner to share your prediction.*

## Engage with the Text

What is another obstacle Nama may encounter? Turn to a partner to share your prediction.

**1.** *The lioness is an unpredictable foe. Un- means "not"; pre- means "before," dict is a root that means "to say," and -able means "able to." So* unpredictable *means that Nama is not able to say before, or predict, what the lioness will do next. (Determine word meaning)*

**2.** *The author uses vivid language to describe the fight between Nama and the lioness. I can hear the lioness cry in pain, feel her claws tear Nama's shoulders, and see him jab the lioness's throat. (Visualize)*

# Thornbush, Part 2

1   For days the warriors returned unsuccessful from the hunt. The lioness, though wounded, still roamed free, more dangerous than ever.

2   Then the women complained, "We have now another fear. A poisonous snake is living in the rocks where thornbush grows."

3   Nama was heartsick. "Has my poison drawn a snake to the path? I must kill it. I will not follow the hunters today."

4   Nama went to the path. "Thornbush, I have made you strong. I have placed a snake at your roots. Today I will right this wrong."

5   Thornbush whispered, "I am your pain. I am your strength. Be brave!"

6   Slowly, cautiously, he began moving all the rocks he had so painfully gathered and placed on the spot where thornbush grew. The snake that slept under them rose angrily and spoke: "Who disturbs my home?"

7   "Snake, I, Nama, have come to destroy your home and you."

8   Snake answered, "I am quick. I work hard. I know well the warrior's ways." It darted out and watched Nama, poised for attack.

9   Nama moved with care. He armed himself as a warrior. With knife and spear he prepared himself for battle.

10  Snake darted forward. Nama threw his knife. It glanced off a rock and fell harmlessly to the ground.

11  Snake moved cautiously, quickly toward Nama, but it attacked the air, for Nama jumped clear.

12  Once more Snake poised for attack. Nama struck swift and true. Snake writhed in pain and then lay still, pinned to the earth with Nama's spear.

13  With Snake dead at his feet, Nama gave the cry of a warrior, but since he was alone, it was not echoed by other hunters. He turned and walked to thornbush. It seemed to whisper to him, "Beware! Be brave!"

14  Then Nama heard a noise in the bush. The sound trembled through the earth, up his feet, to the very top of his head. He knew the sound: the low growl of the lioness! The hunted was now hunting him.

15  He faced her as she stepped from the brush. His mind raced: I cannot look for my knife. I cannot turn my back to reach for my spear. I must not stumble or fail.

16 Nama reached out, never taking his eyes from the wounded lioness, and with both hands tore thornbush from the earth. The thorns stabbed his arms and chest, but he held thornbush, his only weapon against the wounded, dangerous, unpredictable foe. **❶**

17 Her eyes flashing and her snarl vibrating the earth, she attacked. Nama jumped aside and swung thornbush. Sharp thorns tore at her face, and she cried in pain and fury. She turned quickly but now moved more cautiously, warily circling Nama, who dared not take his eyes from her.

18 Furiously, the lioness lunged toward Nama, who clutched thornbush in both hands to defend himself from her attack. As the lioness leaped, Nama thrust thornbush into her face. She screamed in pain as the thorns stabbed her eyes. Her claws reached out and tore down Nama's shoulders and chest, but Nama fought her with thorn bush. A branch broke as he jammed it into her throat. **❷** She gasped, could not breathe, and slowly fell, claws still tearing at the warrior who struggled with her. As she fell, Nama grabbed his spear and, screaming the warrior's cry, ended her suffering.

19 Shouts of warriors echoed his cry as the men appeared around him. Soon women and children were running up the path. Then rejoicing began, for the danger was over and a new warrior was honored.

20 At the initiation celebration Nama danced and enacted his battle, telling how he met and overcame the lioness with thornbush. The thorns and claws left scars that could not be distinguished one from the other. These Nama wore as proudly as he wore the skin of the lioness over his shoulders, the signs of his first victory. **❸**

21 Nama became one of the bravest warriors of his village. He never again walked the path of children, so he never saw the pouch with one thorn that was lost in battle. He never saw the rocks scattered about marking the spot where once a thornbush grew. Thornbush was remembered only as a weapon and shield, as pain and strength in the story of a great warrior. **❹**

---

**3.** *This story has several themes. One is overcoming fears. I know how proud and brave I feel when I succeed at something I am afraid to try at first. So I can understand how Nama feels after he succeeds at killing the lioness and overcomes his fear of the thornbush.* (Make connections)

**4.** *Turn and talk to a partner. Ask: Why is Thornbush no longer at the spot?* (Make inferences/Ask questions)

## Extend Thinking Questions

Pose one or more questions to engage students more deeply with the text.

• *Summarize the obstacles Nama had to overcome and how he overcame them.*

• *What lesson do you think this story teaches?*

### iELD Paraphrase to Support Comprehension

**After paragraph 12:** *A snake comes from the rocks where Nama poisoned the thornbush. The snake and Nama fight. Nama stabs the snake with his spear. The snake dies.*

**After paragraph 19:** *Nama hears the lioness. She attacks him. He uses thornbush to fight her off. He kills the lioness. Nama is honored as a new warrior.*

**After paragraph 21:** *At the initiation celebration Nama acts out his victory over the lioness. The thornbush never grows back. It is remembered as the weapon and shield. It caused the pain and was the strength for Nama.*

**Unit 6**

**CCSS**
**RL.4.1, RL.4.4, SL.4.2, L.4.4b**

**Objective**
• Model fix-up monitoring strategies

**Set the Stage**

**Introduce the Text** *Today I'm going to read aloud an article that relates the song "America the Beautiful" with how immigrants from 1620 to today have enriched America.*

**Engage Thinking** *What contributions made by immigrants do you expect to learn about in this article? Turn to a partner to share your prediction.*

**Engage with the Text**

Read aloud the text at a fluent, expressive pace. Use the suggested prompts to model your thinking, clarify events, and elicit student interaction.

1. *The first paragraph was difficult to understand. I reread it slowly, stopping after each sentence to restate the information in my own words. Now I understand that "America the Beautiful" tells how pilgrims traveled across the wilderness of America in search of freedom.* (Use fix-up monitoring strategies)

2. *In paragraph 6 the synonyms "prodded" and "spurred" are both used to identify "push factors" that encouraged people to move to America.* (Use synonyms)

# Pilgrim Feet

## by Kathiann M. Kowalski

1 Most people probably wouldn't call pilgrims' feet "beautiful." Yet that's the word Katharine Lee Bates used in "America the Beautiful."… Over the centuries, pilgrims and immigrants have contributed a richness to America. People willing to take a chance found great opportunity in this country. Bates saw inspiration in the ways these travelers beat a "thoroughfare for freedom" "across the wilderness." So pilgrims' feet and feats did all that and more from our country's beginnings to today. **❶**

2 Bates' family had lived for eight generations in New England. She grew up in Falmouth, on Cape Cod in Massachusets. She spent her childhood not far from where the first Pilgrims—with a capital "P"— landed in Plymouth in 1620. Those first settlers, a group of religious Separatists, had faced persecution because they did not support the Church of England. They risked a great deal to cross the Atlantic Ocean in the hope that they could make a better life for themselves. With help from the local Wampanoag Indians, their colony took root and grew.

3 The establishment of permanent English settlements in Massachusetts and Virginia encouraged more Europeans to risk the difficult Atlantic crossing in their own quests for better lives. It is important to remember that Native Americans have been here for thousands of years, and African slaves were brought by force. But almost everyone else either came here as an immigrant or is descended from someone who was.

4 America's first wave of immigration spanned the colonial years. Most of these settlers were English. Smaller numbers of Scottish, German, and Irish people also arrived.

5 A second wave of immigration lasted from about 1820 until the mid-nineteenth century. Those travelers mostly came from western and northern Europe. Some people arrived on the West Coast, too, including workers from China. Economic opportunity drew many people to America. Religious and political freedom were also big "pull factors."

6 At the same time, different "push factors" prodded people to move. Starting in 1845, a potato famine in Ireland led more than 1 million people to move. Land seizures and high unemployment made life difficult in Germany. Poverty, political and religious differences, and other factors spurred many Scandinavians to leave their homes. **❷**

7   Newcomers often followed the footsteps of earlier settlers from their countries. For example, Germans and Scandinavians settled along "migration chains." The path eventually led many of them to the Midwest. Many of the second wave of immigrants helped settle America's frontier. Their labor also built the railroads, which connected the East and the West. **3**

8   When Bates first wrote her poem "America the Beautiful" in 1893, a third wave of immigration was in progress in the United States. People still came from western and northern Europe. But huge numbers of immigrants also began arriving from southern and eastern Europe. New York's Ellis Island Station opened in 1892 to process the enormous numbers of newcomers. By 1910, about one seventh of the country's population was foreign-born.

9   Many immigrants faced discrimination. Native-born Americans were prejudiced against southern and eastern Europeans, Chinese, and Japanese newcomers. Nonetheless, the new arrivals forged ahead. They labored for long hours in factories. They built skyscrapers, bridges, and tunnels. They made home in America's new urban landscape. And they helped the country grow. **4**

10  One hundred years after Bates's poem became popular, pilgrims' feet continue to leave their impressions on the country. The fourth wave of immigration to the United States began in 1965 and continues today. In 1965, Congress removed country quotas that had limited arrivals from certain parts of the world. Since then, the face of American immigration has changed dramatically. Now, the largest number of immigrants comes from Mexico, followed by China. The rest of the top ten countries of origin are all in Asia or Latin America.

11  While many Americans celebrate the nation's cultural diversity today, newcomers still face discrimination. Some groups claim that immigration hurts American workers. But researchers feel that immigrants help the economy grow. Newcomers start businesses, which create jobs. Newcomers also are willing to take low-paying physical jobs that other Americans do not want to do.

12  Today's immigrants also include highly skilled talent. They are engineers, mathematicians, computer scientists, and physical scientists. Many immigrants are in the health care field as well.

13  The United States faces new challenges in the twenty-first century. As in the past, the pilgrim feet of immigrants will journey along these new frontiers. The variety of cultures and traditions that immigrants contribute to American society enriches the country. As a result, America can grow and become better. This is indeed beautiful.

3. *Turn and talk to a partner. One main idea is that immigrants came to America for different reasons. Ask: What details support this main idea?* (Summarize/Ask questions)

4. *The fact that some immigrants experience discrimination is caused by the claim that immigration hurts American workers.* (Cause and effect)

## Extend Thinking Questions

Pose one or more questions to engage students more deeply with the text.

• *How did pilgrims and immigrants help America evolve?*

• *Is the author for or against immigration? Give evidence to support your answer.*

### iELD Paraphrase to Support Comprehension

After paragraph 4: *"America the Beautiful" by Katharine Lee Bates celebrates the pilgrims and immigrants who helped build America. The first immigrants were mostly English.*

After paragraph 9: *The second group came from 1820 to mid 1800s. They helped settle the American frontier. They also built railroads to connect East and West. In 1893 a third wave came. Immigrants came for many different reasons. Many faced discrimination.*

After paragraph 13: *A fourth wave began in 1965 and continues to today. Research shows immigrants help the economy grow. Many immigrants are highly skilled. The variety of cultures helps America grow stronger.*

**CCSS**
**RI.4.1, RI.4.2, RI.4.3, RI.4.4, SL.4.2, L.4.5c**

## Set the Stage

**Introduce the Text** *During the 1930s the Midwest suffered a drought, which lasted about ten years. The farmers planted wheat that could not survive the drought. So the wheat roots died and the soil turned to sand. This erosion made farms like deserts. When the winds came, they blew tons of soil into the air.*

*The scene that I will read today takes place during this Dust Bowl. Farmers are going to a meeting to see how the government can help them.*

**Engage Thinking** *How do you think farmers will react to the government's help? Turn to a partner to share your prediction.*

## Engage with the Text

Read aloud the text at a fluent, expressive pace. Use the suggested prompts to model your thinking, clarify events, and elicit student interaction.

1. *Congress declared erosion a national "menace." The next sentence says that it set out to "stop this national disaster." So I think* menace *means "a disaster or threat."* (Determine word meaning)

2. *When Timothy Vane stands up to speak, the farmers look at him and realize he is "not like they are." I think the farmers think he is richer and more educated than they are because of the way he is dressed.* (Make inferences)

3. *Turn and talk to a partner. How do the farmers feel about government help? Support your answer with text evidence.* (Make inferences/Describe characters)

# Before the Rain Came

## SCENE

1   **Sun:** Even after the day of that terrible dust storm—which later came to be known as Black Sunday—in 1935, James still mustered some hope for his farm. About a month after Black Sunday, he called a town meeting, where a representative from the U.S. Department of Agriculture would speak.

2   **Soil:** After Black Sunday, the most terrible of all dust storms, Congress declared erosion a national menace. It passed a law that created the Soil Conservation Service, an organization that set out to stop this national disaster. The hard part was to persuade some very stubborn farmers to change their ways. **❶**

3   **Narrator 2:** People fill every seat. School had been canceled so the town could see the man the government had sent. Dell stands against the wall between Thomas and Rose. He watches his father step onto the pulpit to run the meeting.

4   **James:** Thank you, everyone, for coming. (*coughing*) Today, we have Timothy Vane here to talk about ways we can help keep the topsoil down and prevent massive erosion. Mr. Vane, thank you for being here.

5   **Narrator 1:** The crowd murmurs as a slight man wearing a suit and glasses takes the podium. One glance tells the people that this man is not like they are. **❷**

6   **Timothy Vane:** In this crisis, I'm very glad you've allowed me to speak to you. The black blizzard on April 14 made national headlines. You have the attention of the president. The entire nation is suffering, and we want to help.

7   **Farmer 1:** There's nothing left. Storms have gotten worse year after year. How can you possibly help?

8   **James:** Look here, let the man speak.

9   **Farmer 1:** All right, but I have only so much patience left. There's a car heading out West tomorrow, and I just might be on it.

10  **Timothy:** Look, nothing is going to change for anybody in this country unless we start working together. I've brought some good news. The U.S. government under the great presidency of Franklin Delano Roosevelt has established funds to pay farmers like you to practice new farming techniques.

11 **Farmer 1:** Now it's our fault it hasn't rained in almost five darn years!

12 **Farmer 2:** Pay us? How does a politician over in Washington, D.C., know anything about farming? ❸

13 **James:** Come on, let this man speak. Where are your manners? The president knows just as much as we do right now. Nothing we've done has worked. Let's hear him out.

14 **Timothy:** Thank you, James. We've heard from experts. Do you know that a Mr. Hugh Hammond Bennett has been studying the soil since before some of you were even born? He went to college and became a soil surveyor. He's been trying for years to get the federal government to change farm policy so things like this wouldn't happen. And do you know when the government finally started listening to him? April 14th. It took a disaster, but things are going to change.

15 **Farmer 1:** What can we do to help?

16 **Timothy:** There are methods called crop rotation, strip cropping, contour plowing, and terracing. I've brought information for all of you. I'll also be bringing in some men to help you get started. So here is the first thing…

17 **Narrator 2:** Never in the last handful of years have these people felt anything like hope fill their chests. ❹ There had been despair and sadness, but nothing like this. Proud as they are, their spines straighten. The eyes of more than one shine with hope as they listen.

18 **Narrator 1:** Dell watches his father's face light up.

**4.** *At the end of this scene narrator 2 says: "Never…have these people felt anything like hope fill their chests." I think the people are rejecting what Timothy Vane has to say. I read on to check my understanding. At the end I see I'm wrong. It says, "The eyes of more than one shine with hope."* (Use fix-up monitoring strategies)

## Extend Thinking Questions

Pose one or more questions to engage students more deeply with the text.

• *How did this play show how the nation would come together?*

• *Timothy talks about different kinds of farming methods. How could you learn how each method works?*

**iELD Paraphrase to Support Comprehension**

After paragraph 7: *After Black Sunday, a member of the Department of Agriculture came to speak. He wanted to persuade farmers to change their ways. The crowd did not trust him.*

After paragraph 12: *Timothy Vane tells the people that the government wants to help them. It wants to pay farmers to practice new farming methods. The farmers do not think politicians understand them.*

After paragraph 17: *Timothy Vane tells them about methods studied by experts. Methods such as crop rotation and strip cropping can help stop erosion. The farmers now have hope.*

CCSS
RI.4.1, RI.4.2, RI.4.3, RI.4.4, SL.4.2, L.4.4a

Unit 7

# Dorothea Lange: Witnessing Hard Times

## by Julia LoFaso

1 In a famous photograph from 1936, a mother looks into the distance, her eyes both focused and full of worry. A baby is wrapped in a blanket on her lap and two more children lean on her, burying their faces in her shoulders. The mother's dress is dirty and worn. Her face is tired from long days working in the fields.

2 The photo was taken during a time in American history called The Great Depression, when millions of people across the country were out of work and living in poverty. Its photographer is Dorothea Lange, an adventurous woman dedicated to telling the story of some of America's poorest people. ❶

3 Dorothea Lange was born in 1895, in New Jersey. As a young adult, she briefly attended teaching school, before studying photography at Columbia University. After building her skills in New York City photography studios, she left to travel, selling her photos along the way to earn money. Lange made it as far as San Francisco, California. In 1919, at age twenty-three, she opened her own studio there. ❷

4 Though her studio was a success, Lange grew bored with taking posed portraits of wealthy families. She left to spend some time in New Mexico before returning to San Francisco near the start of the Great Depression. This time, she took her camera onto the streets, turning it toward those who were feeling the most severe effects of the crisis. She took pictures of men who were out of work and sleeping on the streets, and starving families waiting on long lines for free bread. Her camera was large and heavy, but she carried it everywhere.

5 Her photos soon caught the attention of a new government group, the Farm Security Administration. This group was trying to make a record of how the Great Depression had affected farmers in the central United States. This area had gone so long without rain that it became known as the Dust Bowl. Its dry, dusty soil had started to blow away, forming clouds so thick they made day look like night. Dust storms choked the air, and covered homes like snow. With their land destroyed, many farm families left their homes. They went on the road looking for work as migrant farm workers, or workers who moved from farm to farm. In 1935, Lange went on the road, too, and began to photograph them.

6　Lange wanted the people she photographed to feel comfortable in front of her camera. Before she snapped a photo, she often got to know them. She asked questions about their lives, and explained the work she was doing. Details from these conversations appeared alongside her photographs, helping to bring her subjects to life. Lange thought of her photography as a way to make viewers feel for those in need. She hoped that seeing the hardships of these families would lead people to help them. **3**

7　In the process of telling the story of the Great Depression through her photographs, Lange created works of art. In 1965, the year she died, the Museum of Modern Art put on a show with work from her entire life. Lange was the first female photographer to achieve this honor. **4**

**3.** *Dorothea Lange cared a great deal about the people she photographed. Because she wanted people to help the migrant workers, she included details about their lives alongside their photos.* (Make inferences/Cause and effect)

**4.** *Turn and talk to a partner. Ask: What do you think the author's purpose was in writing this article? Give evidence to support your answer.* (Determine text importance/Ask questions)

## Extend Thinking Questions

Pose one or more questions to engage students more deeply with the text.

• *What contributions did Lange make to her community?*

• *What are some questions you have about Lange that were not answered in this article? How could you find the answers?*

### iELD Paraphrase to Support Comprehension

After paragraph 2: *Dorothea Lange photographed America's poorest people. One famous photo from 1936 shows a tired mother with three children—all with worn faces.*

After paragraph 5: *Lange was born in 1895. She eventually took photos of families living on the streets of San Francisco during the Great Depression. She then went on the road to photograph migrant farm workers.*

After paragraph 7: *Lange added details about the poor families she photographed. She hoped this would lead others to help them. In 1965, the Museum of Modern Art displayed her life's work. She was the first female photographer to be honored like this.*

CCSS
RI.4.1, RI.4.3, RI.4.4, SL.4.1c, SL.4.2, L.4.4a

Unit 7

**Objective**

• Model fix-up monitoring strategies

## Set the Stage

**Introduce the Text** *Today I'm going to read aloud the origins of the myth of the flying Africans and how three connected texts relate to it. Next I will read the poem, "O Daedalus, Fly Away Home." This poem, written by African American poet Robert E. Hayden, is based on the myth of flying Africans from 1803.*

**Engage Thinking** *In literature, people often want to fly to escape unbearable circumstances. What circumstances do you think the myth of flying Africans is based on? Turn to a partner to share your prediction.*

## Engage with the Text

Read aloud the text at a fluent, expressive pace. Use the suggested prompts to model your thinking, clarify events, and elicit student interaction.

**1.** *I could not keep track of the connected writings in the introduction. I'll reread this part and list each selection to clarify my understanding. The introduction explains how the Greek myth Daedalus, another myth from the American South, and the poem "O Daedalus, Fly Away Home" are all connected.* (Use fix-up monitoring strategies)

**2.** *The myth of the flying Africans is based on oral tradition. So, unlike the poem "O Daedalus, Fly Away Home," there are probably different versions of the myth because it is oral and not written by one author.* (Make inferences)

# The Legend of the Flying Africans

1   People have always wanted to fly. Especially people trapped in terrible circumstances. In an ancient Greek myth, Daedalus, a master crafter and inventor, is imprisoned by the evil King Minos. Daedalus and his young son Icarus are locked in a tower high up where the birds fly. Gathering feathers, Daedalus crafts wings, and the two prisoners fly away.

2   African American poet Robert E. Hayden refers to that myth in his poem about another myth from the American South. The legend grew out of an actual slave rebellion that took place in 1803 on St. Simon's Island, off the coast of Georgia. A group of captive people from western Africa, newly arrived in America, drowned themselves rather than submit to a life of slavery.

3   Or did they? Over years of telling and retelling, the story changed and expanded—as often happens in oral tradition. The variations grew rich with mystery and magic. According to one tale, rather than drown themselves, the people marched right across the ocean, singing all the way, back to Africa. In the best known version, the people rose up into the sky and flew home.

4   The myth of the flying Africans is an example of the folklore that sustained generations of African Americans. The stories brought people together by helping them understand their shared history. They provided a deep sense of community through hard times. In Hayden's wistful poem, a night of music and dancing conjures up that old African magic, the memories of home, and the dream of flight. The folktale that follows relates the people's yearning for freedom and the solace of even the smallest spark of hope. **❶ ❷**

## O Daedalus, Fly Away Home

by Robert Hayden

    Drifting scent of the Georgia pines,

    Coonskin drum and jubilee banjo.

       Pretty Malinda, dance with me.

    Night is juba, night is conjo,

5       Pretty Malinda, dance with me…

    Night is an African juju man

    weaving a wish and a weariness together

    to make two wings.

    *O fly away home, fly away.*

10  Do you remember Africa?

    *O cleave the air, fly away home.*

    I knew all the stars of Africa.

    *Spread my wings and cleave the air.*

    My gran, he flew back to Africa,

15 just spread his arms and flew away home…

    Drifting night in the windy pines,

    Night is a laughing, night is a longing.

    Dusk-rose Malinda, come to me…

    Night is a mourning juju man

    weaving a wish and a weariness together

20 to make two wings.

    *O fly away home, fly away.* 4

3. *The narrator of the poem asks Malinda to dance with him at night. He says, "Night is juba, night is conjo." So I think "juba" and "conjo" are probably types of dances.* (Determine word meaning)

4. *Turn and talk to a partner. Ask: What mood and emotions are reflected in the poem? How can you tell?* (Ask questions/Determine mood)

### Extend Thinking Questions

Pose one or more questions to engage students more deeply with the text.

• *How does the poem reflect the culture of the African American community?*

• *What is the theme of the poem?*

Unit 7

**CCSS**
**RI.4.1, RI.4.4, RL.4.2, RL.4.4, L.4.4a**

## Set the Stage

**Introduce the Text** *Today I'm going to read aloud the myth on which Robert E. Hayden based his poem. Remember, this is based on oral tradition, so this is just one version of the myth known as "Flying Africans."*

**Engage Thinking** *Some of the events in this myth are based on real events. What events do you think are real? What are myths? Turn to a partner to share your prediction.*

## Engage with the Text

Read aloud the text at a fluent, expressive pace. Use the suggested prompts to model your thinking, clarify events, and elicit student interaction.

**1.** *I think I'll stop after this second paragraph. I'll summarize what I read to check my understanding. This tale has been passed down among Africans and their descendants for generations. It is about African slaves who worked on a Georgia farm picking cotton.* (Use fix-up monitoring strategies)

**2.** *The author provides a definition as a context clue for the meaning of* shaman: *"a holy man."* (Determine word meaning)

# The People Could Fly

## by Deborah Nevins

1   There's a tale they tell down around Georgia. It's been passed on through generations of black folk for about two hundred years, and it goes something like this:

2   Back in the old days, there was a certain plantation on an island off the Georgia coast, where African slaves toiled in the hot sun picking cotton. Let's say that huge farm was owned by a Mr. Butler. He kept some five hundred people, and many had been shipped over from Africa, never to see their beloved homeland again. Others had been born as slaves in America, and never knew freedom. But still, they yearned for it, every last one of them. **❶**

3   Now some masters were kinder than others, but Mr. Butler was a strict man. He had become very wealthy from the sale of Sea Island cotton. With its silky, extra-long fibers, it grew only in what's called the Lowcountry—the coastal regions and Sea Islands of South Carolina and Georgia. So Mr. Butler wanted to protect his treasure—the cotton and the money it brought him. Of course, Mr. Butler's treasure also included those five hundred souls, for without them, he couldn't grow that lovely cotton. So he made sure those people could never escape.

4   Living on a relatively small island, those Africans knew they were trapped. Nevertheless, Mr. Butler hired an overseer just in case. Mr. Butler himself very rarely came out to the fields, so it was the overseer's job to make sure everyone worked hard. Let's say this overseer's name was Mr. Gilbert. Oh, he was a bad one. He rode a horse up and down the fields, carrying a long whip of cowhide. He worked the people eighteen hours a day—even little children as young as five.

5   Now this particular day, when the sun was especially hot, a young slave mother carried her newborn babe on her back as she worked the field. Let's say her name was Abigail. Next to her, her little boy struggled to pick his share of the cotton. As high noon approached, the tiny baby started crying to be fed and the little boy sat down on the warm earth and begged for water. The young mother felt dizzy and faint herself. Mr. Gilbert rode by, and hollered at her to work faster. Abigail begged for water, and asked for a moment to feed the infant. Mr. Gilbert answered with a crack of the whip and poor Abby fell to the ground.

6    "Get up, you lazy, good-for-nothing woman! And make that child of yours work faster or he will also feel this whip!" he cried.

7    Frozen with fear, Abby could only plead with her eyes, but Gilbert's whip lashed out again. Oh, their cries only made that overseer angrier. He was about to strike again when a shadow fell over the huddle of shaking bodies. An old slave man named Moses bent down and offered Abigail his hand.

8    "Stand up now, girl, and gather your children tight," he whispered. Abby did as he told her. Moses was so old that he remembered Africa. Moses also remembered some magical words—he'd thought he'd forgotten them—but now they came whooshing out from his lips as he spoke them into the young woman's ear. Suddenly, Abby, the little boy, and even the tiny babe raised their arms to the sky. "Go home, now, daughter," Moses said. "Fly away home."

9    Abigail and her babes rose into the air as the cruel overseer watched in disbelief. Other slaves came running. They, too, were worn out and battered. "Take me! Take me!" they cried, and Moses whispered the magic words. People rose into the sky, their arms spread wide, until there were hundreds circling, spinning, and soaring on the breeze that carried them out over the Atlantic Ocean and east past the horizon.

10   Moses, you see, had been a shaman—a holy man—back in Africa, before he was sent to America. **2** He carried within him the memory of home, the memory of freedom, and the magic of flight. He knew his people could fly. He had simply forgotten over his long, hard years of captivity. When that baby cried, Moses heard the sound of hope among the most hopeless and wretched of souls. That hope was—and still is— the power of life longing to be free. **3** **4**

**3.** *Turn and talk to a partner. What message does the narrator want to convey in the last line: "That hope was—and still is—the power of life longing to be free"?* (Make inferences)

**4.** *I think the theme of both the poem "O, Daedalus, Fly Away" and this myth is the desire for freedom. The poem presents the theme using rhythm and figurative language. The myth gives description of characters and events.* (Determine theme)

## Extend Thinking Questions

Pose one or more questions to engage students more deeply with the text.

• *How does the myth reflect the history of the African American people?*

• *What are the important events in this myth?*

**iELD** **Paraphrase to Support Comprehension**

After paragraph 4: *In the old days, African slaves picked cotton on an island off the coast of Georgia. Mr. Butler owned the plantation. He hired an overseer to supervise the Africans as they worked.*

After paragraph 6: *A young slave mother, Abigail, worked with her baby and young child in the field. She begged for water. The overseer hit her with the whip.*

After paragraph 10: *Moses, a holy man from Africa, whispered magical words to Abby. Abby and her children flew up to the sky. They flew back home to Africa to freedom.*

Unit 7

**CCSS**
**RL.4.1, RL.4.2, RL.4.4, RL.4.5, RL.4.9, L.4.4a**

# The Kindness of Biddy Mason

## Two Letters from Los Angeles

1   After being freed from slavery, Biddy Mason became a nurse and midwife in Los Angeles. She saved her money and eventually became one of the first African Americans to purchase land in the city. A successful businesswoman, Biddy gave generously of both her time and money. Inspired by historical facts of her time, the following letters imagine how she impacted the people of Los Angeles.

2   **March 10, 1884**

Dear Benjamin,

This week, just when terrible floods had convinced me of the world's unrelenting meanness, I received a powerful reminder of its goodness. Benjamin, you should see what the rain has done to Los Angeles. Houses were filled to the brim with water and mud. So many families are now homeless. For weeks, the water surged so ferociously we could neither send nor receive mail. **❶**

3   Luckily, my store is on high ground, and I was spared the worst of it. I was restocking the shelves last week, stacking bags of rice, when a familiar face appeared. It was Ms. Biddy Mason, known as Grandma Mason for her tendency to take care of everyone. Among the free blacks of our city, Ms. Mason has been uniquely fortunate. Though like many former slaves she suffered greatly, later on she was able to find a well-paying job that allowed her to buy property and become quite prosperous. Since then, she has given much of her money back to the community. **❷** When she isn't bringing food to prisoners at the local jail, she is helping to found the city's first African American church. She even pays the minister's salary!

4   On the day that she came in, she asked me to open an account for her at the store. Ms. Mason explained that she intended to pay for food for everyone who had been left homeless in the flood. Give them food, she told me, and I'll give you the money. Never have I known someone to possess such boundless kindness; the entire city is better for having her in it.

Sincerely,

Abraham

**5**  **February 11, 1877** ❸

Dearest Cousin Susie,

I hope that my mother's last letter did not worry you too badly. When she wrote to tell you of my illness, I was still in bed, fearing the worst. Now, I am happy to send you more uplifting news. I am strong enough to hold a pen, and to write these words. With each day, I feel better, thanks to a kind nurse named Biddy Mason.

**6**  I have heard many people tell of this woman's incredible selflessness, but I had never felt it firsthand until now. Often I've seen her walking through the neighborhood with a large black bag of medical supplies. Sometimes she is rushing to deliver a baby into the world. Other times, at great risk to herself, she is bringing much-needed medicine to a poor soul afflicted with smallpox. Last month, I was that person.

**7**  When my fever was at its worst, all my senses seemed consumed in a raging fire. It was then that I would feel a gentle hand on my forehead, or cool water soothing my throat. Sometimes, a soft hum came from my bedside, drifting me to sleep. After a week of Ms. Mason's attention, my fever broke. I owe her my life, and I shall never forget her kindness. Perhaps when you visit, you will meet her as well.

Fondly,

Annabel ❹

**3.** *I noticed that the second letter was written a few years before the first. In 1877 Biddy was a nurse. By 1884 she was a wealthy landowner. I think the "well-paying job" mentioned in the first letter refers to her job as a nurse.* (Make inferences)

**4.** *Turn and talk to a partner. Take turns summarizing both letters.* (Summarize)

## Extend Thinking Questions

Pose one or more questions to engage students more deeply with the text.

• *How did Biddy Mason help her community grow?*

• *What qualities did Biddy Mason have? What evidence from the letters show these qualities?*

**iELD  Paraphrase to Support Comprehension**

After paragraph 3: *There were terrible floods in Los Angeles. Many people were homeless. Ms. Biddy Mason, a former slave, became wealthy and gave back to this community. She founded the city's first African American church.*

After paragraph 4: *Biddy Mason asked the storekeeper to give food for all who lost their homes in the flood. She will pay for the food.*

After paragraph 7: *Biddy Mason was a nurse. She helped deliver babies and treated people with small pox. She helped save the life of Annabel, who wrote the letter.*

Unit 7

CCSS
RL.4.1, RL.4.2, RL.4.4, SL.4.2, L.4.4a

# Are We There Yet?, Part 1

## by Ellen R. Braaf

1    America's interstate highway system—a network of superhighways like no other in the world—connects our nation coast to coast. We may travel it across town or on a cross-country adventure. It's smooth and fast and gets us where we want to go. But it hasn't always been that way.

## Cars Create Chaos

2    In 1893 Charles and Frank Duryea, bicycle mechanics in Massachusetts, turned a broken-down horse carriage and a one-cylinder gasoline engine into the first gas-powered American automobile. It had no brakes. To stop it, they ran it into the curb. But there was no stopping its popularity. By 1905, 48,000 Americans had cars. Early driving was hazardous. The first cars broke down regularly. People got lost, got stuck ,and got into accidents. Roads were so narrow that cars going in opposite directions couldn't get around each other. Head-on collisions were common. **1** Worst of all, most roads were unpaved, bumpy dirt tracks—dusty when dry, muddy and often impassable when wet. **2**

3    To make things even worse, no one had yet invented driving schools or rules. Traffic in urban areas was chaotic. A hodgepodge of people, bicycles, horse-drawn wagons and carriages, and now the new motorcars and motorized trucks crowded the cobblestone streets. Drivers often settled traffic disputes with fistfights, snarling traffic even more. Pedestrians risked life and limb.

4    In 1908 the police commissioner of New York created the city's first "rules of the road." Slower vehicles were required to keep right, so faster ones could pass on the left. And drivers had to signal with their hands (or buggy whips) to let others know they were about to slow, stop, or turn.

5    The city of Cleveland installed the first electric traffic signals. Red meant stop; green meant go. Other cities used a third colored light—yellow— to signal caution. Some cities installed only red traffic lights, the top one to stop north-south traffic and the bottom one to stop east-west traffic. In New York City, traffic towers flashed the same color at the same time in all directions. Drivers going north or south stopped when the light turned green. Drivers going east or west stopped when it turned red. **3**

6 Outside the cities, driving was no easier. Along the bad roads, few signs guided the way. In an effort to improve car travel, people formed trail associations that adopted roads and named them, printed guidebooks, posted directions, hung cautionary signs, and maintained the roads. Problem was, the associations competed with one another. They sometimes claimed the same roads, gave them different names, and posted a variety of confusing signs anywhere they wanted—on trees, houses, or boulders.

## The Right Direction

7 Clearly, people across the country would have to work together to improve the roads, establish rules everyone could follow, and make a plan for naming and marking highways. To do this, the new Bureau of Public Roads in Washington, D.C., formed partnerships with the forty-eight states (Alaska and Hawaii were not states at this time) to repair old roads and build new, paved ones. They did away with the trail associations and organized the existing jumble of roads into a system. Major roads got U.S. route numbers: odd-numbered routes ran north-south and even-numbered routes ran east-west. They painted lines to mark traffic lanes and posted standard speed limits. Finally, car travel was beginning to make sense. High time, too, since by 1927 Americans owned 20 million cars. **4**

**3.** *I think I read the paragraph about the different kinds of traffic signals too quickly. I'm going to reread this paragraph again. I'll stop after each sentence to be sure I understand it before going on to the next. (Use fix-up/Monitoring strategies)*

**4.** *Turn and talk to a partner. What did the Bureau of Public Roads do to improve driving on the roads? (Summarize)*

### Extend Thinking Questions

Pose one or more questions to engage students more deeply with the text.

- *How do you think the invention of the car and the building of roads affected communities?*

- *How was this article organized? How can you tell?*

**iELD** **Paraphrase to Support Comprehension**

After paragraph 3: *When cars were first invented there were no paved roads. There were no driving schools or rules. Drivers often had fights to settle traffic arguments.*

After paragraph 6: *In 1908, New York created the first rules of the road. Cities began to install traffic signals. People formed trail associations to adopt roads. However, there was confusion because more than one association took on the care of some roads.*

After paragraph 7: *Eventually the federal government organized the existing road system. It made driving rules that all forty-eight states would follow.*

CCSS
RI.4.1, RI.4.2, RI.4.3, RI.4.4, SL.4.2, L.4.4b

Unit 7

## Objective

• Model fix-up monitoring strategies

## Set the Stage

**Introduce the Text** *Today I'm going to read aloud part 2 of "Are We There Yet?" Let's summarize part 1. (Have volunteers summarize part 1.) In part 2 you will learn how today's interstate highway system became a reality. The construction included new highways, bridges, and tunnels.*

**Engage Thinking** *What are some problems engineers designing the highway system had to solve? Turn to a partner to share your prediction.*

## Engage with the Text

Read aloud the text at a fluent, expressive pace. Use the suggested prompts to model your thinking, clarify events, and elicit student interaction.

**1.** *After reading paragraph 2, I was confused. Did President Eisenhower create the new highway system or not? When I reread the first sentence slowly, I realized that he was not the one who first thought of the idea, but he was the one who initiated building it. He "made it happen."* **(Use fix-up monitoring strategies)**

**2.** *One main idea in this article is that preparation had to be done before the highways were built. Details that support this idea are that engineers tested heavy equipment on a 7-mile test strip. They studied bridge and road designs.* **(Determine main idea)**

# Are We There Yet?, Part 2

## My Way Is the Highway

1    In the 1950s the economy boomed, and Americans bought bigger, faster cars. About 16,000 were sold every day—more than double the number sold 50 years before. People wanted to get places fast, and the old two-lane state highways wouldn't do.

2    The idea for a streamlined system of highways connecting every state didn't start with Dwight Eisenhower, America's 34th president, but he made it happen. As a young army officer in 1919, he had crossed the United States in a truck. It took him 62 difficult days, traveling an average of 6 miles per hour. Later, in Europe during World War II, he admired the splendid roads he saw. As president, Eisenhower was convinced that America needed nothing more urgently than a modern, coast-to-coast network of wide, smooth, well-marked highways. It would ease traffic congestion, improve travel safety, and help small towns grow. **1**

3    In 1956 the interstate highway system began to take shape. First, engineers set quality standards for the roads, testing materials on a "road to nowhere." This 7-mile track was built in 836 separate sections. Each section combined different materials such as asphalt and concrete. The builders ran heavy equipment, including army missile carriers packed with concrete blocks, over the sample strips until they crumbled. They studied bridge and road designs to decide which would work best. **2**

4    Planners designed the highways to be the same throughout the system. For instance, each lane is 12 feet wide. In both directions, the divided highway has a 4-foot-wide shoulder on the far left and a 10-foot-wide breakdown lane on the right. Green signs with white lettering mark exits and directions; blue signs with white lettering note services and rest areas. Like the old roads, even-numbered interstates run east-west, and odd-numbered interstates, north-south.

5    Building the U.S. interstate system became one of the largest construction projects ever undertaken. Over nearly 40 years of construction, workers moved trillions of pounds of earth. They built 54,000 bridges across rivers and roads. Interstate 75's Mackinac Bridge links Michigan's upper and lower peninsulas. When completed in 1957, the "Mighty Mac" was the longest suspension bridge in the world. Workers also bored 100 tunnels. In Maryland, Interstate 95's Fort McHenry Tunnel under Baltimore Harbor was actually built elsewhere, in 32 sections, and sunk into an enormous trench—about 200 feet wide and a mile and a half long—that had been dug out of the harbor's floor. **3**

## The Challenge Continues

6    Cars created chaos, but they made people think about how to solve the problems of bad roads and traffic confusion. Cars still challenge us today.

7    Can we find cleaner fuels to burn? Can we keep up with highway repairs? Can we prevent roads and parking lots from taking over the landscape? We aren't there yet, but scientists and citizens alike are working hard to meet the continuing challenge of cars. **4**

**3.** *Turn and talk to a partner. The article said "workers also bored 100 tunnels." Do you think* bored *means "uninterested" or "dug through"? Why?* (Determine word meaning)

**4.** *The author believes that we still have many traffic problems. One reason is that cars still challenge us. The evidence to support this is that we need cleaner fuel and must learn how to keep up with road repairs.* (Cite evidence)

### Extend Thinking Questions

Pose one or more questions to engage students more deeply with the text.

- *How do you think the interstate highway system helped our nation come together?*

- *What signs have you seen on a highway that followed the design the planners made?*

**iELD  Paraphrase to Support Comprehension**

After paragraph 2: *By the 1950s, many cars were being sold. America needed bigger highways. President Eisenhower realized a highway system was needed across the country.*

After paragraph 4: *In 1956 engineers tested materials and designs for the highways. Next planners made uniform designs for the highways to follow.*

After paragraph 7: *Building the U.S. highway system was one of the largest projects ever. It took 40 years. Today we are still working to improve both cars and highways.*

**Unit 7**

CCSS
**RI.4.1, RI.4.2, RI.4.3, RI.4.4, RI.4.8, SL.4.2, L.4.4a**

# Interview with an Earthquake Expert

Lisa Wald is a geophysicist with the United States Geological Survey (USGS). She manages the USGS' Earthquake Hazard Program website. Her job is to present information about earthquakes to other scientists and also to the public.

**1   Earthquakes may be scary, but what else can we think about them?**

When most people think about earthquakes, they think about the shaking and the damage they can cause. But earthquakes are happening all over the earth every day, and most of them are small and go unnoticed. A large earthquake, however, involves the movement of huge blocks of earth in a few seconds, and is an amazing and powerful display of nature! The enormous tectonic plates that cover the earth's surface are constantly moving, causing earthquakes. Earthquakes are reminders that the earth is a single, living planet, and in geologic time, all parts of it are connected and affect each other.

**2   Why don't we hear about small earthquakes more?**

The media tends to report only those earthquakes that are relatively large, are felt by many people, or cause damage or deaths. Most unreported earthquakes are very small and not felt. Many of them are in the middle of oceans, or in other remote areas, so even if they are occasionally large, they may still not be felt.

**3   What do they tell us?**

Most earthquakes occur near the plate boundaries, so they tell us where those boundaries are and how fast and in what direction those plates are moving. Learning about all the earthquakes helps scientists figure out what areas of the earth are more prone to earthquakes, and which areas are more likely to experience a large and potentially damaging earthquake in the future. **❶**

**4   What more should people know about earthquakes?**

The study of earthquakes is a relatively young science, so there are many things about them that even geophysicists still don't understand. The most common misconception is that earthquakes can be predicted by animals, weather, physical symptoms, or any other number of strange and unrelated things. **❷** And there's a lot of confusion about the magnitude of an earthquake and how it relates to the shaking that people feel in different places.

Earthquakes cannot be predicted, and we don't know yet whether it will ever be possible. Many different prediction methods have been tested, and so far not one of them has worked consistently and accurately. A successful method would name the date and time, location, and magnitude. **3**

As for the confusion between the magnitude and the intensity of shaking—the magnitude is the size of the earthquake, and it's related to the size of the fault, the distance that the blocks of earth slip, and the amount of energy that's released. Scientists use different methods to compute the magnitude, depending on what type of earthquake it is and what instruments have recorded it. The magnitude is a single number.

The shaking intensity, on the other hand, varies from place to place. It gets different numbers at different locations. The amount of shaking an area experiences depends on the distance from the earthquake, the depth of it, its type, and the type of geological material near the earth's surface. Many different details affect the seismic waves that radiate from the earthquake source.

**5**   **What is your favorite earthquake story?**

My favorite earthquake story is one that is told entirely by a photograph. The photo was taken after the magnitude 7.1 earthquake near Fairview Peak, Nevada, on December 16, 1954. It shows a fault scarp about 2–3 meters high that was not there before the earthquake. On the down-dropped side of the slope is a small wood-frame house completely intact even though it's only several feet from the fault. Near the edge of the scarp at the top is an outhouse on its side. The picture tells the whole story. **4**

**4.** *Turn and talk to a partner. The photo showed a fault scarp about 2 to 3 meters high. Ask and answer: What do you think a fault scarp is?* (Ask questions/Make inferences)

## Extend Thinking Questions

Pose one or more questions to engage students more deeply with the text.

- *What are some things that scientists can control regarding earthquakes?*

- *What are some things they cannot?*

**iELD  Paraphrase to Support Comprehension**

After question 1: *Lisa Wald is a geophysicist. She gives scientists and the public information about earthquakes. Earthquakes happen all the time. They show how all parts of the earth are connected.*

After question 4: *Many small earthquakes go unnoticed. Earthquakes occur near plate boundaries. So scientists can tell where earthquakes are likely to occur. But earthquakes cannot be predicted.*

After question 5: *The magnitude is the size of an earthquake. One number represents the magnitude. The shaking intensity depends on where it is measured. In an earthquake from 1954, a photo shows a house intact on one side of a fault scarp. On the other, is an outhouse on its side.*

**Unit 8**

CCSS
RI.4.1, RI.4.2, RI.4.3, RI.4.4, RI.4.9, SL.4.2, L.4.4b

# When the Ocean Roars

## by Patricia Barnes-Svarney

1   On April 1, 1946, Marie Morisawa was waiting for a bus along Kuhio Beach, near Waikiki Beach in the Hawaiian Islands. The bus was late, but eventually came to take her to her teaching job in the higher elevations of Honolulu, a thirty-minute ride.

2   "When I reached the school," she recalls, "everyone was talking about the giant wave that had hit around Kuhio Beach about twenty minutes earlier. The huge wall of water had destroyed streets, signs, and homes—even the sidewalk where I had been standing!"

3   Marie's giant wave is known as a tsunami, Japanese for "storm wave." A tsunami is not caused by a storm or the tides (a tsunami is often incorrectly called a "tidal wave"). The majority of tsunamis are caused by submarine earthquakes, while others occur during volcanic eruptions and underwater landslides. **❶**

4   Earthquakes occur when the earth's crust slips along faults, or cracks, near the surface. If the fault moves in a back-and-forth direction, there will be no tsunami. But if the fault slips up and down, giant "ripples" can occur along the surface of the ocean. These "ripples," or tsunamis, can travel at speeds of up to 466 miles per hour. More than one tsunami can strike a low-lying coastal village, with waves reaching as high as 80 feet.

5   Although tsunamis are strong enough to cause extensive damage to coastal villages, ships at sea usually are not harmed by the giant waves. At sea, there may be hundreds of miles between the crests (high points) of the tsunamis, and the waves may be only a little more than a yard in height. It is when a tsunami encounters the shallow coastline that the wave grows in height.

6   Tsunamis can occur in any ocean. The Atlantic coast of the United States has experienced only a few tsunamis, none of which has caused any significant damage. But in the Pacific Ocean, volcanic and earthquake activity produces up to 80 percent of all tsunamis, affecting Hawaii, Alaska, Japan, and the West Coast of the United States.

7   One of the largest tsunamis to strike the West Coast occurred in 1964.

On Good Friday, Alaska experienced a great earthquake that measured 8.6 on the Richter scale. The movement along the fault caused a tsunami that traveled at high speeds to coastal cities from Oregon to southern California. Wave heights in Los Angeles reached 3.2 feet, and in San Francisco waves measured 7.4 feet.

8   Severe damage occurred at Crescent City in northern California. Four large tsunamis struck the town, the largest reaching a height of 13 feet. Logs were carried through the streets at a velocity reaching 33 feet per second. Many homes in low-lying areas were destroyed or badly damaged. Further loss came from oil-tank fires. The estimated cost of damages was more than seven million dollars, and more than a hundred people were killed. **2**

9   To help warn coastal residents of tsunami dangers, the Seismic Sea Wave Warning System, now called the Tsunami Warning System, was organized in 1946. Observatories were established in California and at thirty other stations across the Pacific Ocean. The system provides twenty-four-hour information on earthquakes and tsunamis. In the future, scientists hope to use satellites to track the occurrence and movement of tsunamis all over the world. Laws also prohibit building in some tsunami-prone areas in an effort to save lives and property from these unpredictable events. **3 4**

**4.** *This selection describes the damage tsunamis cause and where they occur. Each paragraph describes a different aspect. So the structure of this selection is a description.* (Determine structure)

## Extend Thinking Questions

Pose one or more questions to engage students more deeply with the text.

• *What changes in the earth cause a tsunami?*

• *Does the Tsunami Warning System control tsunamis? Explain your answer.*

### iELD Paraphrase to Support Comprehension

**After paragraph 3:** *On April 1, 1946, Marie Morisawa took a bus to school. She learned that a tsunami had hit the place where she had just taken the bus. A tsunami is a giant wave. Most are caused by earthquakes or volcanoes.*

**After paragraph 6:** *If a fault moves up and down, giant ripples, or tsunamis can form. They can damage coastal villages. Ships at sea are not harmed by them. Earthquake and underwater volcanoes in the Pacific Ocean cause about 80 percent of tsunamis.*

**After paragraph 9:** *In 1964 one of the largest tsunamis struck the West Coast. Damages were more than $7 million. More than 100 people were killed. The Tsunami Warning System was organized in 1946. It provides information on earthquakes and tsunamis. Some day it might be able to track tsunamis all around the world.*

CCSS
RI.4.1, RI.4.2, RI.4.3, RI.4.4, RI.4.5, SL.4.2, L.4.4a

Unit 8

# A Day at the Beach

## by Jamie McGillian

1   In the face of a disaster, every bit of information makes a difference. Tilly Smith knows that very well. In December 2004, Tilly was ten years old. An English schoolgirl, Tilly was on the coast of Thailand with her family, enjoying a vacation in a beautiful land.

2   On the morning of December 26, 2004, Tilly was on Maikhao Beach, distraught with what she was seeing. "The water was really, really frothy. It wasn't calm and it wasn't going in and out," she said. "It was just coming in and in and in." Everything she was seeing that morning added up to a lesson she had learned in school, just a few weeks prior, taught by her geography teacher, Mr. Andrew Kearney.

3   Tilly was desperately trying to convince her parents that they needed to leave the beach immediately. At one point, when Tilly's mom told her to calm down, Tilly threatened to leave the beach without her. That's how sure she was that something was very wrong. Tilly kept saying, "The bubbles, the water bubbles." When Tilly's parents told her to ignore it and continue walking the shore, she shouted, "There is gonna be a tsunami, listen to me." **❶**

4   Tilly's mom remembers, "The beach was getting smaller and smaller. I felt compelled to look, but I didn't know what was happening. Then Tilly said she'd just studied this at school—she talked about tectonic plates and an earthquake under the sea. She got more and more hysterical. In the end, she was screaming at us to get off the beach."

5   "I didn't know what a tsunami was, but seeing your daughter so frightened, you think something serious must be happening," added Tilly's mom.

6   Her father, Colin Smith, went searching for a security guard after hearing his daughter's pleas. He told the guard what his daughter was saying. "I know this sounds crazy, but my daughter is convinced that there is going to be a tsunami," said Tilly's dad. The guard listened and people were told to get off the beach. **❷**

7   The Smith family made it to the second floor of their hotel just as the tsunami crashed into the building, crushing everything in its path. From the balcony, the Smith family watched the devastation.

8 It was fast thinking that saved Tilly Smith and her family, and 100 other tourists from the 2004 Asian tsunami, which killed at least 200,000 people in 13 countries.

9 So the question is, what if Tilly had been wrong? What if she had spoiled everyone's day at the beach? Most people would agree that these questions are not as relevant as the fact that a young girl was courageous enough to speak up and share what she had learned. That takes guts.

10 Tilly received many accolades and awards for her bravery. **3** **4**

**3.** *Tilly received accolades and awards for her bravery. I think when someone is brave they are praised. So I think* accolades *means "praises or compliments."* (Determine word meaning)

**4.** *Turn and talk to a partner. Ask: What if Tilly had been wrong and there was no tsunami?* (Make inferences/Ask questions)

## Extend Thinking Questions

Pose one or more questions to engage students more deeply with the text.

• *Tilly could not control the tsunami. What could she control? How?*

• *What facts did this account give about changes the tsunami caused?*

### iELD Paraphrase to Support Comprehension

After paragraph 3: *On December 26, 2004, Tilly is on a beach in Thailand. She notices changes in the water that she learned about in school. She tells her parents there is going to be a tsunami.*

After paragraph 7: *Tilly's mom believes something bad is going to happen. Her dad tells the security guard about the tsunami. Tilly's family gets to safety just before the tsunami strikes.*

After paragraph 9: *Tilly saved 100 tourists from the tsunami. It killed at least 200,000 people in 13 countries. Tilly was brave to speak up and share what she learned.*

**Unit 8**

CCSS
**RI.4.1, RI.4.2, RI.4.3, RI.4.4, RI.4.5, SL.4.2, L.4.4a**

- Model asking questions
- Model determining text importance

## Set the Stage

**Introduce the Text** *Haiku is a Japanese form of verse often about nature. A tsunami is a long, high wave that is caused by an earthquake. Today I'm going to read aloud several haiku about the 2011 earthquake that hit Japan and caused a tsunami. The earthquake and tsunami caused a nuclear disaster at the Fukushima Daiichi nuclear power plant in Japan.*

**Engage Thinking** *What events do you think the haiku will describe? Turn to a partner to share your prediction*

## Engage with the Text

Read aloud the text at a fluent, expressive pace. Use the suggested prompts to model your thinking, clarify events, and elicit student interaction.

**1.** *The first two haiku tell about the earthquake and the resulting tsunami. What events will the rest of the haiku tell about? Will I learn about how the tsunami affected the people? Will I learn how big the tsunami was? Will these haiku poems be sad or will they be hopeful?* (Ask questions)

**2.** *The third haiku says that "people have no wings." I think this means that the seagulls escaped the wave, but the people could not.* (Make inferences)

# Tsunami Haiku

1    miles under the sea

     opposing forces collide

     a quiet beach waits

2    Pacific Ocean,

     troubled by a deep earth feud,

     rises in protest **1**

3    standing on the beach

     seagulls blink at the strange wave

     people have no wings **2**

4    on that fateful morn

     a woman dreams of water

     and wakes with a yawn

5    earth quakes six minutes

     wave rises forty meters

     eighteen thousand gone

6   Japan cries hot tears **3**

     for broken Fukushima

     radioactive


7   through vast mounds of muck

     villagers scavenge for signs **4**

     of the lives they lost


8   a child's smiling face

     peers from under the rubble

     it's only a photograph


9   swimming by Japan

     whales sing sadly of the wave

     that reached for the moon

**3.** *The mood of this haiku is very sad. The imagery of the language such as "eighteen thousand gone" and "cries hot tears" evoke sad feelings.* (Determine mood)

**4.** *Turn and talk to a partner. The villagers scavenge for signs of lives they lost. What do you think* scavenge *means? What clues help you figure this meaning? Why did the author choose this word?* (Determine text importance/Ask questions)

## Extend Thinking Questions

Pose one or more questions to engage students more deeply with the text.

- *What does the haiku suggest about the ability to control nature?*

- *What does the haiku suggest about nature's ability to control?*

**iELD** **Paraphrase to Support Comprehension**

After haiku 3: *There is an earthquake. It causes a tsunami in the Pacific Ocean. People cannot escape the tsunami.*

After haiku 6: *No one expected the tsunami that morning. The earthquake lasted six minutes. The wave rose 40 meters. 18,000 people died. The tsunami caused a nuclear disaster at Fukushima.*

After haiku 9: *Villagers look for signs of life. All they find under the rubble is a photograph of a child. Whales swim by Japan. Their voices sing of the huge tsunami wave.*

**Unit 8**

**CCSS**
**RL.4.1, RL.4.3, RL.4.4, RL.4.5, L.4.4a**

# The Legend of Pele, Hawaiian Goddess of Fire

1   On the Big Island of Hawaii, it's not unusual for the earth to start rumbling. At the top of the Kilauea volcano, steam leaks from a crater. Before long, a red fountain of lava bursts into the sky and flows in scorching rivers down the mountain. The red-hot lava hits cool blue ocean water with a sizzle, hardening into new land. Why does the volcano flow with such unending fury? According to Hawaiian beliefs, it's because the fire goddess Pele is angry about something.

2   From the day she was born on the island of Tahiti, Pele had a temper like a roaring blaze. Every time she got mad, a fire broke out, setting aflame the gardenia flowers, the noni fruit trees, and the red bark of the miki miki bushes. Her younger brothers and sisters ran for cover as her cheeks glowed and smoke trickled from her ears. But her older sister, the ocean goddess Namaka, was not so easily scared. For Pele, Namaka was a bottomless well of annoyance. Every time Pele's temper set a fire, Namaka used the ocean to put it out. **1**

3   "If I can't express myself here," Pele thought, "I'll go somewhere else."

4   So she waited until Namaka was sleeping, and set out into the ocean on a canoe. Namaka awoke to find her sister missing and called on the water to bring her back. But by that time, Pele had made it to the islands of Hawaii. There, she dug a fire pit, creating a crater for a volcano. Enraged, Namaka sent the ocean to flood the pit. So Pele moved on to a new island, and dug a new crater. Again, Namaka sent the ocean to drown it. Soaking wet, Pele sputtered with fury. She shook off the water, coughing clouds of smoke. **2**

5   "Some day," she roared at the ocean, "I'll start a fire even you can't put out."

6   Pele's anger fueled her quest. She moved from island to island, setting fires as she went, and every time Namaka doused them. **3** Finally, Pele arrived on Hawaii's Big Island. But this time, she didn't build a fire pit right away. First, she climbed the island's highest mountain. From there, she let loose a blaze so brilliant it lit up the entire night sky. Namaka, alerted by the fireworks display to her sister's latest tantrum, again called on the ocean.

7   With all her strength, Namaka pushed the ocean's water up the mountain, but she couldn't get the waves to go high enough. Over and over, the water rushed partway up, only to flow back down into the ocean. As Pele watched the waves roll away, she knew she'd found a good home. From then on, all Namaka could do was cool her sister's fires once they reached the sea.

8   Deep inside her volcano, Pele still finds plenty to get angry about. Some say nothing bothers her more than when tourists take lava rocks as souvenirs, so she sends her fires flowing down the mountain to keep them away. **4**

**4.** *Turn and talk to a partner. What details did you learn about the setting of this legend?* (Summarize/Describe setting)

## Extend Thinking Questions

Pose one or more questions to engage students more deeply with the text.

• *Was nature able to be controlled in this legend? Explain your answer.*

• *How were Namaka and Pele alike? How were they different?*

### iELD Paraphrase to Support Comprehension

**After paragraph 1:** *Lava erupts often from the Kilauea volcano in Hawaii. It lands in the ocean to harden. According to legend, it is because Pele, the fire goddess, is angry.*

**After paragraph 4:** *Pele was born in Tahiti. Whenever she got angry, a fire would break out. Her sister Namaka would send the ocean waters to put it out.*

**After paragraph 8:** *Pele moved from place to place to avoid Namaka. Eventually she moved high enough away to the volcano in Hawaii. The ocean waters could no longer reach her to put out the fires.*

**CCSS**
**RL.4.1, RL.4.2, RL.4.3, RL.4.4, SL.4.2, L.4.4a**

**Unit 8**

## Objectives

- Model asking questions
- Model summarizing/synthesizing

## Set the Stage

**Introduce the Text** *Today I'm going to read aloud a selection explaining how a disaster might have influenced Edvard Munch to create one of the most famous paintings in the world. The painting is* The Scream. *It depicts a man screaming in the foreground. However, the red sky in the background is the focus of this selection.*

**Engage Thinking** *What disaster may have influenced the painting of the red sky? Turn to a partner to share your prediction.*

## Engage with the Text

Read aloud the text at a fluent, expressive pace. Use the suggested prompts to model your thinking, clarify events, and elicit student interaction.

**1.** *After reading the first three paragraphs, I have many questions. How did Olson learn what inspired the artist? What natural occurrence was it? Why did Munch decide to paint the subject screaming? What made the sky so red?* (Ask questions)

**2.** *In the* New York Times *article, the skies are described as "scarlet", "crimsoned," and "red." I think these are all synonyms for* red. (Use synonyms)

# Krakatoa: The Art of Disaster

## by Hugh Westrup

1 Have you ever held your hands to your cheeks in surprise—or even fright? Or perhaps you've seen a similar expression in one of the world's most famous artworks, *The Scream*. Painted by the Norwegian artist Edvard Munch, it depicts a man standing on a road. Behind him lies a body of water and above it wavy red bands cross the sky. The man is holding his hands to his head while his mouth gapes in horror.

2 When most people look at *The Scream*, they focus on the man's face. But when Don Olson first saw it, his attention was drawn to the wavy red bands. That's natural because Olson is an astronomer. His eyes are always on the sky.

3 The painting's red bands, Olson learned, were inspired by an actual occurrence. In his journal, Edvard Munch wrote, "I was walking along the road with two friends—then the sun set—all at once the sky became blood red—and I felt overcome with melancholy. I stood still and leaned against the railing, dead tired—clouds like blood and tongues of fire hung above the blue-black fjord and the city. My friends went on, and I stood alone, trembling with anxiety. I felt a great, unending scream piercing through nature." **1**

4 Sunsets are often red, of course. But Olson suspected that the "blood red" color that Munch saw had an unusual cause: the eruption of Krakatoa, a volcanic island in Indonesia ten years earlier. On August 26 and 27, 1883, Krakatoa blew its top. It threw 6 cubic miles of dust, ash, and rock into the air. It also triggered a series of tsunamis that engulfed 165 coastal villages, killing 36,000 people. The eruption's roar was heard 3,000 miles away.

5 The mixture of gas and dust that Krakatoa hurled high into the sky drifted through the atmosphere, reflecting sunlight and turning sunsets red around the world for months afterward. On November 28, 1883, *The New York Times* reported: "Soon after 5 o'clock the western horizon suddenly flamed into a brilliant scarlet, which crimsoned sky and clouds. Many thought that a great fire was in progress… The clouds gradually deepened to a bloody red hue." **2**

6   Shortly after that, a newspaper in the city of Oslo, Norway, reported: "A strong light was seen yesterday and today around 5 o'clock to the west of the city. People believed it was a fire: but it was actually a red refraction in the hazy atmosphere after sunset." **3**

7   Munch didn't paint *The Scream* until 1893, as part of a series of artworks called *The Frieze of Life*. But the artist said that his inspiration for *The Frieze of Life* came much earlier—in 1884, not long after Krakatoa's eruption.

8   To learn more about Munch and *The Scream*, Don Olson and a team of researchers traveled to the city of Oslo. Munch was living there when Krakatoa erupted. Olson and his team went through letters, journals, and maps in search of clues. Eventually, they found the exact location depicted in the painting. From that spot, a spectator can clearly see the southwestern sky where the twilights were so brilliantly red during the winter of 1883–84.

9   Altogether, the evidence strongly suggests that the wavy red bands in *The Scream* are indeed features of a Krakatoa sunset, concludes Olson.

10  When Krakatoa blew its stack in 1883, the volcano collapsed, leaving a submerged caldera (crater) in its place. In 1927, an underwater eruption in the crater gave birth to a new volcano. Its name is Anak Krakatoa, which is Indonesian for "Child of Krakatoa." Since then, the volcano has erupted regularly, sometimes hundreds of times a day. All of the eruptions have been small expulsions of fumes, dust, and lava. In time, though, the ejected material will build up and up, forming a much larger mountain. Many thousands of years from now, Anak Krakatoa might explode with the same force that its parent did in 1883. Once more, sunsets may catch fire around the world. **4**

3. *Newspapers from New York and Oslo reported the red skies months after the eruption at Krakatoa. I know these cities are thousands of miles from Indonesia. So I think that the powerful eruption of Krakatoa affected countries all over the world.* (Summarize/Synthesize)

4. *Turn and talk to a partner. How did the author relate art with science?* (Make connections)

## Extend Thinking Questions

Pose one or more questions to engage students more deeply with the text.

• *What are some changes the eruption of Krakatoa caused to the earth?*

• *What changes do scientists expect Anak Krakatoa to make?*

### iELD Paraphrase to Support Comprehension

After paragraph 3: The Scream *is a famous painting by Edvard Munch. Most people look at the man screaming. Don Olson focused on the red sky, which he learned was inspired by a real event.*

After paragraph 6: *Olson believed the red sky was based on the eruption of Krakatoa. Newspaper articles confirm skies were red as far away as New York and Oslo.*

After paragraph 10: *Munch was in Oslo when Krakatoa erupted. So Olson concludes evidence shows the red sky is from the Krakatoa sunset in Oslo. Krakatoa left behind a crater. In 1927 a new volcano erupted in the crater. Anak Krakatoa continues to have small eruptions.*

**Unit 8**

CCSS
RI.4.1, RI.4.2, RI.4.3, RI.4.4, SL.4.2, L.4.5c

# Popocatepetl and Iztaccihuatl

## A Mexican Volcano Myth

1   In Puebla, Mexico, two snow-covered volcanoes named Popocatepetl (poh-puh-KAY-tuh-puh-tul) and Iztaccihuatl (ees-tah-SEE-wah-tul) stand starkly against the vast sky. One, low and long, resembles a sleeping woman, while the other is known to spew plumes of smoke into the air. This is the legend of how those two great mountains came to be.

2   War had come to the ancient city, and its people, the Aztecs, had gathered an army to fight their enemies. Down on the streets, log drums pounded and the footsteps of the departing army beat out their own deafening rhythm. Princess Iztaccihuatl, nicknamed Izta, watched the warriors with a mix of worry and hope. Down in the crowd marched her beloved, Popocatepetl, known as Popo to the many who admired him.

3   As soon as the marigolds bloom," Popo had told Izta, "I will be back to marry you."

4   Popo was a brave fighter, and Princess Izta had high hopes that he would return safely. Every morning, as the green-feathered quetzal birds sang in the trees, she daydreamed of their wedding day. Every night she listened for the stamp of returning footsteps, and the blare of a conch-shell trumpet used in battle. Soon spring crept in, and new shoots poked up from the dark earth. Daily, the princess watched, waiting for the flowers to appear.

5   But what Princess Izta didn't know was that Popo had a rival, the cowardly and jealous Tlaxcala. Tlaxcala wanted Princess Izta for himself, but his hard-hearted nature assured he'd never win her love. Full of envy, he climbed her lookout post one night. There, he twisted his face into a sorrowful frown.

6   "Princess," he said, in a mock-mournful tone, "Forgive me, but I must tell you the tragic truth. Popo has fallen in battle. He died a hero, but he is lost to us."

7   Poor Princess Izta was beside herself. ❷ Her sobs echoed through the streets, and her tears were endless. No healer could cure her, and no friend could console her. The idea of living without Popo was more than the sweet princess could endure, and she soon died of a broken heart.

8    But the truth was that Popo was alive and well. As Princess Izta mourned, he raced through rivers and forests, traveling day and night to reach her. He arrived to find her lying lifeless on a bed of flame-colored marigold flowers.

9    Popo dropped his spear, lifted the princess, and carried her to the top of a nearby hill. There, he knelt by her side and lit a smoking torch, vowing to always watch over her. **3**

10   Though Popo felt as if the whole world had died with Princess Izta, the sun continued to rise, the wind continued to blow, and the seasons continued to change. Winter came, and mounds of fresh snow whispered down from the sky to cover the warrior and the princess, forming the two volcanoes that bear their names today. **4**

11   Even now, smoke puffs into the sky from the top of Popocatepetl to show the world that Popo still keeps watch. Nearby, Princess Izta sleeps peacefully, finally reunited with her beloved.

**4.** *The next to last paragraph contains sensory language that helps me visualize the setting. I can see the sun, hear the wind, and feel the snow covering the warrior and the princess.* (Use figurative language)

## Extend Thinking Questions

Pose one or more questions to engage students more deeply with the text.

• *Based on this legend, how did Popo and the princess change the earth?*

• *What is the purpose of this legend?*

**iELD  Paraphrase to Support Comprehension**

After paragraph 4: *The legend is about how the volcanoes Popocatepetl and Iztaccihuatl came to be. Popo was going to war in Puebla. His beloved Princess Izta will wait for him to return to marry her.*

After paragraph 7: *Jealous Tlaxcala told the princess that Popo died in battle. The princess did not know that this was a lie. She died of a broken heart.*

After paragraph 11: *Popo returned. When he found the princess dead, he carried her to the top of a hill. He knelt by her side and lit a smoking torch. Snow covered them. They formed the two volcanoes. Smoke puffs out of the top of Popocatepetl, which demonstrates that Popo still watches over his princess.*

**Unit 8**

CCSS
**RL.4.1, RL.4.3, RL.4.4, SL.4.2, L.4.5b**

# Mapping Disaster

## by Mike Weinstein

1 One of the scariest phone calls you might have to make is only three numbers: 9-1-1. Imagine calling for help. You give your location clearly. But what if the 9-1-1 dispatcher still doesn't know where you are? Maps are helping to solve that problem. **1**

2 In many small towns, landmarks are used instead of exact addresses. Rather than saying, "Come to 242 Elm Street," you might say, "Take a right turn two miles past the grocery store. Our house is on the right, opposite the lake."

3 You understand these directions. But they can be confusing for emergency workers hurrying to find you at night. So towns around the country are computerizing their maps. When you call 9-1-1, the dispatcher can look at a map that shows your exact location based on your phone number. Using the same map, the dispatcher can plot the fastest route to your house and the quickest way from your house to the hospital.

4 Such fancy maps are not limited to personal disasters. They can also help with enormous natural disasters. In 1900, for example, the citizens of Galveston, Texas, were caught unawares by a fierce hurricane. It killed more than 5,000 people. Researchers at Texas A&M University have developed special maps to help people avoid such surprises.

5 These disaster maps show roads and important places like police stations and hospitals. The maps also show flood levels for hurricanes with different strengths. If weather forecasters predict a hurricane, the maps help people know which places are at risk. So people can be warned to flee before their lives are in danger. **2**

6 In California, earthquakes are a major worry. In 1989, an earthquake struck San Francisco. It destroyed buildings and highways and disrupted baseball's World Series.

7 The California Office of Emergency Services has developed maps to help people prepare for earthquakes. Using the Internet, a resident can view a map of his or her town. The map will show the possible damage from earthquakes of different strengths. In one town, a medium-strong earthquake might rattle dishes. In another town, the same quake might bring down walls.

8 With the spread of computers, more people are moving into far-off, country areas. Many of these places suffer from tornadoes, forest fires, floods, or blizzards. As the population increases, so do the risks. Researchers are developing maps to help people predict the effect of all types of natural disasters.

9 Some disasters happen when people's efforts to control nature don't work out. For example, more than 2,000 people died in the famous 1889 Johnstown Flood when a reservoir collapsed. Trying to prevent disasters like this, California has developed "dam inundation" maps. These maps show which roads and buildings would be flooded if each dam failed. **3**

10 No map can control a flood or a tornado. But a good map can help people cut their losses and maybe save their lives. **4**

4. *Turn and talk to a partner. One main idea of this selection is that disaster maps can help save lives. Ask: What details support this main idea? (Ask questions/Summarize/Synthesize)*

**Extend Thinking Questions**

Pose one or more questions to engage students more deeply with the text.

• *Can these maps help control nature? Explain your answer.*

• *How are these maps related to earth changes?*

**iELD** **Paraphrase to Support Comprehension**

After paragraph 3: *Sometimes emergency workers cannot find the location of an emergency. So towns are using computers to make maps to show locations based on a phone number. They can also be used to plot fast routes to get to the emergency and then to a hospital.*

After paragraph 7: *Disaster maps show which places are at risk when a hurricane or flood hits. They also show the possible damage from earthquakes of different strengths in different places.*

After paragraph 10: *As people move to far-off country areas, disaster maps help them predict what can happen in disasters. Disaster maps cannot control nature. But they can help save lives.*

Unit 8

CCSS
RI.4.1, RI.4.2, RI.4.3, RI.4.4, RI.4.5, SL.4.2, L.4.4a

## Objectives

- Model making connections
- Model making inferences/predictions

## Set the Stage

**Introduce the Text.** *Today I'm going to read aloud an article about a group of people who still follow in their ancestors' footsteps. "Coming Through the Clouds" is about people in northern Mongolia who herd cattle over mountains and pastures as the seasons change.*

**Engage Thinking** *Why do you think the herder must move the cattle when seasons change? Turn to a partner to share your prediction.*

## Engage with the Text

Read aloud the text at a fluent, expressive pace. Use the suggested prompts to model your thinking, clarify events, and elicit student interaction.

**1.** *I wasn't sure what* migration *meant, so I reread the sentences before it. The author says that people "move to a warmer southern home. This is a kind of migration." So now I know that* migration *is a move from one place to another.* (Determine word meaning)

**2.** *I try to understand how cold -65 degrees must be, so I think of the coldest weather I have ever been in. I remember one winter it was -5 degrees. I couldn't stay outside for more than 5 minutes. My face was stinging. So, it must be impossible to be outside in a temperature of -65 degrees. What is the coldest weather you remember being in?* (Make connections)

**3.** *In this last part, the author writes that everyone helps in the migration. Some details that support this main idea are: Dogs protect flocks from wolves; Men and boys keep animals moving forward; Women and girls herd and manage the family.* (Summarize)

# Coming Through the Clouds

## by Meg Moss

1 During the hot summer months, some people stay comfortable in a place like Denver, and, when the winter comes, they move to a warmer southern home. This is a kind of migration that some humans make, following the good weather from north to south. **❶**

2 Other people around the world make a living by migrating with the seasons. They move from place to place to pick fruits and vegetables. Some migratory workers travel with their farm equipment, harvesting wheat in different areas. One of the oldest reasons for humans to migrate is to move herds of animals from summer to winter pasture lands. And, though this way of life is growing less common, cultures around the world still practice it, including the people of northern Mongolia's Darhad Valley.

3 The ancient country of Mongolia is located at the heart of Asia, between China and Russia. In the north, tall, forested mountain ranges and large lakes punctuate the broad grasslands. During the long, cold winters, temperatures dip as low as -65 degrees Fahrenheit, locking the land in a frozen grip. Though short, the summers can be hot, sometimes reaching into the nineties. **❷**

### Over the Top of the World . . .

4 People in this rugged landscape make their living by herding sheep, cattle, goats, yaks, and horses. To do so, they must migrate with the seasons. Having lived here for centuries, the herders know that by autumn, their animals will have nibbled the valley grasslands down to nothing. So, each October, when the bitter winds begin to blow from the north and the grass is running out, the people prepare to leave the Darhad Valley and move across the mountains to the protected shores of Lake Hovsgol. They walk up and over the mountain range that soars into the clouds nearly two miles high. With babies, belongings, herds, and homes in tow, these nomads travel for a week, covering up to 70 miles and camping along the way. They brave frostbite, blizzards, deep and dangerous ravines, and wolves to arrive safely.

5 At Lake Hovsgol, they hope to find fresh grass, water, and warmer temperatures to see them and their herds through the winter. In good years, there will be enough grass here to fatten the animals. But dry summers and harsh winters—the combination is called a zud—mean

that grass will be scarce, even at the lake, and many animals will die. Several years ago, a zud killed over six million animals in Mongolia. This created a terrible hardship for the herders, who flooded the towns and cities in search of work.

### . . . And Back Again

6    The return trip to the Darhad Valley in the spring can be extremely difficult. Blizzards in the high mountains make the going tough, especially if the herd has been weakened by a rough winter. But in the valley, the grasslands are renewing themselves, promising good grazing all summer.

7    Hard though the trek may be, the people look forward to each migration. For them, these journeys are as much a part of life as breathing and eating. Everyone from kids to grandparents helps. Dogs protect the flocks from wolves, and oxen or camels carry the loads. Men and boys ride their prized horses like cowboys, keeping the animals, perhaps as many as 400, orderly and moving forward. Women and girls are tough and able herders, too. They also manage the family and keep everyone fed. **3**

8    While some children remain behind to attend boarding school during the winter, efforts are underway to establish schools on both ends of the migration so that families can stay together and children can learn the herding life. Though herding is in their blood, some kids plan to go to college and live in the city, and many Mongolian parents heartily approve.

9    Can this ancient way of life survive the modern world? Twenty-first-century herders face the challenges of changing weather, overgrazing, and land disputes. But, if enough young Mongolians are willing, they'll continue to migrate back and forth through the clouds. **4**

**4.** *Turn and talk to a partner. The author asks: Can this ancient way of life survive the modern world? What do you think will happen to this culture in the future?* (Make inferences/predictions)

## Extend Thinking Questions

Pose one or more questions to engage students more deeply with the text.

• *How does the access to pastures influence the lives of both ancient and present-day people of Mongolia?*

• *What resources do the people who migrate from Darhad Valley to Lake Hovsgol and back look for? Why?*

### iELD Paraphrase to Support Comprehension

After paragraph 4: *People migrate, or move from one place to another for different reasons. People in the Darhad Valley of Mongolia move herds of animals to find green pastures.*

After paragraph 5: *The herders of Darhad Valley move their animals to Lake Hovsgol when winter comes. Sometimes at the lake, dry summers and hard winters cause grass to not grow. This is called a "zud." If a zud happens, many animals will die.*

After paragraph 9: *When the herders, families, and animals return to Darhad Valley in the spring, everyone helps. Dogs protect flocks from wolves. Adults and children keep animals orderly as they move. There are efforts to build schools on both ends of the journey so children can stay with their families and still get an education.*

Unit 9

**CCSS**
**RI.4.1, RI.4.2, RI.4.3, RI.4.4, RI.4.8, SL.4.3, L.4.4a**

## Objectives

- Model making inferences/predictions
- Model making connections

## Set the Stage

**Introduce the Text** *Today I'm going to read aloud part 1 of a short story about a father and daughter and their struggles to live on limited resources. In this first part, the main characters, Roberto Ignacio Torres and his daughter Lita, start their Sunday with Lita trying to wake up her father to go food shopping.*

**Engage Thinking** *Lita's father does not want to get up and go shopping with her. What do you think Lita does? Turn to a partner to share your prediction.*

## Engage with the Text

Read aloud the text at a fluent, expressive pace. Use the suggested prompts to model your thinking, clarify events, and elicit student interaction.

**1.** *Papi tells Lita "Times are hard." I'm not sure what this phrase means. As I read on, I learn that people cannot afford to stay in their houses, so Papi cannot get work building new ones. So I can tell that the phrase "Times are hard" means at this period, people are having trouble earning money and getting jobs. This seems like realistic fiction, as I recall a friend recently had a hard time getting a job. (Determine phrase meaning/Make connections)*

**2.** *Lita told Gilberto that her father was working, but he was not. I think she said this to help her father keep his pride. Gilberto's brother is also in construction. She didn't want him to think her father could not get work and just stayed in bed. (Make inferences)*

# Roberto Ignacio Torres Bakes, Part 1

## by Steven Frank

1   Papi won't wake up.

2   I go to the window and tug on the bottom of the shade. Sunlight lands on Papi's cheek.

3   "Come on, sleepyhead," I tell him, "or we won't get the good persimmons."

4   Papi tucks his head under the pillow like a turtle. Then he pokes it out again. "Go without me, Lita," he says, "just this time. You know where the money is."

5   I pull down the shade and go out of his room.

6   In the kitchen, I open the drawer where we keep the forks, knives, and spoons. I lift their tray, and that's where the money is. Papi keeps it in envelopes. One says "rent," one says "food," another "clothes." There's one at the bottom of the pile. "Just for fun," it says.

7   That one's been empty since last Christmas.

8   "Times are hard, Lita," Papi told me. "People can't afford to stay in their houses, so who's going to build new ones? If they don't build new ones, they don't need framers like me to turn sticks into homes." **❶**

9   I take two twenties from the food envelope and push my bicycle out the door.

10  From our apartment on Addison, it's only a 20-minute ride. Twenty there and 25 back. Back is when we have to take it slow, our bicycles all wobbly from the bags of fruits and vegetables we hang from the handlebars. Sometimes, when the "just for fun" envelope is full, we balance bags of kettle corn on our laps too.

11  Today is my first ride alone, but I know the way. I've known it since I was a baby in Mamma's sling. Since they took turns pushing me in a stroller and the bag of oranges got to sit in my seat. After Mamma died, it was Papi and me riding side by side.

12  By the time I get there, Jacques and Pierre, the French guys who sell pastries and always say "'Ow many dozens would you like?" are all sold out of chocolate croissants, and the lines for burritos are 20 people long. Ted, the organic guy, smiles at me as I push my bike past his stall. Me and Papi always make one pass up the market, to see what's good along the way and to visit the flowers at the end. Then we come back down, and our handlebars start to grow plastic bags.

13  Gilberto, who sells lettuce, broccoli, zucchini, carrots, and onions—the stuff we mostly buy—asks where Papi is today.

14  "He's working," I say. Gilberto's brother works in construction too.

15  "On Sunday?"

16  "On any day he can." ❷

17  He takes his hand out from under the scale. I know he's been keeping it light for me.

18  "Five dollars, Lita," he says. And he takes it out of the twenty.

19  I tell him I'll see him next week, but he says, "Not unless you're coming to Mexico. Mi'ito's getting married, and we're all going. My stall will be empty." ❸

20  "See you in two Sundays, then," I say, and he says, "Sí, you will."

21  After I buy the oranges, the avocados, the apples, and the persimmons—I get lucky and pay half the price for the bruised ones—I'm down to $3.00. I know I should just take it home to Papi, but there's the stand from Rockenwagner's Bakery, and they make this chocolate streusel cake that can send a girl to heaven and home again in just one bite.

22  But at $2.75 a slice I decide to skip heaven and ride straight home.

23  Where I find Papi still asleep.

24  They say that teenagers sleep in really late, maybe past noon, because their brains are still growing. But what's my Papi's excuse? I'm the one who's supposed to be sleeping like a teen, not him. I can't get mad at him, though. He's not sleeping because he's tired. Or not just because he's tired, anyway. He's sleeping because, as Mamma would say, he's blue in the heart.

25  I know *just* how to wake him.

© Benchmark Education Company, LLC

---

3. *It's interesting that the author chose to let readers know that Gilberto will not be at his stand next Sunday. I predict this information will be important to the plot later on in the story.* (Make predictions)

4. *Turn and talk to a partner: Why did Lita go to the market alone? What happened at the market?* (Summarize)

## Extend Thinking Questions

Pose one or more questions to engage students more deeply with the text.

• *Money is an important resource. How does Lita and her father's access to money affect their lives in this part of the story?*

• *At the end Lita says, "I know just how to wake him." What do you think will happen next in the story?*

### iELD Paraphrase to Support Comprehension

After paragraph 4: *Lita tries to wake her father up. He does not want to get up. He tells her to get the money and go to the market on her own.*

After paragraph 11: *Her father explains he cannot get work building houses because people cannot afford new houses. Lita gets the money from the silverware drawer and goes to the market alone. Her father and mother used to take her there. But her mother has died.*

After paragraph 25: *At the market Lita buys food. She learns that Gilberto, who sells vegetables, will not be at his stand next Sunday. He will be back in two Sundays. She decides her father should wake up and she knows "just how to wake him."*

CCSS
RL.4.1, RL.4.2, RL.4.4, RI.4.9, SL.4.2, L.4.5b

**Unit 9**

## Set the Stage

**Introduce the Text** *Today I'm going to read aloud part 2 of "Roberto Ignacio Torres Bakes." Let's review what happened so far in part 1.* (Have volunteers summarize part 1.) *In part 2 Lita wakes up her father in an unusual way. She then starts to act a "crazy idea" she has to help her father and her make money.*

**Engage Thinking** *How do you think Lita might wake up her father? Turn to a partner to share your prediction.*

## Engage with the Text

Read aloud the text at a fluent, expressive pace. Use the suggested prompts to model your thinking, clarify events, and elicit student interaction.

**1.** *Papi used to bake "meringue" cookies. I don't know how to pronounce this word or what it means. I know that Lita beat egg whites and added sugar. I think this may be what meringue is. When I check the pronunciation and definition in a dictionary, I learn that meh-RANG is a mixture of well-beaten egg whites and sugar.* (Determine word meaning)

**2.** *I can hear the conversation Papi has with Lita about Lita's mother. I can see them talking to each other. I can hear how Lita finishes each sentence for her father.* (Visualize)

# Roberto Ignacio Torres Bakes, Part 2

1 He used to bake those meringue cookies that made our apartment smell like a chocolate factory. The recipe's so easy you can't give it away because then everyone's apartment will smell like a chocolate factory. I drape a towel over the bowl when I beat the egg whites. I want Papi to wake up by smell, not sound. The chocolate chips in the pantry have little gray specks on them like the spots on an old man's hand. I toss them in anyway because the oven'll make them young again. Then I spoon the whipped egg whites with the sugar and chocolate chips and cocoa powder onto the parchment paper. The oven's ready now, and in they go. **1**

2 Papi comes out of his room nose first. His hair looks like it's windy in the apartment. His arms look tiny inside his robe.

3 "Your mamma married me for these cookies," he says. "She invited me to a barbecue in the park. 'What can I bring?' I said, and she said, 'Just pick up some cookies at Von's.' Store-bought cookies? Does Roberto Ignacio Torres ever bring store-bought cookies to a party?"

4 "No, Papi."

5 "Roberto Ignacio Torres bakes! You should've seen her, Lita, sitting on a blanket under a tree, taking her first bite of Roberto's chocolate meringues. Her hair was—"

6 "—pulled around to one side and falling over her shoulder—"

7 "—like something you'd want to pet."

8 "Her eyes were deep cocoa brown—"

9 "—like something rich you'd want to sip on a cold day. **2** **3**

10 "I've told you the story."

11 "Yes, Papi."

12 "Her father tasted them too. He gave me his blessing that very day."

13 "Papi," I say, "what did you want to be when you grew up?"

14 "A papi."

15 "No, I mean, what did you want to do?"

16 "Do? What do you mean, do?"

17 "For life."

18 "Oh. I did what my daddy showed me to do. Construction. Framing."

19 "But what was your dream?"

20 Papi's big hand comes out of his sleeve and plucks the cookies from the parchment. He doesn't even need the spatula because they pop right off. He takes a bite, smiles, and says, "I dreamed to be a papi."

21 But I, Carmelita Consuela Torres, don't believe him. I think he had a dream that he let go. And as I watch his face still crusty with too much sleep starting to wake up with each bite of his own cookie, I get an idea. A crazy idea…

22 Later that day, when Papi's napping, I climb on top of a chair and open the cabinet above the fridge. There's a huge pile of paper, scraps mostly, and all in a big mess. The papers are crinkly, like something spilled on them a long time ago and dried. This heap of papers is Papi's cookbook. His recipes to make a dream—is it his dream or mine?—come true.

23 I put them all in a folder, alphabetically by name, just in case.

24 I make a deal with myself: If Papi gets a job by Saturday, I won't try my crazy idea. ❹ I'll put it back up there with the scraps of paper and never take it out again. But if he doesn't…

25 Tuesday, Wednesday, and Thursday go by. No job yet for Papi.

26 Friday morning he sleeps in. I leave early to go to school and watch the clock the whole day. At 3:20 I race home. Papi left me a note to say he has an interview with Jim Montana to give Papi a job, and I grab the two hundred.

27 At Von's I'm a smart shopper. I look at the price per pound, the instant coupons, the specials if you're a Von's Club member. I already did the math on the ingredients, multiplying everything by 10. Ten batches of meringues. Ten fruit tarts. Ten dozen red velvet cupcakes. My magic number is 10.

28 The lady says my total is $243.75. My brown skin turns bleach white.

29 "Is that after the Von's Club discount?" I ask.

30 "Oh," she says, "I forgot to swipe your card."

31 She does, and the total does gymnastics on the screen: from $243.75 to $202.75. I'm left with a lucky quarter.

© Benchmark Education Company, LLC

---

3. *Lita being able to finish each sentence her father begins means he must have told her these stories many times. This helps me understand how close Lita is to her father, as well as how much Roberto loved his wife.* (Make inferences)

4. *Turn and talk to a partner. Ask: What do you think Lita's crazy idea is? What would you do?* (Make predictions/ Make connections)

## Extend Thinking Questions

Pose one or more questions to engage students more deeply with the text.

• *Lita uses resources such as food and money. How do these resources impact her actions?*

• *What is an idea you had to help someone that seemed difficult to do? What happened?*

### iELD Paraphrase to Support Comprehension

After paragraph 5: *Papi wakes up to the smell of the chocolate meringue cookies that Lita baked. He reminds Lita of when he baked the cookies for the first time for her mother.*

After paragraph 21: *Lita asks Papi what he always dreamed to do. He says he dreamed to be a papi, but Lita does not believe him. She gets an idea.*

After paragraph 31: *Lita gathers Papi's recipes. She organizes them into a folder. She waits to see if Papi gets a job by Friday. When he doesn't, she works on her idea. She takes $200 and goes to Von's. She buys ingredients for ten batches of meringues, tarts, and cupcakes.*

CCSS
RL.4.1, RL.4.4, SL.4.2, L.4.4c

Unit 9

## Objectives

- Model visualizing
- Model making inferences/predictions
- Model making connections

## Set the Stage

**Introduce the Text** *Today I'm going to read aloud part 3 of "Roberto Ignacio Bakes." Let's review what happened in part 2. (Have volunteers summarize part 2.) In part 3 we learn what Lita's "crazy idea" is and if it is successful.*

**Engage Thinking** *What resources do you think Lita will use to implement her "crazy idea"? Turn to a partner to share your prediction.*

## Engage with the Text

Read aloud the text at a fluent, expressive pace. Use the suggested prompts to model your thinking, clarify events, and elicit student interaction.

1. *Papi is holding the rent envelope when he asks Lita what she did. I realize what happened. That's where Lita got the $200. She used the rent to buy food supplies. I think she and Papi will use them to bake items to sell at the farmers' market.* (Make inferences/predictions)

2. *Lita says that Papi told her she has her mamma's eyes. I know this cannot mean that her eyes are actually her mother's. It is an idiom that means Lita's eyes look like her mother's eyes.* (Use idioms)

# Roberto Ignacio Torres Bakes, Part 3

1   I walk into the kitchen with my arms full of shopping bags.

2   Papi's holding the rent envelope in his hand.

3   "What did you do, Lita?"

4   I talk fast, the way my mamma used to when she and Papi disagreed. The words pop off my tongue like kettle corn. I tell Papi how Gilberto's stand will be empty tomorrow and how they charge $2.75 for one square of chocolate streusel and how the croissants always sell out but that Papi's baking, the thing about him that Mamma fell in love with and that the whole world would too if they could taste it, is better, and isn't that his dream? To be a baker?

5   He looks at me icy cold. "Did you keep the receipt, Carmelita?"

6   "Yes, Papi."

7   "Go back to the store. Return everything."

8   One more word comes out of my mouth, this time real slow.

9   "No."

10   I drop the bags, take out the folder of his recipes, and lay them on the kitchen table. "We'll start with the dough for your fruit tarts," I say, "and while it's chilling, we'll make 10 batches of meringue cookies. Then we'll do your flourless chocolate cakes—we can sell those for $5.00 a slice, I know we can. We'll bake all night, Papi, and all day tomorrow."

11   "Give me the receipt Carmelita."

12   "Did Jim Montana have work for you?

13   "No," he says, "not this month."

14   We look at each other. Papi's eyes are so tired. And mine? They start to fill up with tears. He once told me that I have my mamma's eyes. And she once told me that he could never stand to see her cry. ❷

15   He looks at the bags of groceries on the floor.

16   "Did you buy vanilla?" he asks.

17  On Sunday morning, Papi wakes me before dawn. It takes us 25 minutes there and 20 back. I make three trips while Papi sets up. Ted, the organic guy, loans us a table, and we make one stop at Smart 'N Final to buy paper plates, napkins, and bags.

18  The market opens at 8:00. At 8:30, I get there with the last batch. Only I panic because I can't find Papi. There's a wall of people in front of Gilberto's produce stand, which isn't selling any produce today. As I make my way forward, I see people standing off to the side with their eyes closed and their tongues licking their lips, and that's when I know something good is going on. I push my bicycle through, and when everyone sees what I'm bringing, they make way like I'm Moses, and soon I find Papi serving slices of his fruit tart with one hand and taking in money with the other.

19  "Lita," he says, "I could use a little help back here."

20  I crawl under the table, pop up on the other side, and get to work.

21  That night Papi and me stay up late telling stories about the people who lined up all day for his baking. He tells me that when he was a boy he had dreamed of what he wanted to be when he grew up. He doesn't have to say what it was. **3**

22  Later, after Papi goes to bed, I finish cleaning up the kitchen. I put away the forks, knives, and spoons, and I peek under the tray. The rent envelope is full again. There's money for food and clothes.

23  And the last envelope, the one that says "just for fun," holds a crisp $100 bill. **4**

3. *Lita and Papi sold lots of baked goods at the market. People were lined up to buy them. They must feel both excited and proud of their success. I remember feeling the same way when I participated in a successful fundraiser.* (Make connections)

4. *Turn and talk to a partner. Describe in as much detail as you can what happened to Lita and Papi at the marketplace.* (Summarize/Visualize)

## Extend Thinking Questions

Pose one or more questions to engage students more deeply with the text.

• *How did a lack of resources affect Lita and Papi in the beginning of the story?*

• *How did access to resources impact their lives at the end of the story?*

**iELD Paraphrase to Support Comprehension**

After paragraph 9: *Papi learns that Lita spent the rent to buy baking goods. He tells her to return all of the food. Lita tells him no. She wants to sell Papi's baking at Gilberto's stand, which will be empty tomorrow.*

After paragraph 16: *Lita tells Papi they can bake all night to make his recipes. He still wants her to return the food. When he sees Lita start to cry, he gives in.*

After paragraph 23: *Lita and Papi set up their bakery at Gilberto's stand. People line up to buy the baked goods. That night Lita finds that they now have money for the rent, food, clothes, and even $100 "just for fun."*

**Unit 9**

CCSS
RL.4.1, RL.4.3, RL.4.4, SL.4.2, L.4.5b

# Art Is Everywhere

## by Maureen Ash

1 Artists don't always have studios and they don't always go to art school. They make art out of all kinds of things. Sometimes they don't even really think they are making art. They are just making something they need.

2 For more than 200 years the women in Gee's Bend, Alabama, have worked hard. As small children, they went to the fields to play while their parents worked. But soon they had to work in the fields themselves. Some of them had to work so much that they could not go to school very often. Before long they were mothers and had to take care of their own children—who went with them to the fields to play while their parents worked.

3 The cabins they lived in were cold in winter and hot in summer. In many, the floors were made of dirt. There was no glass in the windows, just shutters to close when it got cold. The families pasted pages from newspapers and magazines on the walls to keep the drafts out. The women used fabric scraps and old clothes to sew quilts that kept their children warm in their beds at night. ❶

4 Other than singing, going to church, and sewing quilts, there wasn't much to do except work. The work was hard—chopping cotton with a heavy hoe, or picking cotton, or getting the fields ready to plant more cotton. The women's hands and bodies were busy all the time. ❷

5 But their minds were free. Often they thought about the quilts they were making. What would look good with that red corduroy fabric? Now that all the fancy print was used up, what could be used to finish the edges?

6 When they could get together, the women met to work on each other's quilts. Each one did the top piece, the part with the fabric blocks on it, at home by herself. But the quilters worked as a group to add the cotton batting for warmth, and the back piece, and then they sewed the pieces together so the cotton batting wouldn't shift around when the quilt was washed. ❸

7 Each time they met, the women exclaimed over each other's patterns. They decided to try something like what the other had done, but with a different twist.

8  They had their own ideas about what looked best, and the quilts were their chance to see their ideas in the light. Their daughters worked with them and learned to make quilts, too.

9  Years went by. The women lived in better houses. They still made quilts, and many of those quilts are now considered to be some of the most important art ever made in America. They hang in museums and have even been pictured on U.S. postage stamps. They are called American treasures.

10  What is it about these quilts? Some of them are ragged. Most are not perfectly square or rectangular, but seem kind of twisted or kinked to the side. A lot of them don't follow a pattern, or one that we recognize. Some of them have such crazy colors put together in crazy ways! Others are made from worn, tired work clothes. In places, the faded denim is suddenly bright because that's where there used to be a pocket.  Can great art come from scraps and old clothes? We have only to look at the quilts to know that the answer is Yes! **4**

**3.** *At first I thought quilters might be some kind of quilting tools. But then I remembered that the suffix "-er" usually means "a person who." The text says that the quilters "worked as a group." So the suffix and the context clues show that quilters were the people who made the quilts.* (Build vocabulary)

**4.** *Turn and talk to a partner. Talk about what the quilts looked like. Imagine one and describe it aloud. If you were making a quilt, what would yours look like?* (Visualize/Make connections)

## Extend Thinking Questions

Pose one or more questions to engage students more deeply with the text.

• *How did the resources available to the women of Gee's Bend impact their lives?*

• *Describe in your own words the process the women followed to make a quilt.*

### iELD Paraphrase to Support Comprehension

After paragraph 4: *For over 200 years women in Gee's Bend, Alabama, worked hard. They worked in fields chopping or picking cotton. Their cabins were cold in winter and hot in summer. They sewed quilts to keep their children warm.*

After paragraph 8: *Women got together to help work on each other's quilts. They came up with new ideas on how to make the quilts better.*

After paragraph 10: *Years passed. Women continued making the quilts. Today they hang in museums. Some have been pictured on stamps. Some quilts have no patterns, are not square, and are made from old work clothes.*

CCSS
RI.4.1, RI.4.2, RI.4.4, SL.4.2, L.4.4a, L.4.4b

Unit 9

## Objectives

• Model making connections

• Model making inferences/predictions

## Set the Stage

**Introduce the Text** *Today I'm going to read aloud part 1 of a biography about the famous leader Cesar Chavez. Listen closely to learn how Cesar Chavez grew from a young farm worker to an organizer and union leader.*

**Engage Thinking** *Chavez went on a hunger strike for twenty-five days to protest poor conditions for farm workers. What effect do you think this hunger strike had? Turn to a partner to share your prediction.*

## Engage with the Text

Read aloud the text at a fluent, expressive pace. Use the suggested prompts to model your thinking, clarify events, and elicit student interaction.

**1.** *I wonder why the author began this selection with an event in Chavez's adult life rather than with his date of birth. Did she want to show what Chavez was like? Did she want to capture the readers' interest? What other questions do you have about this introduction?* (Ask questions)

**2.** *Some of the workers were illegal immigrants. I know il- means "not" and -leg- is a root that means "law." So illegal must mean "not lawful or not following the law." This helps me understand why these workers were afraid they would be sent back to Mexico.* (Determine word meaning)

**3.** *I remember reading about Cesar Chavez. I understand that he helped workers. That information made me curious to learn more about Chavez. Having a background about who Chavez was helped me to better understand this selection.* (Make connections)

# Cesar Chavez: His Fight for the Farm Workers, Part 1

## by Barbara Bloom

1   Inside the old gas station, Cesar Chavez lay fasting as he had for twenty days since February 14, 1968. Outside, migrant workers, dusty from their hard work in the fields, stood keeping watch over their leader. Many of these crop pickers had brought gifts or charms to give Chavez luck; others had painted the windows with brightly colored designs to make them look like stained glass. One television reporter said the site was "like a shrine to nonviolence at which the followers of Cesar Chavez have come to worship." ❶

2   Each day Chavez's wife and children came to see him and check his health. At first Chavez thought only of food, but gradually he no longer dreamed of eating. He grew thin and weak, yet his mind remained clear.

3   As head of the National Farm Workers, he continued to hold meetings, sign papers, and plan. Chavez hoped that his sacrifice would help the cause (La Causa). He fasted because of his commitment to his people, the poor farm workers, and to his belief that they should have higher wages, decent working conditions and housing, health care benefits, and a life without violence. He wanted to show those who thought they had to fight to gain these ends that nonviolence took courage, too. Twenty-five days after beginning, Chavez ended his fast, having won respect for his peaceful methods.

4   Cesar Chavez was born near Yuma, Arizona, in 1927 on his family's farm. His grandfather had come there from Mexico in the 1880s. He and his family lived there until Cesar was ten years old, growing fruits and vegetables. They lost their land during the Depression and headed for California to join the thousands of other migrant farm workers who traveled up and down the state following the crops and working in the fields. ❷

5   Moving often, Cesar, his five brothers and sisters, and his parents labored long hours under the hot sun, barely earning enough money to get by. Sometimes they slept in their car, sometimes in the fields, and sometimes in tumble-down shacks provided by the farmers. Always they hoped for a better life. By the time Cesar had finished eighth grade, he had attended more than thirty schools and had picked crops throughout California. His formal schooling was over, and his experience had taught him that farm workers received little justice or respect.

6   Cesar Chavez began talking with fellow pickers, trying to get them to join him in demanding improvements. Most of the workers were afraid. Some were illegal immigrants from Mexico who were afraid of being sent back to a life that was even more difficult. Others spoke little English and knew the farm owners had the power on their side.

7   The chance for Chavez to do something came in 1951. Fred Ross, an organizer for the Community Service Organization (CSO), a private group helping migrants get food, medical care, legal aid, and housing, came to see him. Ross asked Chavez if he wanted to work with the CSO to register migrants to vote. Voting, he said, could give Hispanics power. Chavez, just twenty-four and shy and unsure of his abilities, agreed to help. All day he picked apricots, and at night he registered voters and organized classes in English. Within two months, he had registered more than four thousand workers. When his boss found out, he fired Chavez.

8   The CSO then hired him and gave him a steady income. He studied labor laws and led meetings of his fellow migrants. The migrants listened to him. Most trusted him, for he was one of them, but they feared the landowners and the loss of their jobs.

9   After nine years, Chavez believed farm workers needed to form a union to lobby for decent wages and working conditions. The CSO disagreed. On September 30, 1962, Chavez quit the CSO, and using his own savings to live on, he started the National Farm Workers Association, later called the United Farm Workers of America. **3** **4**

4. *Turn and talk to a partner. Ask: What effect do you think the National Farm Workers Association will have?* (Make inferences/predictions)

## Extend Thinking Questions

Pose one or more questions to engage students more deeply with the text.

• *Are unions helpful? Why or why not?*

• *How did a lack of economic resources affect farm workers?*

### iELD Paraphrase to Support Comprehension

After paragraph 3: *Cesar Chavez was the head of the National Farm Workers Association. He went on a hunger strike for twenty-five days to show a peaceful way to protest. He wanted to get farm workers higher pay and better benefits.*

After paragraph 6: *When Cesar was ten years old, his family lost their farm. They became migrant farm workers. Working conditions were hard and pay was low. He tried to get other workers to demand improvements, but they were afraid they would be sent back to Mexico.*

After paragraph 9: *When he was twenty-four, Cesar began working for the Community Service Organization. He worked to get migrant workers to vote. After nine years there, Cesar wanted farm workers to form a union. In 1962 he started the National Farm Workers Association.*

**Unit 9**

**CCSS**
**RI.4.1, RI.4.3, RI.4.4, RI.4.9, SL.4.1c, L.4.4b**

## Objectives

- Model making inferences/predictions
- Model making connections

## Set the Stage

**Introduce the Text** *Today I'm going to read aloud part 2 of an article about Cesar Chavez. In this part we will learn what Chavez and the farm workers did to convince the farmers to pay them a living wage and to treat them more fairly.*

**Engage Thinking** *What actions do you think the migrant farm workers took to convince farmers to raise their pay? Turn to a partner to share your prediction.*

## Engage with the Text

Read aloud the text at a fluent, expressive pace. Use the suggested prompts to model your thinking, clarify events, and elicit student interaction.

**1.** *The text says "he could organize a boycott." At first I didn't know what a boycott was, but when I read on it says "asking people not to buy or sell grapes." So I think a boycott is when people stop buying and selling a certain product. Have you ever participated in a boycott?* (Determine word meaning/Make connections)

**2.** *Turn and talk to a partner. Ask: How do you think the grape growers will react to a boycott? Why?* (Make inferences/predictions)

**3.** *One main idea throughout this selection is that Cesar Chavez believed that the best way to win rights for farm workers was through nonviolent methods. Details that support this main idea are: he fasted; he used strikes; he supported boycotts.* (Summarize/Synthesize)

# Cesar Chavez: His Fight for the Farm Workers, Part 2

1   In 1964, the [National Farm Workers Association] took a farmer to court for paying less than minimum wage. The court found the farmer guilty and forced him to pay the minimum wage. The first victory in the fields came in May 1965. The nursery industry in Delano, California, offered one wage to rose grafters at the beginning of the week but less at week's end. When the workers asked Cesar Chavez for help, he convinced them to go out on strike. After a four-day strike, the nursery owners gave in to the workers' demands.

2   Chavez hoped one day to have enough members to make all growers pay decent wages, but he felt that would take years. In the summer of 1965, some grape pickers went out on strike against the grape growers. They asked Chavez to join them, but he felt that his group was not ready. At a meeting on September 15, the group's two thousand members disagreed, shouting "Huelga! Huelga!" ("Strike! Strike!")

3   They quit picking grapes and picketed the vineyards, warning others not to work until the grape growers recognized their right to a union and fair pay. After a few weeks, two vineyards agreed, and the workers returned to those vineyards. Other growers still refused. Chavez realized he had to find new ways to oppose the powerful growers.

4   Perhaps, Chavez thought, he could organize a boycott, asking people not to buy or sell grapes. In November, he called for a nationwide boycott. The following spring, he led a three-hundred-mile march through California's farmland to the state capital, Sacramento. People all over the nation heard about the migrants' problems. Students, nuns, lawyers, doctors, and ministers came to help. Others sent money, food, and clothing for the strikers. As more people boycotted grapes, more growers signed contracts with the workers. **1** **2**

5   At some vineyards, migrants resorted to violence to make their point. Chavez disagreed with this tactic, preferring instead the nonviolent means favored by the former Indian leader Mohandas Gandhi and American civil rights leader Martin Luther King Jr. After much thought and prayer, he began his fast, which stopped most of the violence among his followers. **3**

6    By 1970, most vineyards were paying fair wages, and the grape boycott ended. The American Federation of Labor and Congress of Industrial Organizations (AFL-CIO) chartered the United Farm Workers in 1972. Until his death in 1993, Chavez presided over many victories and defeats and continued to lead farm workers, using fasts, strikes, marches, and boycotts to dramatize their plight. Although changes came slowly, Cesar Chavez continued to support nonviolence and to dream. He said, "Our struggle is not easy...we are poor. But we have our bodies and spirits and the justice of our cause as our weapons." **4**

**4.** *This selection begins in 1964. The events are then told in time order. The other dates such as 1965 and 1970, and time order words such as "September 15," "after a few weeks," and "the following spring" help me understand the sequence of the events.* (Determine structure)

## Extend Thinking Questions

Pose one or more questions to engage students more deeply with the text.

• *How did the boycott of grapes impact the grape growers? Why?*

• *Do you think Cesar Chavez was an effective leader? Why or why not?*

### iELD Paraphrase to Support Comprehension

After paragraph 2: *The National Farm Workers Association won a court case that got a worker a minimum wage. In another case, nursery workers went on strike and the owners gave in to their demands. In 1965 grape pickers went on strike.*

After paragraph 4: *Two vineyards agreed to the grape pickers' demands. To get others to agree, Chavez organized a nationwide boycott of grapes.*

After paragraph 6: *Some pickers used violence, but Chavez disagreed. Instead he began a fast. By 1970 most vineyards were paying fair wages. The boycott ended. Chavez continued to use nonviolence to help workers be treated fairly.*

Unit 9

CCSS
RI.4.1, RI.4.2, RI.4.4, RI.4.5, SL.4.2, L.4.4a

# I'd Rather Not Be on Relief

## by Lester Hunter Shafter, 1938

We go around all dressed in rags

While the rest of the world goes neat,

And we have to be satisfied

With half enough to eat.

5   We have to live in lean-tos, **1**

Or else we live in a tent,

For when we buy our bread and beans

There's nothing left for rent.


I'd rather not be on the rolls of relief,

10   Or work on the W. P. A.,

We'd rather work for the farmer

If the farmer could raise the pay;

Then the farmer could plant more cotton

And he'd get more money for spuds,

15   Instead of wearing patches,

We'd dress up in new duds. **2**


From the east and west and north and south

Like a swarm of bees we come; **3**

The migratory workers

20   Are worse off than a bum.

We go to Mr. Farmer

And ask him what he'll pay;

He says, "You gypsy workers

Can live on a buck a day."

25  I'd rather not be on the rolls of relief,

    Or work on the W. P. A.,

    We'd rather work for the farmer

    If the farmer could raise the pay;

    Then the farmer could plant more cotton

30  And he'd get more money for spuds,

    Instead of wearing patches,

    We'd dress up in new duds.


    We don't ask for luxuries

    Or even a feather bed.

35  But we're bound to raise the dickens

    While our families are underfed.

    Now the winter is on us

    And the cotton picking is done,

    What are we going to live on

40  While we're waiting for spuds to come?


    Now if you will excuse me

    I'll bring my song to an end.

    I've got to go and chuck a crack

    Where the howling wind comes in.

45  The times are going to better

    And I guess you'd like to know

    I'll tell you all about it,

    I've joined the C. I. O. **4**

**4.** *Turn and talk to a partner. The CIO stands for Congress of Industrial Workers. It was a union that helped organize workers to fight for rights. What caused migratory workers to join? Would you ever join a union?* (Summarize/Make connections)

## Extend Thinking Questions

Pose one or more questions to engage students more deeply with the text.

• *What resources were destroyed by the Dust Bowl? How did their destruction affect farm workers?*

• *Why does the narrator believe that times are going to get better?*

### iELD Paraphrase to Support Comprehension

**After line 16:** *The farm workers are very poor. They do not want government help or work. They would rather work for farmers, but farmers pay too little.*

**After line 32:** *Workers migrate from all over the country. They work on a farm, but the farmer pays too little. If the farmer could pay more, the workers would not have to work for the W.P.A., the Works Progress Administration, a government agency established to pay workers to build roads, dams, along with other public works projects.*

**After last line:** *The end of farming season comes. The workers protest the poor living conditions. They believe things will now get better because they joined the C.I.O.*

Unit 9

**CCSS**
**RL.4.1, RL.4.4, RL.4.5, RI.4.9, L.4.4c, L.4.5a**

## Objectives

- Model asking questions
- Model determining text importance

## Set the Stage

**Introduce the Text** *Today I'm going to read aloud a free verse poem about electricity coming to a village in the Caribbean.*

**Engage Thinking** *How do you think electricity might come to a small village in the Caribbean? Turn to a partner to share your prediction.*

## Engage with the Text

Read aloud the text at a fluent, expressive pace. Use the suggested prompts to model your thinking, clarify events, and elicit student interaction.

1. *I wasn't sure what kling-klings were. They swooped down and landed in trees. So they can fly. They may be insects or birds. When I check the Internet I found they are birds also known as Great Antillean Grackles.* (Determine word meaning)

2. *The way the author uses language to evoke emotions and images is more typical of poetry than prose. For example, "a breeze coming home from sea held its breath" gives a human quality to the breeze. Why would the author choose to use personification here?* (Determine text importance)

# Electricity Comes to Cocoa Bottom

## by Marcia Douglas

Then all the children of Cocoa Bottom

went to see Mr. Samuel's electric lights.

They camped on the grass bank outside his house,

their lamps filled with oil,

5   waiting for sunset,

watching the sky turn yellow, orange.

Grannie Patterson across the road

peeped through the crack in her porch door.

The cable was drawn like a pencil line across the sun.

10   The fireflies waited in the shadows,

their lanterns off.

The kling-klings swooped in from the hills, **1**

congregating in the orange trees.

A breeze coming home from sea held its breath; **2**

15   bamboo lining the dirt road stopped its swaying,

and evening came as soft as chiffon curtains:

Closing. Closing.

Light! Mr. Samuel smiling on the verandah –

a silhouette against the yellow shimmer behind him –

20 and there arising such a gasp,

such a fluttering of wings,

tweet-a-whit,

such a swaying, swaying.

Light! Marvellous light!

25 And then the breeze rose up from above the trees,

swelling and swelling into a wind such that the long grass bent forward

stretching across the bank like so many bowed heads.

And a voice in the wind whispered:

Is there one among us to record this moment?

30 But there was none – ❸

no one (except for a few warm rocks

hidden among mongoose ferns) even heard a sound.

Already the children of Cocoa Bottom had lit their lamps for the dark journey home,

and it was too late –

35 the moment had passed. ❹

**3.** *I wonder why no one recorded the moment? Couldn't any of the children write? Did they have pencils or paper? Weren't there news people there? How long after did the poet record this moment?* (Ask questions)

**4.** *Turn and talk to a partner. Ask: What do you think the theme of this poem is? What details support that theme?* (Ask questions/Summarize)

## Extend Thinking Questions

Pose one or more questions to engage students more deeply with the text.

• *What do you think will happen in Cocoa Bottom with the introduction of electricity?*

• *How can you retell the events of this poem in prose form?*

### Paraphrase to Support Comprehension

After line 5: *Children, animals, and nature gather outside of Mr. Samuel's house. They wait and watch as night comes.*

After line 30: *The lights in Mr. Samuel's house are turned on. Everyone is thrilled. But no one records this important moment.*

After line 35: *The children head for home. They use their oil lamps to light the way. The moment has passed.*

# Turning on the Light

## by Kathiann M. Kowalski

1  We come home to a dark house, but with the flick of switch, there is light. Until the late 1800s, however, light came from candles and oil or gas lamps. These light sources came with the danger of fire or accidental explosion. Thomas Alva Edison's incandescent lightbulb offered a safer, steadier way to light up homes and businesses. **❶**

2  Incandescent light works when an electric current flows through a fine material, called a filament, and makes it glow. Edison's journals noted that effect in 1876 after some experimentation with carbonized paper. But Edison did not become serious about developing an incandescent lightbulb until a physicist friend, George Barker, encouraged him to explore the possibilities of an electric lighting system. Upon his return home to New Jersey from a vacation out West, Edison visited an electric arc light factory in Connecticut. Edison was intrigued by how the owner, William Wallace, made eight lamps glow at once with one generator, or dynamo.

3  In September 1878, Edison caused a sensation when he declared to the press, "With 15 or 20 of these dynamo-electric machines...I can light the entire lower part of New York City." He added, "[T]he same wire that brings the light to you will also bring power and heat."

4  Edison's self-publicity had its desired effect: It attracted financial backers. But actually making a practical and reliable bulb took far longer than the "few weeks" Edison originally had predicted. Finding the right material for the filament turned out to be a huge problem. Edison's first bulbs used carbonized paper in partial vacuum jars. They glowed, but for only about eight minutes. Edison and his team then tested other materials. They rejected iron, cobalt, nickel, silicon, boron, and others because they either melted or burned out too quickly.

5  Edison decided he needed the thinnest possible filament. A thin filament would raise the electrical resistance, which would let Edison bring down the current. Edison also found a better vacuum pump for his glass bulbs. With less oxygen present, the wires could not burn as easily. Edison found more efficient ways to seal the bulbs and keep the oxygen out, too. **❷**

6   By the spring of 1879, Edison had a lightbulb working with a platinum filament. But platinum was very expensive, and the bulb still was not reliable enough. Then, while working in the lab one fall evening, Edison began playing with a piece of lampblack and tar that was there for the lab's telephone project. After rolling it into a thin thread, Edison later said that he decided on carbon as his new filament. After all, something that was already carbonized was not likely to burn much more.

7   But what kind of carbon? Edison's team tried carbonizing all sorts of things, including wood, fishing line, and even coconut hair. On October 21, 1879, they tried a lightbulb with carbonized cotton sewing thread. It glowed for more than thirteen hours! Over the following weeks, the team had even more success with a carbonized cardboard filament shaped like a horseshoe, which glowed for more than 100 hours. **3**

8   News of Edison's invention became public in December. Crowds thronged to his laboratory in Menlo Park for a special New Year's Eve demonstration of the new incandescent lightbulbs.

9   Edison had promised to light up lower Manhattan, however, and that took longer. Finally, on September 4, 1882, Edison's Pearl Street Power Station lit up about 200 homes and businesses in New York City. In 1889, Edison's electric companies joined together as Edison General Electric. After merging with another firm in 1892, the company became simply the General Electric Company (GE), which still exists today.

10  Over time, alternating current (AC) power systems prevailed over Edison's direct current (DC) system. And lightbulb manufacturers eventually switched to tungsten filaments. But Edison's incandescent light bulb and his foresight to create an electrical delivery system remain among his brightest inventions and one that provided light to the world. **4**

---

**4.** *Turn and talk to a partner. Ask: What are some problems Edison encountered? How did he solve them? (Ask questions)*

## Extend Thinking Questions

Pose one or more questions to engage students more deeply with the text.

- *What other scientific discoveries did Edison's lightbulb lead to?*

- *How has Edison's technology been changed and improved?*

### iELD Paraphrase to Support Comprehension

**After paragraph 2:** *Before the lightbulb, light came from candles and oil or gas lamps. In 1876 Thomas Edison began experimenting with incandescent lightbulbs.*

**After paragraph 7:** *Edison worked to find the right material to make a filament that glows for a long time. By 1879 he found the best material: a carbonized cardboard filament shaped like a horseshoe. It glowed for more than 100 hours.*

**After paragraph 10:** *In 1882 Edison's Power Station lit up about 200 homes in New York City. By 1892 his electric companies merged with another company to become General Electric. Eventually lightbulbs changed to using tungsten filaments.*

CCSS
RI.4.1, RI.4.2, RI.4.4, RI.4.5, RI.4.9, SL.4.2, L.4.4a

**Unit 10**

# Winds of Hope, Part 1

## by Katy Duffield

1 Parched red dust swirled on the wind as William Kamkwamba stooped between rows of chimanga, or maize, near his family's mud-brick thatched home in Malawi, Africa. **❶** As the searing sun scorched his back, the fourteen-year-old wrapped his hand around a withered stalk. Instead of being plump and green, the maize was dry and brittle. It had grown barely knee-high. The maize should have been up to his father's chest by that time, but the rains had not come to nourish it.

2 William saw the worried look in his father's eyes. His family depended on the maize for the thick, pasty nsima they ate each day. (William liked to eat his nsima with roasted grasshoppers or dried fish and tomatoes.) How would they live if the maize did not grow?

3 But the drought of 2001 dragged on and on. For many months, William's family had only enough maize for one meal each day. And then, for just a small handful at night; and finally, for only four mouthfuls. As they grew thinner and thinner, William feared they all would die of starvation.

4 The following spring, William and his father knew that all they could do was begin again. They planted a new maize crop. This time, the rains came. The maize grew—ankle-high, knee-high, chest-high. At harvest time, William's family feasted, breathing sighs of relief. They had survived the terrible years of famine. Thousands of others in Malawi, including many in William's village of Wimbe, had not.

5 William hoped that life could now return to normal. He'd worked hard to pass the exams to enter high school. When the term began, however, William's father explained that, because of the drought, there was no money to pay his school fees. It appeared that William's education would end at eighth grade. **❷**

6 Though he could not attend school, William still wanted to learn. He was curious about many things. He took apart radios, trying to discover how they made music. One day, turning a bicycle upside down and cranking the pedals by hand, he figured out that the dynamo that generated electricity for the headlight could be wired to power a radio instead. **❸** He asked how gasoline made cars run and how CDs stored songs. No one knew, or even cared much about his questions.

7  Some days, William visited the village library. It had only three shelves, but William found books that interested him—science books about how things worked. William would check out *Explaining Physics* or *Integrated Science*, plop under a mango tree, and pore over the drawings and diagrams inside. Since his English was not very good, he often looked up words in the dictionary or asked the librarian. He wondered if something in these books might be useful to his family.

8  One day, while looking for a dictionary on the bottom shelf, he found a book he hadn't seen before pushed behind the others. It was an American school textbook called *Using Energy*. On the book's cover was a picture of a row of windmills, tall steel towers with blades spinning like giant fans. They reminded William of the toy pinwheels he'd made with his friends.

9  From this book William learned that wind—something of which Malawi had plenty—could produce electricity. William was delighted! Only 2 percent of the houses in Malawi have electricity. After the sun sets, everyone stops what they're doing, brushes their teeth, and goes to sleep—at seven in the evening! If William could build a windmill, his family could have lights in their home. And a windmill could be used to pump water to irrigate the family's maize fields. If another drought came, the windmill could provide the water for life. ❹

**4.** *Turn and talk to a partner. Ask: What are some advantages a windmill might have for William's family? (Summarize/Ask questions)*

## Extend Thinking Questions

Pose one or more questions to engage students more deeply with the text.

• *Where do you think the scientific discoveries that William learned about in* Using Energy *will lead him?*

• *How was the account of the drought in this selection like the account of the drought in "Before the Rain Came"? How did the accounts differ?*

**iELD  Paraphrase to Support Comprehension**

After paragraph 5: *The drought of 2001 caused a famine in William's village of Wimbe, Africa. The following year the rains came and maize grew. But because of the drought, William's father could not pay school fees. William could not go to high school.*

After paragraph 7: *William wanted to learn about science. He read books and learned how things worked.*

After paragraph 9: *William read the book* Using Energy. *He learned that windmills can generate electricity. If he could build a windmill his family could have lights. He could have water if another drought occurred.*

**CCSS**
**RI.4.1, RI.4.3, RI.4.4, RI.4.6, SL.4.2, L.4.4a, L.4.4c**

**Unit 10**

## Objectives

- Model determining text importance
- Model asking questions

## Set the Stage

**Introduce the Text** *Today I'm going to read aloud part 2 of "Winds of Hope." Let's review what we learned in part 1. (Have volunteers summarize part 1.) In this part we will read about William's struggle to build the windmill and the results of the struggle.*

**Engage Thinking** *Do you think William will be able to build a working windmill? Why or why not? Turn to a partner to share your prediction.*

## Engage with the Text

Read aloud the text at a fluent, expressive pace. Use the suggested prompts to model your thinking, clarify events, and elicit student interaction.

1. *The first four paragraphs contain many facts about the parts William collected and how he put them together. Although these facts are important, the most important information is that he was able to collect all the parts he needed and he then put them together to build the windmill.* (Determine text importance)

2. *When William removed the spoke to unlock the wheel he "held his breath." I think this means he was nervous and worried that the windmill might not work.* (Make inferences)

3. *The TED conference featured innovators. The root nov means "new." The suffix -or means "people." So innovators are people who develop new products and ideas.* (Determine word meaning)

# Winds of Hope, Part 2

1   William could picture in his mind the windmill he wanted to build, but collecting the parts and tools he needed would take months. In a junkyard across from the high school, William dug through piles of twisted metal, rusted cars, and worn-out tractors, searching for anything that might help him construct his machine. He took a ring of ball bearings from an old peanut grinder and the cooling fan from a tractor engine. Cracking open a shock absorber, he removed the steel piston inside. He made 4-foot-long blades from plastic pipe, which he melted over a fire, flattened out, and stiffened with bamboo poles.

2   Earning some money loading logs into a truck, he paid a welder to attach the piston to the pedal sprocket of an old bicycle frame. This would be the axle of the windmill. When the wind blew, the rotating blades would turn the bicycle wheel, like someone pedaling, and spin a small dynamo. Although he had no money for a dynamo, a friend came to the rescue and bought one from a man in the road, right off his bike.

3   Village kids laughed at William when they saw him scrounging in the scrap yard. They called him *misala*, which means crazy. But William was too focused on his idea to care.

4   When he had collected all the parts, William took them out of the corner of his bedroom, laid them outside in the shade of an acacia tree, and began putting them together. Since he did not have a drill to make bolt holes, he pushed a nail through a maize cob, heated it in the fire, then pushed its point through the plastic blades. He bolted the blades to the tractor fan, using washers he'd made from bottle caps. Next he pushed the fan onto the piston welded to the bicycle frame. With the help of his two best friends, William built a 16-foot-tall tower from trunks of blue gum trees and hoisted the 90-pound windmill to the top. ❶

5   Shoppers, farmers, and traders could see William's tower from the local market. They came in a long line to find out what the "crazy" boy was up to. "What is it?" they all asked. Since there is no word for "windmill" in Chichewa, the language of Malawi, William answered with the phrase *magetsi a mphepo*—"electric wind." From the top of the tower he explained that, by using the power of wind, his machine could create electricity. No one believed him.

6  William knew this was his moment—his moment to show everyone he wasn't crazy, to find out if his experiment would work. He connected two wires from the dynamo to a light socket he'd made from a reed and that held a small bulb. As the wind whipped around him, he removed the bent spoke he'd jammed into the wheel to lock it. Then he held his breath. **2**

7  The blades began to turn, slowly at first, then faster and faster. The lightbulb flickered, then flashed to life. The crowd cheered from below. "Wachitabwina! Well done!" A month later William found enough wire to reach from the windmill into his house. His family crowded around to marvel as the small bulb lit up in William's room. Reading *Explaining Physics* by its light, he stayed up long after others had gone to bed.

8  In 2006, a school inspector saw the windmill and informed his head office. William's machine now powered four lights and two radios in his house. He'd added a storage battery with homemade switches and a circuit breaker. He also recharged village cell phones.

9  Soon William was being interviewed on the radio and photographed for the newspapers. The story of the boy with only an eighth grade education who'd built "electric wind" spread across the Internet. In 2007, the nineteen-year-old who had not attended school for five years was flown to Tanzania to speak at the prestigious TED conference, featuring innovators from around the world in Technology, Education, and Design. **3** Nervously struggling with his English, William received a rousing ovation from the auditorium of inventors and scientists when he modestly described what he had done. "After I drop out from school I went to library and I read a book titled *Using Energy*, and I get information about windmill. And I try and I made it."

10  Today William attends Dartmouth College, where he studies environmental sciences and engineering. William is dedicated to bringing wind- and solar-powered electricity and water pumps to impoverished villages in rural Africa. His *Moving Windmills Project* sponsors high school scholarships and is rebuilding William's primary school in Wimbe. It is also adding books to the village library. **4**

---

**4.** *Turn and talk to a partner. Ask: What were some of William's accomplishments?* (Ask questions)

## Extend Thinking Questions

Pose one or more questions to engage students more deeply with the text.

• *How did the power of electricity change the lives of the people in Malawi?*

• *Where did William's scientific discoveries lead him?*

**iELD  Paraphrase to Support Comprehension**

After paragraph 4: *William collected all the parts he needed and put them together to build the windmill.*

After paragraph 8: *People from all over the village came to see if William's windmill would work. It did. He lit a lightbulb. Eventually he ran electricity to his house.*

After paragraph 10: *In 2007, William spoke at the TED conference. Later he went to Dartmouth College. He is working to bring wind and solar powered electricity to rural Africa.*

**Unit 10**

**CCSS**
**RI.4.1, RI.4.2, RI.4.3, RI.4.4, SL.4.2, L.4.4b**

# Sweat Power!

1   Wait! Don't shower just yet. Your sweat could be useful! Scientists have created a product that uses body sweat to charge batteries. **1**

2   The product is like a stick-on tattoo. You may have even worn one like it before. But this one goes on your arm while you play a sport or exercise. As you sweat, the tattoo gets a charge. When you peel it off, you can use it to charge a watch. Maybe you can charge a smartphone or iPad one day! **2**

3   "I've worn it myself," Wenzhao Jia told BBC News. "You don't even feel it," she said. Dr. Jia is one of the scientists who developed the sweat-loving product. She and her team presented it in San Francisco, California.

4   "Our device is the first to use sweat," said Dr. Jia. "At the moment, the power is not that high," she added. "But we are working on enhancing it so it can power small electronic devices."

# Student Gym Rats Help Power Texas State University Campus

5  Texas State University is now home to the world's largest human power plant.

6  The university has unveiled exercise equipment at the Student Recreation Center that will generate electricity when students use it. **❸**

7  The equipment, produced by a Florida company called ReRev, was placed on 30 elliptical machines that are feeding electricity back into the campus power grid.

8  Other universities have installed the system, but Texas State's rec center is using more ReRev machines than any other.

9  "And we're the first in Texas" to install the system, said Glenn Hanley, director of campus recreation.

10  A typical 30-minute workout on the elliptical produces 50 watt-hours of electricity, enough to power a lightbulb for 2 ½ hours and a desktop computer for 30 minutes.

11  The system cost about $20,000 to install, Hanley said, and could pay for itself in seven or eight years.

12  But Blair Hartley, a recreation management graduate student in charge of the project, said powering the grid isn't the point. It's making students more aware of how much power it takes to run their devices and encouraging them to use less electricity.

13  "When you realize, 'I just worked out for 30 minutes, and it's only enough to power a lightbulb for about two hours,' it gives you some perspective." **❹**

---

**4.** *Turn and talk to a partner. Ask: Do you think the ReRev machines are worth the cost? Why or why not?* (Ask questions/Make connections)

## Extend Thinking Questions

Pose one or more questions to engage students more deeply with the text.

• *Where does Blair Hartley hope the discovery of the power generating elliptical machine will lead?*

• *Which discovery do you think is more important: the stick-on tattoos or the ReRev machines? Why?*

### iELD Paraphrase to Support Comprehension

After paragraph 4 of "Sweat Power!": *Dr. Jia and her team are working on using body sweat to charge batteries. The product is a stick-on tattoo. So far it can only produce a small charge.*

After paragraph 6 of "Student Gym Rats": *Texas State University is using ReRev elliptical machines to generate electricity. A 30-minute workout produces enough electricity to power a lightbulb for 2 1/2 hours.*

After paragraph 9 of "Student Gym Rats": *Blair Hartley runs the project at Texas State. He hopes it will help students realize how much power it takes to run devices. He hopes they will conserve electricity once they realize this.*

**CCSS**
**RI.4.1, RI.4.2, RI.4.3, RI.4.4, SL.4.2, L.4.4a**

**Unit 10**

# The Rise of Solar Farms

1   When you hear the word farm, what kind of picture pops into your head? Chances are, you see a sheep or two. Or maybe you envision rows of soil, with green plants shooting up from it. Now imagine that a farm isn't trying to raise animals or grow vegetables, but to harvest energy from the glowing ball of fire that gives life to all these things: the sun. This would be a solar farm, and it would look very different. On one kind of solar farm, rows of shiny rectangles called solar panels tilt toward the sun. Each panel is full of solar cells, which absorb sunlight and change it into electricity. The cells work best in areas where the sun is strong, such as deserts, and they face toward the places where it shines the brightest. A solar farm that collects the sun's energy using these kinds of cells is called a photovoltaic solar farm. **1**

2   Photovoltaic is a word you might start hearing a lot more often. That's because right now the United States is building the largest photovoltaic solar farm in the world. This farm, called Agua Caliente, is in the sunny state of Arizona. The farm is gigantic, stretching over 2,400 acres. The cells it uses are made to absorb as much sunlight as possible. Once sunlight enters the cells, it breaks down into different types of particles. Some of these particles can be conducted, or moved, through the cell. From there, they go toward a device that needs power. **2** Tiny solar cells can be used to power small devices, like watches. Large solar farms pull in enough energy to heat and light homes. Agua Caliente will produce enough electricity for 230,000 homes in California.

3   A company called NRG Energy started building the farm in 2010, and the U.S. Government provided money to help. Why did they support this project? **3** Well, solar energy has many advantages over other types of power. Unlike coal power or oil power, solar power doesn't make any air pollution. It also uses up fewer nonrenewable resources. People who install solar panels on their homes may also save money over time. After all, sunlight is free.

4    Agua Caliente isn't the only solar farm baking under the hot Arizona sun. A farm called Solana also has a home in the state. California has solar farms too, including Ivanpah and Genesis. All of these solar farms were helped with loans from the U.S. Government's Energy Department. Unlike Agua Caliente, they are thermal solar farms, which means they collect energy a bit differently. Instead of solar panels, they have trenches covered with mirrors. These collect sunlight and use it to heat water. The water gets so hot it turns to steam. The steam powers generators that produce electricity.

5    As more people learn about the benefits of solar power, we may see a lot more thermal and photovoltaic farms popping up in our country's sunniest states. Maybe someday all our homes will be fueled by that glowing fireball in the sky. **4**

**4.** *Turn and talk to a partner. How are thermal and photovoltaic farms alike? How are they different?* (Compare and contrast)

## Extend Thinking Questions

Pose one or more questions to engage students more deeply with the text.

- *What influenced scientists to develop ways to use solar power to produce electricity?*

- *Where do you think using solar power to produce energy will lead us?*

**iELD  Paraphrase to Support Comprehension**

After paragraph 2: *A photovoltaic solar farm uses solar panels with cells. The cells change the sun's energy into electricity. The largest photovoltaic solar farm is Agua Caliente in Arizona.*

After paragraph 3: *Solar power has many advantages. It does not cause air pollution. It uses few nonrenewable resources. It can save money over time.*

After paragraph 4: *California has thermal solar farms. Instead of solar cells, the farms have trenches covered with mirrors. They collect sunlight. The sun heats water. Water turns to steam. Steam powers generators. Generators produce electricity.*

CCSS
RI.4.1, RI.4.2, RI.4.3, RI.4.4, RI.4.8, SL.4.2, SL.4.3, L.4.4.a

**Unit 10**

## Objectives

- Model determining text importance
- Model asking questions
- Model fix-up monitoring strategies

## Set the Stage

**Introduce the Text** *Today I'm going to read aloud an article about a successful business leader. Elon Musk has always had an interest in three major areas: space, the Internet, and renewable energy. Listen to how he pursued each.*

**Engage Thinking** *How do you think Elon Musk was able to pursue all of his interests? Turn to a partner to share your prediction.*

## Engage with the Text

Read aloud the text at a fluent, expressive pace. Use the suggested prompts to model your thinking, clarify events, and elicit student interaction.

**1.** *There is some interesting information up to now. But I think the important information is about the Internet companies Musk created: the video game at age twelve, the maps and city guides at age twenty-four, and PayPal.* (Determine text importance)

**2.** *In 2012 SpaceX hit a milestone. I wasn't sure what a "milestone" is. I read on to learn about the achievement SpaceX made. So I think* milestone *means a "big achievement" or "target."* (Use fix-up monitoring strategies)

**3.** *Tesla cars can drive longer distances than other electric cars. So I think this means their batteries can hold a charge longer than batteries in other electric cars.* (Make inferences)

# Elon Musk: Exploring Earth, Space, and the Internet

1   Innovator and billionaire Elon Musk has never thought small. When he was still in college, trying to decide what to do with his life, he asked himself a big question. What can I work on that will affect how people live in the future? Musk believed the answer could be found in three categories: the Internet, space exploration, and renewable energy.

2   Back in 1995, when Musk had just started graduate school, the Internet was still new. Two days into classes, he decided to take some time off to make his mark on the Web. Musk's plan didn't come out of nowhere. Since his childhood in South Africa, he had a gift for computer programming. By age twelve, he had created and sold his first computer game. At age twenty-four, he made a name for himself on the Internet by starting a company that provided maps and city guides for online newspapers. Next, he used his profits to create the website he became famous for: PayPal. PayPal gave Internet shoppers a safe way to pay for items online. It was a website they could trust to keep their credit card information private. **1**

3   With PayPal a success, Musk moved on to his next area of interest: space. In 2002, he founded a company called SpaceX. SpaceX is a private company that builds spacecraft, a job that the government had usually handled. Since 2008, the company has been launching rockets into space. In 2012, it hit a milestone. It became the first private spacecraft company to make a delivery to the International Space Station. Though thrilled with this achievement, Musk is thinking even bigger. Eventually, he'd like to put people on Mars. **2**

4   As SpaceX launched rockets, Musk also had his mind on Earth's problems. He wanted to make a difference in the third category he'd named back in college: energy. Like many environmental scientists, Musk believes we need to use more renewable energy sources, such as sunlight, water, and wind. That also means using fewer nonrenewable resources, like coal and gas.

5   To work toward this goal, Musk focused his efforts on a big user of gas: cars. In 2003, he cofounded an electric car company called Tesla. Unlike gas-run cars, electric cars run on batteries, which charge at electrical outlets. Tesla didn't invent electric cars, but it did improve how they work. Compared to other electric cars, Tesla batteries charge more quickly. The cars can also drive longer distances. **3**

6   The electricity for charging cars comes from many places. While some electricity plants run on gas, others use wind, water, and solar power. So even though electric cars still rely on some gas, they don't rely on nearly as much as gas-run cars. As more electricity plants turn to renewable energy, Tesla cars will help the environment even more.

7   And who better to speed up that process than Musk? One of his newest projects is SolarCity, a company that provides solar energy products and services. After reaching Earth and space, Elon Musk has set his sights on the sun. **4**

---

**4.** *Turn and talk to a partner. Ask each other about Elon Musk's major achievements.* (Ask questions)

## Extend Thinking Questions

Pose one or more questions to engage students more deeply with the text.

• *Where do you think Elon Musk's projects at SolarCity will lead?*

• *What examples of the power of electricity are contained in this article?*

### iELD Paraphrase to Support Comprehension

After paragraph 2: *Elon Musk had three main interests: the Internet, space, and renewable energy. His main Internet company was PayPal. It allowed customers to buy things online safely.*

After paragraph 5: *Musk's interest in renewable energy is demonstrated with his electric car company, Tesla. The electric cars run by battery instead of gas. Tesla batteries charge more quickly and longer than other electric car batteries.*

After paragraph 7: *Musk hopes more companies will use renewable energy. Musk's company, SolarCity provides solar energy products.*

**CCSS**
**RI.4.1, RI.4.2, RI.4.4, SL.4.2, L.4.4a**

Unit 10

# Let There Be Light!

## by Stephen James O'Meara

1  Without wires or cords that is. Welcome to the wild and wacky world of "WiTricity"—wireless power! **1**

2  According to ScientificAmerican.com, physicists vow to cut the cord between your laptop battery and the wall socket—with just a simple loop of wire. In fact, it's already been done by physicists at the Massachusetts Institute of Technology (MIT). They successfully lit a 60-watt lightbulb by transferring energy through the air from one specially designed copper coil to the bulb, which was attached to a second coil 7 feet away.

3  In essence, the wireless lightbulb works like a rechargeable electric toothbrush. **2** When you place an electric toothbrush into its station, there are small coils of wire in the end of the toothbrush and in the base of the charger. The moving electric charge in the station base creates a moving magnetic field, which in turn transfers, or induces, a smaller electric charge in the toothbrush. Here the objects must be in contact for the recharging to work. The MIT physicists' challenge was to extend the charge's reach. To generate wireless electricity (WiTricity), they used coupled resonant objects.

4  Resonance is a type of vibration, or back-and-forth motion. The natural frequency of a resonant object is how fast it will vibrate if a force acts on it. Coupled resonant objects both have the same natural frequency. If one of them starts vibrating, it will transfer energy to the other object, which will get that object vibrating, too. It's a safe way to transfer energy because energy can only move to other nearby objects with the same natural frequency. **3**

5  You may have heard that an opera singer can shatter a wine glass. This happens because sound energy (the opera singer's voice) vibrates at the same natural frequency as the glass. When the glass receives the energy, it also starts to vibrate, until it absorbs more energy than it can handle, and it shatters. But the eyeglasses of someone in the audience remain intact because the lenses have a different natural frequency. The same principle holds true for transmitting energy across the air from a power source. **4**

6    The resonant nature of the process ensures the strong interaction between the sending unit and the receiving unit, while the interaction with the rest of the environment remains weak.

7    These experiments in wireless energy transfer could pave the way for a plugless world, and extend the meaning of wireless computing.

**4.** *Turn and talk to a partner. Ask: How is an opera singer shattering a glass similar to wireless electricity?* (Ask questions/Summarize)

## Extend Thinking Questions

Pose one or more questions to engage students more deeply with the text.

• *What benefits do you think the discovery of wireless electricity will lead to?*

• *Think about what you learned in "Turning on the Light." How did the information about electricity differ from the information about wireless electricity?*

### iELD Paraphrase to Support Comprehension

After paragraph 2: *Physicists at MIT discovered wireless power. They found a way to light a bulb by transferring energy through the air from one coil to another.*

After paragraph 3: *The wireless lightbulb works like a rechargeable electric toothbrush. The toothbrush sits on the station. The electric charge in the station transfers to the toothbrush. Wireless electricity extends the charge's reach.*

After paragraph 5: *An opera singer can shatter a glass that has the same natural frequency. With wireless electricity, the sending unit, like the opera singer's voice, sends the energy across the air to the receiving unit, like the glass.*

**Unit 10**

CCSS
**RI.4.1, RI.4.2, RI.4.3, RI.4.4, RI.4.9, SL.4.2, L.4.4b**

# Grade 4 Passage Matrix

| Unit | Unit Topic | Title | Author/Source |
|------|-----------|-------|---------------|
| 1 | Government and Citizenship | Hail to the Chief | John P. Riley |
| 1 | Government and Citizenship | Give the People What They Want, Part 1 | Dan Gutman |
| 1 | Government and Citizenship | Give the People What They Want, Part 2 | Dan Gutman |
| 1 | Government and Citizenship | Let Your Voice Be Heard! | Ann Jordan |
| 1 | Government and Citizenship | The Quilt | Sachi Oyama |
| 1 | Government and Citizenship | Mariano Vallejo: A Californio for Statehood, Part 1 | Diane Brooks |
| 1 | Government and Citizenship | Mariano Vallejo: A Californio for Statehood, Part 2 | Diane Brooks |
| 1 | Government and Citizenship | And the Citizenship Award Goes To… | Jamie McGillian |
| 2 | Characters' Actions and Reactions | An excerpt from Out of My Mind, Part 1 | Sharon Draper |
| 2 | Characters' Actions and Reactions | An excerpt from Out of My Mind, Part 2 | Sharon Draper |
| 2 | Characters' Actions and Reactions | Mirror, Mirror! | Jamie McGillian |
| 2 | Characters' Actions and Reactions | Let's Go! | Jamie McGillian |
| 2 | Characters' Actions and Reactions | The King of the Polar Bears, Part 1 | L. Frank Baum |
| 2 | Characters' Actions and Reactions | The King of the Polar Bears, Part 2 | L. Frank Baum |
| 2 | Characters' Actions and Reactions | Ode to La Tortilla | Gary Soto |
| 2 | Characters' Actions and Reactions | Peter and Wendy | Jamie McGillian |
| 3 | Observing Nature | Three Bird Summer excerpt | Sara St. Antoine |
| 3 | Observing Nature | I Wandered Lonely as a Cloud/To a Butterfly | William Wordsworth |
| 3 | Observing Nature | A Famous Secret Valley | Jerry Miller |
| 3 | Observing Nature | Portrait of An Artist: Grafton Tyler Brown | Deborah Nevins |
| 3 | Observing Nature | The Secret Garden, Part 1 | Frances Hodgson Burnett |
| 3 | Observing Nature | The Secret Garden, Part 2 | Frances Hodgson Burnett |
| 3 | Observing Nature | Rachel Carson's World of Wonder | Sylvia Salsbury |
| 3 | Observing Nature | Kindness to Animals/Delight in Nature | Anonymous |
| 4 | Different Points of View | The Spider and the Fly | Mary Howitt |
| 4 | Different Points of View | Capture! a chapter from Akimbo and the Snakes, Part 1 | Alexander McCall Smith |
| 4 | Different Points of View | Capture! a chapter from Akimbo and the Snakes, Part 2 | Alexander McCall Smith |
| 4 | Different Points of View | The Dreams of a Dog | Deborah Nevins |
| 4 | Different Points of View | Doctor Dolittle, Part 1 | Hugh Lofting |
| 4 | Different Points of View | Doctor Dolittle, Part 2 | Hugh Lofting |
| 4 | Different Points of View | Doctor Dolittle, Part 3 | Hugh Lofting |
| 4 | Different Points of View | We Are the Geese | Amy Imbody |
| 5 | Technology for a green future | Blam It on the House | Carmelle LaMothe |
| 5 | Technology for a green future | How Green Is My City? | Marcia Amidon Lusted |
| 5 | Technology for a green future | Innovative Packets Save Lives | Hugh Westrup |
| 5 | Technology for a green future | The Clean Power of Wind | Amber Lanier Nagle |
| 5 | Technology for a green future | Intruders, a chapter from Operation Redwood, Part 1 | S. Terrell French |
| 5 | Technology for a green future | Intruders, a chapter from Operation Redwood, Part 2 | S. Terrell French |
| 5 | Technology for a green future | Researchers Develop a Cheap Battery to Power Your House–and It's Organic | Kristine Wong |
| 5 | Technology for a green future | The Latest Smog-Eating Weapon Might Just Be Your Roof | Liz Dwyer |

| Lexile® | Text Type | Genre | CCSS-ELA | HSS | NGSS |
|---|---|---|---|---|---|
| 930L | Informational | Social Studies | RI.4.1, RI.4.2, RI.4.3, RI.4.4, SL.4.2, L.4.4a | 4.5 | |
| 540L | Literary | Realistic Fiction | RL.4.1, RL.4.3, RL.4.4, L.4.4b | | |
| 530L | Literary | Realistic Fiction | RL.4.1, RL.4.3, RL.4.4, L.4.4a, L.4.5b | | |
| 930L | Informational | Social Studies | RI.4.1, RI.4.2, RI.4.4, RI.4.8, SL.4.2, L.4.4a | 4.5 | |
| 950L | Informational | Social Studies | RI.4.1, RI.4.2, RI.4.3, RI.4.4, RI.4.8, SL.4.2, L.4.4b | 4.5 | |
| 970L | Informational | Biography | RI.4.1, RI.4.3, RI.4.4, SL.4.2, L.4.4a | 4.3.5 | |
| 980L | Informational | Biography | RI.4.1, RI.4.2, RI.4.3, RI.4.4, RI.4.5, SL.4.2, L.4.4a, L.4.4c | 4.3.5 | |
| 790L | Literary | Realistic Fiction | RI.4.1, RL.4.2, RL.4.3, RL.4.4, SL.4.2, L.4.4a, L.4.5b | | |
| 790L | Literary | Realistic Fiction | RL.4.1, RL.4.3, RL.4.4, L.4.4b | | |
| 670L | Literary | Realistic Fiction | RL.4.1, RL.4.2, RL.4.3, RL.4.4, L.4.5b | | |
| NP | Literary | Drama | RL.4.1, RL.4.3, RL.4.4, RL.4.5, SL.4.2, L.4.4 | | |
| NP | Literary | Drama | RL.4.1, RL.4.3, RL.4.4, RL.4.5, SL.4.1c, L.4.5b | | |
| 800L | Literary | Fantasy | RL.4.1, RL.4.3, RL.4.4, SL.4.2, L.4.4a, L.4.4b | | |
| 900L | Literary | Fantasy | RL.4.1, RL.4.3, RL.4.4, SL.4.2, RL.4.4b, RL.4.5a | | |
| NP | Literary | Free Verse Poetry | RL.4.1, RL.4.3, RL.4.4, RL.4.5, L.4.4a | | |
| NP | Literary | Fantasy | RL.4.1, RL.4.3, RL.4.4, RL.4.5, SL.4.3, L.4.4b | | |
| 1080L | Literary | Realistic Fiction | RI.4.1, RL.4.2, RL.4.3, RL.4.4, L.4.4a, L.4.5c | | |
| NP | Literary | Rhythmic poetry | RL.4.1, RL.4.2, RL.4.4, RL.4.5, RL.4.6, SL.4.2, L.4.4a, L.4.5a | | |
| 1040L | Informational | Social Studies | RI.4.1, RI.4.2, RI.4.3, RI.4.4, SL.4.3, L.4.4b | 4.1.3 | |
| 930L | Informational | Biography | RI.4.1, RI.4.2, RI.4.4, RI.4.5, L.4.4a | | |
| 830L | Literary | Realistic Fiction | RL.4.1, RL.4.3, RL.4.4, L.4.4c | 4.4.9 | |
| 940L | Literary | Realistic Fiction | RL.4.1, RL.4.3, RL.4.4, L.4.4a | | |
| 940L | Informational | Biography | RI.4.1, RI.4.2, RI.4.3, RI.4.4, SL.4.1c, L.4.4b | | |
| NP | Literary | Rhythmic/Free Verse Poetry | RL.4.1, RL.4.2, RL.4.3, RL.4.4, SL.4.2, L.4.4a, L.4.5b | | |
| NP | Literary | Poetry | RL.4.1, RL.4.3, RL.4.4, RL.4.5, L.4.4a | | |
| 740L | Literary | Realistic Fiction | RL.4.1, RL.4.2, RL.4.3, RL.4.4, SL.4.2, L.4.4a | | |
| 780L | Literary | Realistic Fiction | RL.4.1, RL.4.2, RL.4.3, RL.4.4, SL.4.2, L.4.4a | | |
| NP | Literary | Rhythmic Poetry | RL.4.1, RL.4.2, RL.4.4, RL.4.5, L.4.4a, L.4.5c | | |
| 630L | Literary | Animal Fantasy | RL.4.1, RL.4.3, RL.4.4, L.4.4a | | |
| 700L | Literary | Animal Fantasy | RL.4.1, RL.4.2, RL.4.3, RL.4.4, SL.4.2, L.4.4a, L.4.4b | | |
| 1140L | Literary | Animal Fantasy | RL.4.1, RL.4.2, RL.4.3, RL.4.4, SL.4.2, L.4.4a | | |
| NP | Literary | Poetry | RL.4.1, RL.4.2, RL.4.4, RL.4.5, L.4.4b | | |
| 790L | Informational | Science | RI.4.1, RI.4.2, RI.4.3, RI.4.4, SL.4.2, L.4.4a | | |
| 960L | Informational | Science/Social Studies | RI.4.1, RI.4.2, RI.4.3, RI.4.4, SL.4.2, L.4.4a | | 3-5-ETS1-2 |
| 910L | Informational | Science | RI.4.1, RI.4.2, RI.4.3, RI.4.4, SL.4.2, L.4.5c | | 3-5-ETS1-2 |
| 1210L | Informational | Science | RI.4.1, RI.4.2, RI.4.3, RI.4.4, RI.4.8, SL.4.2, SL.4.3, L.4.4b | | 3-5-ETS1-2 |
| 810L | Literary | Realistic Fiction | RL.4.1, RL.4.2, RL.4.3, RL.4.4, SL.4.2, L.4.4a, L.4.5b | | |
| 490L | Literary | Realistic Fiction | RL.4.1, RL.4.2, RL.4.3, RL.4.4, SL.4.2, L.4.4a | | |
| 1200L | Informational | Science | RI.4.1, RI.4.2, RI.4.4, SL.4.2, L.4.4a | | 3-5-ETS1-1 |
| 1240L | Informational | Science | RI.4.1, RI.4.2, RI.4.4, SL.4.2, L.4.4a | | 3-5-ETS1-1 |

| Unit | Unit Topic | Title | Author/Source |
|------|-----------|-------|---------------|
| 6 | Confronting Challenges | Ordinary, a chapter from Wonder | R.J. Palacio |
| 6 | Confronting Challenges | The Grand Tour, a chapter from Wonder | R.J. Palacio |
| 6 | Confronting Challenges | Hercules and the Lion | Deborah Nevins |
| 6 | Confronting Challenges | The Inca Chasqui, Part 1 | Wendi Silvano |
| 6 | Confronting Challenges | The Inca Chasqui, Part 2 | Wendi Silvano |
| 6 | Confronting Challenges | The Inca Chasqui, Part 3 | Wendi Silvano |
| 6 | Confronting Challenges | Thornbush (Part 1) | Carrel Muller |
| 6 | Confronting Challenges | Thornbush (Part 2) | Carrel Muller |
| 7 | A Nation Comes Together | Pilgrim Feet | Kathiann M. Kowalski |
| 7 | A Nation Comes Together | Before the Rain Came | Alicia Zadrozny |
| 7 | A Nation Comes Together | Dorothea Lange: Witnessing Hard Times | Julia LoFaso |
| 7 | A Nation Comes Together | The Legend of the Flying Africans/O Daedalus, Fly Away Home | Robert Hayden |
| 7 | A Nation Comes Together | The People Could Fly | Deborah Nevins |
| 7 | A Nation Comes Together | The Kindness of Biddy Mason: Two Letters from Los Angeles | Julia LoFaso |
| 7 | A Nation Comes Together | Are We There Yet? Part 1 | Ellen R. Braaf |
| 7 | A Nation Comes Together | Are We There Yet? Part 2 | Ellen R. Braaf |
| 8 | Earth Changes | Interview with an Earthquake Expert | Lisa Wald |
| 8 | Earth Changes | When the Ocean Roars | Patricia Barnes-Svarney |
| 8 | Earth Changes | A Day at the Beach | Jamie McGillian |
| 8 | Earth Changes | Tsunami Haiku | Deborah Nevins |
| 8 | Earth Changes | The Legend of Pele: Hawaiian Goddess of Fire | Julia LoFaso |
| 8 | Earth Changes | Krakatoa: The Art of Disaster | Hugh Westrup |
| 8 | Earth Changes | Popocatepetl and Iztaccihuatl: A Mexican Volcano Myth | Julia LoFaso |
| 8 | Earth Changes | Mapping Disaster | Mike Weinstein |
| 9 | Resources and Their Impact | Coming Through the Clouds | Meg Moss |
| 9 | Resources and Their Impact | Roberto Ignacio Torres Bakes, Part 1 | Steven Frank |
| 9 | Resources and Their Impact | Roberto Ignacio Torres Bakes, Part 2 | Steven Frank |
| 9 | Resources and Their Impact | Roberto Ignacio Torres Bakes, Part 3 | Steven Frank |
| 9 | Resources and Their Impact | Art Is Everywhere | Maureen Ash |
| 9 | Resources and Their Impact | Cesar Chavez: His Fight for the Farm Workers, Part 1 | Barbara Bloom |
| 9 | Resources and Their Impact | Cesar Chavez: His Fight for the Farm Workers, Part 2 | Barbara Bloom |
| 9 | Resources and Their Impact | I'd Rather Not Be on Relief | Lester Hunter Shafter |
| 10 | The Power of Electricity | Electricity Comes to Cocoa Bottom | Marcia Douglas |
| 10 | The Power of Electricity | Turning on the Light | Kathiann M. Kowalski |
| 10 | The Power of Electricity | Winds of Hope, Part 1 | Katy Duffield |
| 10 | The Power of Electricity | Winds of Hope, Part 2 | Katy Duffield |
| 10 | The Power of Electricity | Sweat Power!/Student Gym Rats | News-O-matic/Austin American-Statesman |
| 10 | The Power of Electricity | The Rise of Solar Farms | N/A |
| 10 | The Power of Electricity | Elon Musk: Exploring Earth, Space, and the Internet | Julia LoFaso |
| 10 | The Power of Electricity | Let There Be Light! | Stephen James O'Meara |

| Lexile® | Text Type | Genre | CCSS-ELA | HSS | NGSS |
|---|---|---|---|---|---|
| 630L | Literary | Realistic Fiction | RL.4.1, RL.4.2, RL.4.3, RL.4.4, L.4.4b | | |
| 560L | Literary | Realistic Fiction | RL.4.1, RL.4.2, RL.4.3, RL.4.4, SL.4.2, L.4.5b | | |
| 920L | Literary | Myth | RL.4.1, RL.4.2, RL.4.3, RL.4.4, L.4.4a | | |
| 970L | Literary | Historical Fiction | RL.4.1, RL.4.3, RL.4.4, RL.4.5, SL.4.1c, L.4.5b | | |
| 750L | Literary | Historical Fiction | RL.4.1, RL.4.2, RL.4.3, RL.4.4, RL.4.9, L.4.4a, L.4.4c | | |
| 780L | Literary | Historical Fiction | RL.4.1, RL.4.2, RL.4.3, RL.4.4, L.4.4a | | |
| 530L | Literary | Fable | RL.4.1, RL.4.2, RL.4.4, RL.4.9, L.4.4a | | |
| 740L | Literary | Fable | RL.4.1, RL.4.4, SL.4.2, L.4.4b | | |
| 900L | Informational | Social Studies | RI.4.1, RI.4.2, RI.4.3, RI.4.4, SL.4.2, L.4.5c | | |
| NP | Literary | Drama | RI.4.1, RI.4.2, RI.4.3, RI.4.4, SL.4.2, L.4.4a | | |
| 990L | Informational | Biography | RI.4.1, RI.4.3, RI.4.4, SL.4.1c, SL.4.2, L.4.4a | 4.4.9 | |
| NP | Literary | Free Verse Poetry | RI.4.1, RI.4.4, RL.4.2, RL.4.4, L.4.4a | | |
| 880L | Literary | Legend | RL.4.1, RL.4.2, RL.4.4, RL.4.5, RL.4.9, L.4.4a | | |
| 920L | Literary | Historical Fiction | RL.4.1, RL.4.2, RL.4.4, SL.4.2, L.4.4a | 4.3.4, 4.4.4 | |
| 950L | Informational | Social Studies | RI.4.1, RI.4.2, RI.4.3, RI.4.4, SL.4.2, L.4.4b | | 3-5-ETS1-1 |
| 1010L | Informational | Social Studies | RI.4.1, RI.4.2, RI.4.3, RI.4.4, RI.4.8, SL.4.2, L.4.4a | | 3-5-ETS1-1 |
| 1100L | Informational | Interview | RI.4.1, RI.4.2, RI.4.3, RI.4.4, RI.4.9, SL.4.2, L.4.4b | | |
| 1160L | Informational | Science | RI.4.1, RI.4.2, RI.4.3, RI.4.4, RI.4.5, SL.4.2, L.4.4a | | 4-PS4-1 |
| 880L | Informational | Profile | RI.4.1, RI.4.2, RI.4.3, RI.4.4, RI.4.5, SL.4.2, L.4.4a | | 4-PS4-1 |
| NP | Literary | Rhythmic Poetry | RL.4.1, RL.4.3, RL.4.4, RL.4.5, L.4.4a | | |
| 950L | Literary | Myth | RL.4.1, RL.4.2, RL.4.3, RL.4.4, SL.4.2, L.4.4a | | |
| 970L | Informational | Art History | RI.4.1, RI.4.2, RI.4.3, RI.4.4, SL.4.2, L.4.5c | | 4-ESS1-C |
| 1000L | Literary | Myth | RL.4.1, RL.4.3, RL.4.4, SL.4.2, L.4.5b | | |
| 870L | Informational | Science/Social Studies | RI.4.1, RI.4.2, RI.4.3, RI.4.4, RI.4.5, SL.4.2, L.4.4a | | 4-ESS2-2 |
| 1110L | Informational | Geography | RI.4.1, RI.4.2, RI.4.3, RI.4.4, RI.4.8, SL.4.3, L.4.4a | | 4-ESS3-2 |
| 800L | Literary | Realistic Fiction | RL.4.1, RL.4.2, RL.4.4, RI.4.9, SL.4.2, L.4.5b | | |
| 690L | Literary | Realistic Fiction | RL.4.1, RL.4.4, SL.4.2, L.4.4c | | |
| 740L | Literary | Realistic Fiction | RL.4.1, RL.4.3, RL.4.4, SL.4.2, L.4.5b | | |
| 850L | Informational | Social Studies | RI.4.1, RI.4.2, RI.4.4, SL.4.2, L.4.4a, L.4.4b | | |
| 1060L | Informational | Biography | RI.4.1, RI.4.3, RI.4.4, RI.4.9, SL.4.1c, L.4.4b | 4.4.4 | |
| 1020L | Informational | Biography | RI.4.1, RI.4.2, RI.4.4, RI.4.5, SL.4.2, L.4.4a | 4.4.4 | |
| NP | Literary | Ballad | RL.4.1, RL.4.4, RL.4.5, RI.4.9, L.4.4c, L.4.5a | | |
| NP | Literary | Free Verse Poetry | RL.4.1, RL.4.2, RL.4.4, RL.4.5, SL.4.2, L.4.4a, L.4.4c | | |
| 1080L | Informational | Science | RI.4.1, RI.4.2, RI.4.4, RI.4.5, RI.4.9, SL.4.2, L.4.4a | | 4-PS3-2 |
| 900L | Informational | Profile | RI.4.1, RI.4.3, RI.4.4, RI.4.6, SL.4.2, L.4.4a, L.4.4c | | 4-PS3-4 |
| 1040L | Informational | Profile | RI.4.1, RI.4.2, RI.4.3, RI.4.4, SL.4.2, L.4.4b | | 4-PS3-4 |
| 1040L | Informational | Science | RI.4.1, RI.4.2, RI.4.3, RI.4.4, SL.4.2, L.4.4a | | |
| 910L | Informational | Science | RI.4.1, RI.4.2, RI.4.3, RI.4.4, RI.4.8, SL.4.2, SL.4.3, L.4.4a | 4.4.6 | 4-PS3-4 |
| 900L | Informational | Science | RI.4.1, RI.4.2, RI.4.4, SL.4.2, L.4.4a | | 4-PS3-4 |
| 1170L | Informational | Science | RI.4.1, RI.4.2, RI.4.3, RI.4.4, RI.4.9, SL.4.2, L.4.4b | | 4-PS3-2 |

**Notes:**